The Appraisal Interview:
Three Basic Approaches

The Appraisal Interview:
Three Basic Approaches

A revision of
The Appraisal Interview:
Objectives, Methods, and Skills

Norman R.F. Maier

University Associates, Inc.
8517 Production Avenue
P.O. Box 26240
San Diego, California 92126

*There is no abstract art. You must always
start with something. Afterwards you can
remove all traces of reality . . .*

PABLO PICASSO

Preface to the Revised Edition

Attempting to improve the interviewing skills of a group of executives, I became aware of a special difficulty in the appraisal interview. An interviewer often began with the best intentions to be permissive and to respond to feeling, yet before long found himself in a position where he felt the need to defend himself or justify his evaluation. In most cases, the cause of his defensive behavior could be traced to the tendency of the subordinate to question the fairness of the appraisal, his first line of defense.

It had been expected that the subordinate would resist accepting unfavorable evaluations, but the inability of the interviewer to cope with this resistance had not been foreseen. No matter how much the need to accept resistance was stressed in training, defensiveness invariably worked its way into the interviewer's remarks. Often his initial defensive reaction was so slight that it was imperceptible to the untrained observer. Frequently, the interviewer himself was entirely unaware of attempts to justify his position and felt that he was only explaining. But from the moment that such behavior appeared, the interview would progressively deteriorate and all evidence of human relations training would disappear. During experiments with such interactions in training, the interview was interrupted as soon as the superior's defensive behavior became obvious, in order to permit an analysis of what was happening. After the analysis, the interview would be resumed at a point just preceding the beginning of the breakdown in constructive interaction. In this way, the interviewer was given the opportunity to take advantage of the analysis and try a different way to avoid an obstacle. Despite precautions of this kind, new difficulties would come up, defensive reactions would be expressed, and again the deterioration in human relations skills would set in.

Because so much difficulty was encountered in training interviewers to be permissive during an appraisal interview, the conviction began to grow that appraisal interviewing and permissive behavior were in conflict. This theory sounded even more likely when it was found that persons trained as clinicians completely abandoned their permissive skills when conducting appraisal interviews in role-play situations.

Experiences of this kind finally led to the conclusion that objectives, methods, and skills can not properly be studied and evaluated separately, because each is related to and, in part, determines the nature of the others. A demonstration and analysis of these three dimensions of appraisal interviewing is the purpose of this book.

Perhaps the book's major contribution lies not so much in the separation of objectives, methods, and skills, but in the isolation of some principles of problem solving. Although these principles initially were designed to meet some of the difficulties encountered in appraisal interviewing, it was apparent that they had a much broader application.

Three basically different methods of interviewing were used to study the interrelationships among objectives, methods, and skills. Each method was demonstrated twice so that six unrehearsed role-playing interviews of the same case study were recorded. Chapters 3 through 8 are edited transcriptions of these recordings, accompanied by analytical comments. A count of the number of words spoken was made from the transcriptions, although the length of the various speeches may deviate slightly from the edited transcriptions because editing changes were made to make the interactions more readable and understandable. Original tape recordings of the interviews in Chapters 4, 6, and 8, with commentary, are now available from University Associates, Inc. They reveal how realistic simulated case studies can be.

A demonstration is not scientific proof. The exact extent to which the interview objective influences the method chosen, the way the method calls for the selection of certain skills from an interviewer's repertoire, and the extent to which training can be facilitated by these differences are problems that can be accurately answered only by research. Until that time, we must be satisfied with approximations and insightful hunches, rather than scientific laws. The interactions reported in this book will permit the reader to reach his own conclusions about cause and effect and the validity of some of the human relations principles set forth.

Work with groups has made it clear to me that a great deal can be learned by working with specific experiences and that discussions at the conceptual level lead to disagreements without adequate understanding of the points of view that are expressed. Concepts are difficult to communicate and attempts to express them lead to agreements without understanding, disagreements about semantics, and misunderstandings.

For purposes of learning and communication it is best to deal with specifics. What happened in a particular interview is raw, live data that can be used for discussion and analysis. If a superior asks a question and a subordinate becomes defensive, the cause-and-effect relationship can be explored whether or not it conforms with generally accepted concepts. A particular event can be more clearly communicated and discussed than a generalization because there are fewer possible meanings for the event. For example, a group of executives might agree that the concept of delegation of authority is a good thing and advocate that it be stressed in a training program. However, when a case study about the concept is under discussion, the same group may disagree on the question of whether the supervisor in the case took too much or too little freedom when a particular emergency condition arose. Causes for disagreements must be sought out and clarified to permit accurate communication; by a discussion of particular incidents, differences in viewpoint are made clear. Once there is communication at the level of particulars, it is possible to formulate and communicate generalizations.

The quotation from Picasso that was selected as the motto for this book, though it refers to painting, can be applied to role playing certain specific cases. There is basic truth in Picasso's saying that effective art can best be achieved by starting with the concrete and moving to the abstract. So it is with effective communication.

The discussion of cause-and-effect relationships in role-playing case material permits a degree of involvement that can never be achieved in textbook-type treatments. After actual incidents have been discussed, generalized statements and principles can be formulated and communicated. The six transcriptions in this book of the same problem situation offer a great deal from a study of particulars.

The question of whether role-playing cases adequately reveal the same principles as real-life situations must be raised. Some evidence supporting the view that the basic dynamics of interpersonal relations are present in role playing can be marshalled. Perhaps the most convincing observation, however, is that role-playing experience reduces rather than increases skepticism about the validity of role-playing interactions. Those who participate in role-playing situations experience real emotions, although the intensity may not be as great as in real-life situations. Skepticism, however, is desirable; we do not recommend gullibility.

After many years of study and observation of the appraisal-interview styles presented in this volume, it was apparent that the three basic interview styles are actually three ways in which two human beings interact when one attempts to influence the other. Thus, supervisor-employee, teacher-pupil, parent-child, salesman-customer interactions seem to follow the three patterns of interaction described in the book.

The Tell and Sell, the Tell and Listen, and the Problem-Solving approaches may be considered three models of influence. When a power factor is present, the persuasion approach, typified by the Tell and Sell method, predominates. The Tell and Listen method requires training to be effective; its value became apparent in the celebrated Hawthorne studies (Roethlisberger & Dickson, 1939). The Problem-Solving approach seems most natural in a setting in which power does not play a part in the inter-action and in which two people respect each other and search together for a better way to do something. Although certain skills are helpful in the Problem-Solving approach, this type of interaction can be encouraged by giving small groups a problem to solve. Problem solving is least likely to occur when one person already has a solution and wishes others to adopt it.

Since the book first appeared, a number of real-life studies of the appraisal interview as practiced by various organizations have been reported (Burke & Wilcox, 1969; Kay, Meyer, & French, 1965; Meyer & Walker, 1961; Meyer & Kay, 1964). The findings of these studies support the conclusions reached in our simulation experiments, which show the ineffectiveness of persuasion approaches by revealing the hostility generated and the failure to make satisfactory changes in behavior. It was thus unnecessary to modify the conclusions previously drawn from the simulation studies.

I am indebted to a number of individuals who have contributed knowingly and unknowingly to the development of the book; they are too numerous to mention. This revision has greatly benefited from the editorial suggestions and contributions of University Associates staff members Rebecca Taff and Dr. Anthony J. Reilly. I am especially indebted to the men who played the roles in the transcriptions and cooperated in the project for which the demonstrations were made: Dr. L. E. Danielson, Dr. L. R. Hoffman, Dr. R. A. McCleary, Dr. V. H. Vroom, Dr. James Dent, and Dr. L. M. Lansky. Dr. R. W. Heyns assisted me in planning the program and in training the role players. I appreciate the generosity of these associates and former students. As usual, my wife, Ayesha, gave liberally of her time and comments.

Norman R. F. Maier

Ann Arbor, Michigan
April 1976

Contents

CHAPTER ONE

The Appraisal Interview and Its Objectives

One of the most common executive development procedures is for the supervisor to appraise an employee's performance and interview the employee in connection with the appraisal. This procedure may be set up in various ways, but it is always adapted to the line organization and requires interviews.

Some Possible Problem Areas

The Need for Skill

Unless skillfully conducted, the interview may be an unpleasant experience for supervisor and employee, and the person interviewed may lose the motivation to improve. The skill of the interviewer is an important factor in the success of an interview; because interviews are conducted by supervisors at all levels, interviewing skill is a general managerial requisite. Fortunately, an interview that is satisfactory to the interviewer is likely to satisfy the one interviewed and can be a constructive experience for both.

The Need for Accuracy

One way to increase the success of appraisal programs is to improve the accuracy of the appraisal, assuming that a person will accept criticism that is constructive and true.[1] To achieve greater accuracy, committee appraisals, standardized rating procedures, and training programs for raters have been developed. These modifications make ratings more objective and less dependent on individual differences. Unfortunately, the desire to avoid unpleasantness in interviews actually introduces one of the major sources of error: the appraiser makes an evaluation generous to avoid hurt feelings and resistance in the interview. Thus, inaccuracy rather than accuracy may be encouraged by the interview, which, incidentally, is an unpleasant experience whenever a subordinate questions the appraisal.

The tendency to be generous, particularly among supervisors who are human relations oriented, means that appraisals have little value for decision making for promotions and transfers. Proponents of appraisal plans regret that evaluations so painstakingly made are not more widely used by higher management, but they do not realize that value judgments made with the coming interview in mind are bound to be quite different from those made with a promotion in mind.

Method vs. Skills

If a successful interview can not be achieved by improving the evaluation and appraisal procedures, it may be that the answer lies in the *type* of interview that is conducted or in the interviewer's skills. Two skilled interviewers may practice quite *different methods*. It may be that each method has its own specific skills and that more can be accomplished with whatever method is superior, even when skills are equal.

Once an interviewer differentiates between skill and method, the problem of developing skills is greatly simplified. No longer is it necessary to attempt to reconcile apparently contradictory skills, and the goals or objectives that the skills are intended to accomplish are also clarified. The problem of developing skills in any activity is simplified when the objective is made clear. For example, if the objective when driving a golf ball is direction rather than distance, the orientation of the body while swinging, rather than the force of the stroke, takes on meaning as a skill.

---

[1]See Chapter 12 for a more complete treatment of the need for accuracy in appraisal.

Conflicting Objectives

Management supervisors conduct appraisal interviews with subordinates to (a) let them know where they stand; (b) recognize good work; (c) communicate directions for improvement; (d) develop employees on their present jobs; (e) develop and train them for higher jobs; (f) let them know how they may make progress within the company; (g) serve as a record for assessment of the department or unit as a whole, showing where each person fits into the larger picture; and (h) warn certain employees that they must improve. It is frequently supposed that several or all of these objectives may be achieved by a single interview plan, but this is not true.

The differences among these objectives are slight in some cases, but even minor differences may affect the course of the interview. For example, "letting an employee know where he stands" suggests that a rather complete report should be given, but "recognizing an employee for good work" suggests that the interview should be favorable and more selective in content.

Another factor that sometimes affects the outcome is a discrepancy between the goals of the interviewer and those of the subordinate who is being evaluated. For example, a very superior employee has many virtues and few faults. The interviewer may make a minor criticism or pass off something as "satisfactory" in light of the praise given, forgetting that the superior person may see even the "satisfactory" category as a criticism and may feel crushed by any suggestion for improvement.

A very weak subordinate may be treated rather carefully by a supervisor because the latter does not wish to hurt the employee's feelings. The supervisor may call the employee's best point "quite satisfactory" although it is about average and then spend time praising the person for trying. Such an employee may emerge from the interview greatly relieved and perhaps more secure than he is entitled to feel.

When an appraisal interview is to serve as a warning that an employee has failed to improve, it is necessary to keep a record of the interview. Borderline employees frequently say, "No one has ever told me that I was doing an unsatisfactory job." As evidence that the employee has been warned, some companies require the employee to sign the appraisal. If a signature is required, an objective inconsistent with those of most of the other appraisal interviews has been injected into the plan.

Three Methods with Specific Objectives

The three interview methods used in this book have specific and slightly different objectives. The differences are highly important to determine the skills required by an interviewer, and to a great extent the methods need different skills from the interviewer's repertoire, as a very unique interaction sequence characterizes each of the methods. This qualitative difference makes the skill requirements for each interview specific to the method. The three appraisal interview methods described and demonstrated in this book are Tell and Sell, Tell and Listen, and Problem-Solving.

The Tell and Sell Method

Objectives

The initial objective of the Tell and Sell method is to communicate the employee's evaluation as accurately as possible. The accuracy and fairness of the evaluation are assumed. The supervisor must (a) let the employee know how he is doing; (b) gain the employee's acceptance of the evaluation; and (c) have the employee agree to follow a plan for improvement. The three objectives seem, at first glance, to be consistent with each other and attainable through a single method.

If it is also assumed that a person has a desire to correct his faults, that the judgment of the superior is acceptable to the subordinate, and that the subordinate has the ability to change in the direction specified, it is reasonable to suppose that the desired objectives can be achieved. However, it is not uncommon for subordinates to think that supervisors' expectations are unreasonable and their criticisms are unjustified or to think that the methods of work suggested are inefficient. It may not be reasonable, either, to expect a person to improve just because he wishes he could. Abilities to make wise decisions, to be patient, to get along with people, to conduct conferences, and to stand up under strain may be sought, but may not be subject to voluntary control, although abilities such as getting to work on time, turning in honest expense accounts, and doing more work are usually considered to be matters of volition. However, even some of these may require more than the desire to change them, and frequently they are as much a problem of emotional adjustment as of motivation. Emotional maladjustment may require therapy, and improper attempts on the part of an employer to make improvements may aggravate rather than correct the condition.

For purposes of discussion, we will assume that extreme and difficult cases are exceptions and that the interviewer has to deal with management personnel who probably are above average in their ability to take criticism.

Skill Requirements

The skills required for success in the Tell and Sell interview are considerable. They include the ability to persuade the person to change in the prescribed manner (and this may require the development of new needs in the person), as well as an ability to make use of the kinds of incentives that motivate each particular individual. The salesperson must know a client in order to influence him, and selling an evaluation makes the same demands on a supervisor who attempts to upgrade an employee.

The method is especially difficult if the supervisor encounters resistance. Because the interviewing supervisor sees himself as doing something for the good of the employee, failure on the part of the latter to appreciate this gesture places the supervisor on the defensive, and from this point on, the situation becomes strained or deteriorates into obvious hostility. This result, of course, is not part of the interviewing plan, and yet it sometimes happens despite anything the interviewer can do.

Usually, however, the employee senses the supervisor's increased aggression before actual hostility is apparent and refrains from questioning the evaluation. The passive resistance and verbal agreement that follow are often seen by the interviewer as acceptance of the evaluation. A failure to allow the subordinate to discuss the evaluation introduces a different difficulty. When the subordinate ceases to talk, the supervisor feels more obligated to talk and, consequently, lectures or preaches. This is something the supervisor does not plan to do during the session, and yet he may find himself dominating the discussion and unable to stop.

Potential Reactions

Defensive Feelings. Whether expressed through docility or overt behavior, defensive feelings are a natural reaction to the Tell and Sell interview situation, because the supervisor is cast in the role of a judge who has the diagnosis and the remedy. However, the person who is being judged is motivated to make as good a showing as possible. The employee would like to conceal any weaknesses and, if he feels the criticism is severe or the praise faint, is inclined to protest. If the criticism appears unjust (and this is bound to happen because the judge never knows all the circumstances and provocations) defensive responses are impossible to repress.

Face Saving. Once the subordinate questions the superior's evaluation, a face-saving situation is created and, unless the interviewer is very patient or something happens to break the chain of events that naturally comes from this type of conflict, the relationship continues to deteriorate. Without unusual interviewing skill or a salvaging event, someone must lose face. Because the superior usually has some degree of power, it is the subordinate who invariably learns to give in. Actually, subordinates often can develop a degree of insensitivity and not become unduly disturbed by criticism on these occasions. The employee's viewpoint can be expressed as "everybody gets criticized during appraisal interviews, so you just take it with a grain of salt." Some interviewers attempt to comfort their subordinates by saying that they themselves are also evaluated and criticized.

Motivational Factors

Although an appraisal interview of the Tell and Sell type may be unpleasant for both parties, this does not mean that it lacks merit. It may be that correction is necessarily unpleasant. Most of us can recall ways in which we have discarded faults because of criticisms that once were painful. There is no question but that faulty behavior can be inhibited or replaced when someone points out a better way. The crucial issue is to find the most effective way or the most dependable approach. Both training and motivation are essential to any change.

When an employee lacks the ability to do a job in the way a superior desires, the problem is whether to train or transfer. If the person is worthy of being developed on the present job, then the interviewer needs to clarify the job demands so that the subordinate knows what is expected. He also must indicate where and how the subordinate can acquire the desired knowledge or skills.

Because people usually want to do a job in an effective way and behave in the proper fashion, there is motivation to adopt correct methods and habits. Even approval from the boss may be an important source of motivation.

Sometimes, however, employees have their own views about a job or are inclined to continue as they have previously because they do not wish to show a lack of ability to change. If employees have "bad habits" or are negligent in certain respects, they may resist the change because the undesirable behavior is attractive to them. Whenever one kind of behavior is more attractive to an employee than another, motivational conditions must change to produce a modification. One way to make the old behavior unattractive is to use punishment and threats of discharge. This is similar to removing an undesirable growth through surgery. The *operative* approach is unpleasant for the employee, who must either do without the desired behavior or suffer undesirable consequences.

A second method is to make another behavior attractive by rewarding it or promising a better future for the person if a given change is made. This is the *substitution* approach and it is usually more pleasant and effective than the *operative* approach, not only because the threat of punishment is unnecessary, but also because an alternative is supplied. For example, a child's emotional disturbance will be reduced if a toy that has been removed is replaced by another, and a smoker will find it somewhat easier to give up cigarettes by substituting gum. However, something pleasant (a reward) must be added to the alternative to make the choice attractive and voluntary.

Both approaches require that an external motivating factor be added to one of the alternatives; a negative incentive (punishment) must be connected with the undesirable behavior, or a positive incentive (reward) must be connected with the acceptable alternative. This form of motivation is *extrinsic*, or external to the activity itself, in contrast to *intrinsic* motivation, where the activity itself is satisfying and is chosen for its own sake (e.g., the motivation for walking to reach a restaurant is extrinsic; the motivation for walking for pleasure is intrinsic). When extrinsic motivation is used to correct behavior, the new way is not accepted for its own sake, but for the products of the activity. Undoubtedly, if an employer knows an employee's needs, he can find highly effective incentives, but such an approach can only lead to extrinsic forms of motivation.

Because of the limited motivation and the defensive attitudes that are aroused, the Tell and Sell method lacks effectiveness. A selling situation permits two possibilities: either the product is bought or it is not, although the product may be accepted with limited enthusiasm. Frequently, the subordinate buys the evaluation, or says he does, in order to get out of the interview situation. Regardless of the degree of acceptance a subordinate has for a supervisor's judgment or plan, a selling situation permits only two possibilities: continue as before or change to the superior's plan. However, plans for improving a work situation and ways of dealing with a behavior problem can seldom be reduced to two possibilities.

When To Use Tell and Sell

Favorable Conditions. No plan can be expected to be satisfactory in all situations, and an approach that is effective in one situation may fail in another. The Tell and Sell method has its greatest potential with young and/or new employees, who may be inexperienced and insecure and want the advice and assurance of an authority figure. The superior is likely to be respected, not only because of position, but also because knowledge and experience are so obviously greater. To a considerable degree, this same favorable condition prevails when the employee is new on an assignment; mutually recognized inexperience with a given assignment of any kind tends to assure a favorable reaction to the Tell and Sell method.

Individual differences also play a part in reactions to the Tell and

Sell method. Persons who are easygoing, uncritical, and somewhat un-imaginative, and who accept authoritarian leadership should be most able to profit from the method.

From a company's point of view, it is an efficient method, providing it works. It takes less time to present an evaluation than to discuss one and, if the person interviewed accepts the presentation, a fairly complete evaluation can be covered in fifteen minutes. However, if the subordinate resists the appraisal, the time required may be considerable.

Unfavorable Conditions. Although the Tell and Sell method may pro-duce positive results under favorable conditions, it also may be harmful. The method becomes undesirable if the harmful effects exceed the gains. For this reason, an interviewer must examine the possible gains in light of the price that must be paid for them.

When subordinates perceive appraisals as unfair, they may feel unappreciated and think that their interests and those of the company are no longer the same. Loyalty depends on *mutual interests* and both super-visors and the company may lose employees' loyalties in the process of conducting appraisal interviews.

If the exchange becomes personal, face-saving problems come up; these may extend beyond an interview and strain the day-to-day relation-ship between superior and subordinate. If each finds the relationship un-pleasant and stressful, these feelings depress job satisfaction for both.

The greatest risk, particularly where appraisals include middle and top management, occurs when the subordinate accepts the judgment of the superior and tries to please him rather than give his own best think-ing to the job. Every language has a word for a "yes man" and no superior wishes to develop one, yet the Tell and Sell method is bound to encourage this kind of reaction. Using the method, the superior assumes that he knows best; he is the parental figure and the dispenser of rewards and punishments. An executive who relies on Tell and Sell expects employees to want to please him, and they soon learn to know what is expected of them. Often, they compete with each other to gain favors. Although the boss may ask subordinates to make independent judgments and take the initiative, the fact that the boss appraises and recommends motivates the weaker among them to find out what the boss wants and then do it his way. Even adopting the boss's manners and dress can forestall criticism, be-cause no executive can criticize a person for following in his footsteps. Dependent and docile behavior is likely to be developed in those with whom the method works best; individualistic and rebellious behavior may be produced in those who are least able to profit. Neither extreme is desirable.

Underlying Organizational Philosophy. Organizations vary in the extent to which they are conservative at one extreme and receptive to new methods, fads, and ideas at the other. When decisions are made from the top down, it is difficult for anything new to enter the organization, except at the top. New values can enter the organization if top personnel are recruited from outside, but this requires overcoming resistance to change down the line. Because the Tell and Sell interview is a form of downward communication that makes no provision for upward communication, the perpetuation of existing values is one of its pronounced effects. Although changes can occur effectively when initiated from the top or when approved by the proper superiors, methods for stimulating and discovering new ideas are not built into the plan. The Tell and Sell method of developing employees promotes conservatism rather than change, and insofar as conservatism has merit, the Tell and Sell method is effective in assuring it.

The Tell and Listen Method

Objectives

The Tell and Listen method is somewhat unnatural for an interviewer and he often views it with skepticism because he must be a bit ambiguous about authority to use it. The general idea of the Tell and Listen interview is to communicate the evaluation to the employee and then wait for a response. This means that the interviewer covers the strong and weak points of a subordinate's job performance during the first part of the interview and avoids interruption and controversy by postponing any points of disagreement for later consideration. The second part of the interview is devoted to thoroughly exploring the subordinate's feelings about the evaluation. The superior is still in the role of a judge, but he always listens to disagreement and defensive behavior without attempting to refute any statements. Actually, the interviewer encourages the employee to disagree and to express feelings, because he sees the objective as not only to communicate an appraisal, but also to allow the release of feelings aroused by the evaluation. The value of catharsis, that the verbal expression or release of frustrated feelings tends to reduce or remove them, is assumed.

Skill Requirements

Accepting Defensive Reactions. Initially, reactions to the Tell and Listen method are similar to those for the Tell and Sell method because both begin with the presentation of the evaluation. However, they differ radically in the way disagreement and resistance are handled. Instead of dominating the discussion to clarify his views, the interviewer encourages the subordinate to disagree with the evaluation and to relate his own feel-ings. Thus, the interviewer is a nondirective counselor (Rogers, 1942) during the second part of the interview.

The skills of the Tell and Listen approach are (a) *active listening*—to refrain from talking and to accept and try to understand the employee's attitudes and feelings; (b) effective *use of pauses*—to wait patiently and avoid embarrassment, knowing that a pause will cause the other person to talk; (c) *reflection of feelings*—to respond to feelings to show under-standing; and (d) *summarizing of feelings*—to indicate progress, to show understanding, and to point up aspects of the problem, as well as to wrap up the interview. None of these skills requires that the interviewer either agree or disagree with what is said. Rather, he strives to communicate that he understands the subordinate's position; he entertains the possibility that the evaluation may be unjust and even incorrect; and he reveals that he wants the employee to take from the appraisal only ideas that may be helpful.

Potential Reactions

Face Saving Reduced. Because it is assumed at the outset that there are two sides to the appraisal, face-saving issues are not aggravated and the superior is not caught in a situation where he feels the need to defend his evaluation. He does not expect the subordinate to agree and is not disappointed when the employee resists. The unpleasant aspects of the appraisal interview are reduced when the superior has a method for dealing with defensive responses and when he is in a better position to under-stand and respect feelings. For this reason, the manager who is able to practice the Tell and Listen method is less inclined to avoid appraisal interviews than is the Tell and Sell interviewer, who may be overanxious and overprepared to fend off signs of resistance.

Motivational Factors

The motivational factors in the Tell and Listen interview are complex. Fears of reprisal and of displeasing the superior are reduced, so most motivational factors associated with fear of displeasing the superior are weakened, if not lost. Unadaptive defensive behavior fanned in part by these same fears is also reduced. Thus, *resistance to change* is over-come or reduced by the counseling process, and the desire to change to avoid displeasing the boss is sacrificed. Which of these two opposed motivations is of greater value undoubtedly varies from one individual to another.

The positive motivation that is created by having a pleasant exper-ience with the boss is undoubtedly greater for the Tell and Listen type of interview than for the Tell and Sell type, because the former reduces any hostility that may have been engendered. In addition, it makes the subordinate feel accepted and even important. This is conducive to the formation of a constructive attitude—so essential to growth. A subordinate is more likely to want to please a supervisor he likes than one he fears. When fear is the dominant motive, a person, at best, shies away from wrongdoing but does not extend himself to perform beyond the call of duty.

Up to this point, the motivational factors discussed have been *extrinsic*—that is, the incentives lie outside the job activity but the task or work itself has not been made more interesting, although some increase in job satisfaction may come about. Interest in a job depends on the work itself and on the social climate in which it is performed. An employee who likes the boss will find the job more satisfying than an employee who fears or dislikes the boss. Other employees also influence job interest, and a supervisor who respects and knows how to deal with feelings is able to reduce strains in interpersonal relationships and create a relaxed and friendly social climate. Any change in job interest represents a form of *intrinsic motivation*.

A more important intrinsic motivation is present if the interview results in (a) solving some job problems; (b) clarifying certain misunderstandings between supervisor and subordinate; or (c) solving a personal problem. The motivational possibilities vary from individual to individual and are greater when an employee's performance shows deficiencies that can be corrected.

If the superior listens and learns from the interview, additional intrinsic motivational gains are possible. The superior can modify job assignments and expectations; alter his evaluation; perceive the subordinate's job differently; and discover his own negligence in training and assisting. These gains tend to depend upon an exceptional interviewer, however, because the appraisal has been made prior to the interview and a previous commitment reduces the interviewer's ability to see inaccuracies or injustices in the appraisal (Maier, 1973a).

When To Use Tell and Listen

Favorable and Unfavorable Results. The result that the Tell and Listen interview is most likely to produce is a good relationship between superior and subordinate during the interview. The employee is likely to leave with a positive feeling and with a favorable attitude toward the supervisor. He is likely to regard the interview as worthwhile and feel important to the company as an individual. The superior can profit from what he learns about the employee's needs and aspirations and should not be misled by a defensive attitude or feelings expressed emotionally.

There is a risk, however, that the interview may not achieve its first objective, letting the employee know where he stands. Although the employee may change, depending on new insights, he is not likely to discover ways to improve the job. An employee may leave the interview with satisfaction, but not necessarily with a program for developing on the job.

Underlying Organizational Philosophy. The values promoted by the Tell and Listen interview are tolerance and respect for the dignity of the individual. Any supervisor who tries to understand a subordinate's viewpoint experiences an increased respect for the employee, so the method tends to make management personnel employee minded rather than production minded. Because supervisors who are employee centered tend, in general, to stimulate higher morale than others (Katz, Maccoby, & Morse, 1950) this influence may be a constructive one. However, simply because high morale and higher productivity frequently are related, it does not mean that there may not be variations in productivity among groups that have equally high morale.

The fact that the interviewer may profit from the appraisal interview is one of the greatest potential values of the Tell and Listen method. Change initiated from below can occur because a subordinate is able to influence a superior's views on how the job may be improved by changes in (a) supervision; (b) work methods; (c) job assignments; and (d) job expectations. Very often the people who supervise the work of others once performed the jobs of those they now supervise. This causes them to expect the job to be performed much as they themselves did it (Read, 1962). Because individuals differ, and times as well as jobs change, this expectation may be unreasonable, impractical, or biased—yet it is most understandable. The expectations of a superior, under the best circumstances, tend to restrict freedom, stifle initiative, and inhibit improvements that have their origin with subordinates. Although some of the loss in new ideas from below may be recaptured by suggestion boxes, it is important not to stifle new ideas through an appraisal program that was designed to develop employees. A supervisor who listens and learns may encourage upward communication in deed as well as in word; the belief that constructive forces for change can come from below may be an important part of organizational philosophy.

The Problem-Solving Method

Objectives

The Problem-Solving approach to an appraisal interview is a product of the author's research on problem solving and his studies of executive development. Of the three methods presented in this book, it deviates the most from commonly held management views. It is the only method that takes the interviewer out of the role of a judge and makes him a helper. Although the interviewer may always wish to be a helper to a subordinate, he can not escape retaining the role of a judge in the other two types of interview because the process of appraising is inconsistent with helping. Because an appraisal, by its nature, is an evaluation or judgment, it may appear that the purpose of the interview has been lost if the evaluation is not directly communicated to the subordinate. However, the development of the employee's performance often is the primary reason for conducting an appraisal interview and this objective may be lost in the process of communicating the evaluation directly.

Although the two methods discussed in the preceding sections communicate the appraisal to the subordinate, they do not assume his understanding and acceptance. The Problem-Solving approach, in contrast, has no provision for communicating the appraisal, and indeed it may not be essential to do so. If the appraisal is required for other purposes, it may be desirable to delay making it until after the interview.

The soundness of having the development of the employee's performance serve as the objective of the interview is apparent; this establishes a *mutual interest* between the interviewer and his subordinate. Both would like the employee to improve on the job and both would agree that the boss could assist in this improvement. When the subordinate accepts the supervisor as a helper, he is more willing to describe the nature of his difficulties. When the boss passes judgment on job performance, however, the interests conflict. The employee wants to impress his boss favorably and is motivated to cover up any weaknesses. The interviewer, on the other hand, would like to avoid being deceived and is inclined to discuss weaknesses that have come to his attention. The mutual interest factor in the traditional appraisal interview, therefore, is present only as long as the employee's merits are extolled and ends when the interviewer indicates that he is not satisfied.

Because job performance can also be improved by changes in the job itself, problem solving places attention on the situation, not on the individual. Subordinates are not on the defensive when discussing how their jobs can be made more satisfying and efficient. "Changing the job" explores an entirely different dimension of job performance and avoids the implication that individuals must change, which invariably leads to defensiveness.

Another way to improve job performance is to change the nature of the supervision. Superiors have great influence on the productivity of their subordinates, but subordinates are reluctant to be critical of their superior's style of supervision. Discussion of job-related factors can reveal problems in this area.

The Problem-Solving approach may show four ways in which the performance of subordinates can improve: (1) changing the subordinate's behavior; (2) changing the job duties or the job procedure; (3) changing jobs; and (4) changing the pattern of supervision. The Tell and Sell and the Tell and Listen approaches tend to limit improvement to the first of these four changes and this change is often the least acceptable to the subordinate.

Essential Attitudes

Although the objective of the Problem-Solving approach is improved job performance, the interviewer can not specify the area in which this development should take place because this constitutes diagnosis and judgment. The interviewer must limit his influence to stimulating thinking, rather than supplying remedies or solutions. He must be willing to accept for consideration all ideas on job improvement that the employee brings up. It is his function to discover the subordinate's interests so that he can respond to them and cause the employee to examine himself and his job duties. To accomplish these things, the interviewer must forget his own viewpoint and try to see the job as the employee sees it. If the employee's ideas seem impractical, the interviewer should explore the views expressed more thoroughly, using questions to learn more specifically what the employee has in mind. Often the ideas that are difficult to accept are ones that are misunderstood or viewed with a different mental set. Each person speaks from his own frame of reference, but each listener has a different frame of reference. Communication is faulty until the backgrounds, attitudes, and experiences of each are mutually understood.

When the interviewer finds that a subordinate's thinking is naïve and in need of upgrading, he must be willing to assume that a problem-solving discussion is the best way to stimulate growth and sophistication. If an employee can grow in this way, it is never necessary that he know he has had weaknesses and faults. The process may be analogous to the training of children; to learn to be graceful and skilled, they never need to know that they once were gawky and uncoordinated. As a matter of fact, they might improve more if left to themselves and not exposed to too much faultfinding. These assumptions are not easily converted to practice, largely because discriminating adults are so concerned with the faults they observe that it is difficult for them to suppress comments and advice. Wisdom and experience can be a handicap to an individual who directs the work of others, unless he knows how to share them in an acceptable manner.

Problem-solving behavior is characterized by the exploration and evaluation of a variety of solutions. It is inhibited whenever one person feels threatened by an evaluation, because this directs attention to the person rather than the situation. When people are placed in the spotlight, they are motivated to hide defects and alerted to protect themselves. Defensive behaviors are attempts to justify old behaviors, and as long as people defend their past actions they are not searching for new or better ways to perform. If an evaluation is very threatening it may induce frustration, which not only arouses hostile and childish behavior, but also promotes stubbornness. These behavior characteristics also delay problem solving because they are in direct opposition to rational thinking.

Skill Requirements

The skills associated with the Problem-Solving approach are consistent with the nondirective procedures discussed in connection with the Tell and Listen method: listening, accepting, and responding to feelings. The interviewer needs to be especially alert and notice any expression of concern during the introductory period. A remark such as, "Well, this is the day we get overhauled, I suppose," should be answered with a statement such as, "You consider these interviews somewhat rough on people in some ways, I suppose."

However, the objective of the Problem-Solving interview is to go beyond an interest in the subordinate's feelings. As soon as he is ready to discuss the job situation (and this may be at the very outset if the employee is not anxious about the interview), the interviewer can ask questions about the job. Such questions are directive in order to channel the subject of conversation, but nondirective about feelings that an employee can express.

In some situations, the employee's job description should be explored and its importance discussed. The interviewer may find differences in perceptions of what the job is that may account for some of the unfavorable points in the evaluation. For example, the interviewer may be surprised to learn that the subordinate sees the job as "getting an assignment finished on time, regardless of the feelings of others" and that he has this mistaken emphasis because of a previous reprimand. These differences should be passed over and should serve to enlighten the interviewer about misunderstandings and the need for better job descriptions, training, or communication.

In the typical appraisal interview with an employee of long standing, the job analysis may be omitted because it can be assumed that this understanding has been accomplished with previous interviews. The employee can be asked to review the year's progress and discuss the problems, needs, innovations, satisfactions, and dissatisfactions he has encountered. The idea is to make this interview the employee's opportunity to get the boss's ear.

To help a subordinate talk freely, it is desirable for the superior to consider all problems the employee wishes to raise. Restating ideas in somewhat different words is an effective way for the interviewer to test his understanding, and it demonstrates that the superior is interested in considering changes that are important to the subordinate. An interviewer need not agree or disagree with ideas to accept them. Understanding or accepting ideas is an important neutral position between agreeing and disagreeing.

When the employee's ideas are numerous, it may be wise for a supervisor to jot them down so they can be referred to later. Making a record of ideas is an act of accepting and considering without taking a stand for or against. Later, these same ideas can be evaluated to pick out the best ones.

Skillful questioning is an effective way for an interviewer to stimulate a subordinate to evaluate his own ideas. Questions should not be used to put an employee on the spot or indicate the weakness of a plan, but should indicate that the listener wants to hear the complete story. The following examples illustrate stimulating exploratory questions:

Can this plan of yours deal with an emergency situation, in case one arose?

Would you have other people at your level participate in the plan?

Could your own employees be induced to go along with the change?

What kinds of problems do you anticipate with a changing market?

Have you examined the plan from the point of view of quality control?

Nonthreatening exploratory questions are effective for drawing an employee out and making him think more clearly; in addition, they may serve to direct attention to areas that have been overlooked. The last two questions above are examples of broad questions, and the first three stimulate more detailed examination of a delineated area.

Skillful summarizing serves a variety of purposes, and opportunities for useful summaries usually occur several times during an appraisal interview. Effective summaries may be used to accomplish the following:

1. To restate the points already covered in a broader sense;

2. To demonstrate that the interviewer understands the ideas expressed up to the point at which the summary occurs;

3. To facilitate communication by creating opportunities to check and refine ideas; and

4. To separate what has been covered from the problems that remain unexplored.

The effective *use of pauses* is one of the most subtle skills and is useful in connection with the Problem-Solving method, as well as the Tell and Listen method. Ideas require thought, and if the interviewer interrupts the employee he disturbs a train of thought. By waiting patiently he gives the subordinate time to explore and evaluate. This is in contrast to the cross-examination some interviewers practice.

Motivational Factors

Problems offer opportunities to explore the unknown, and their solutions lead to new experiences. The statement of a problem can cause a group to engage in a lively problem-solving discussion. Curiosity is a strong drive and, as long as fear is not aroused, it leads to exploratory behavior. Children, for example, have a strong motivation to explore their surroundings when they are in a free and secure environment, but the exploration ceases when danger or threats of punishment are introduced. If a subordinate is free to analyze the job and expects to have an influence on any improvements that are made, he is immediately motivated to think constructively, rather than defensively. Some *extrinsic* motivational factors, such as gaining approval or avoiding failure, may be present, but essentially the problem-solving activity itself has interest value and is a form of *intrinsic* motivation. Intrinsic motivation is present in many of the things we like to do and is an important aspect of play. If intrinsic motivation could be made a larger part of the job, then work would become more like play and the problem of gaining acceptance of any changes would be nonexistent because employees would be carrying out their own solutions.

Sources of Job Satisfaction. An examination and a re-evaluation of the job description are bound to suggest some changes, because there always are aspects of the job that give more satisfaction (or less dissatisfaction) than others. Usually, how to maximize the best features and how to minimize the poorer ones are topics of mutual interest for the interviewer and the subordinate.

When the job itself is a topic for consideration, it is apparent that there are four distinctly different ways in which job satisfaction may be improved. These are (a) the job itself may be reorganized, enlarged, subdivided, or rescheduled; (b) the subordinate's perception of the job and the meanings of its various aspects may be changed; (c) the superior's understanding of the job problems may be increased so that he will relate differently to his subordinates, supply assistance in the form that is needed, or improve communication; and (d) the opportunity may be created for solving problems that are of a group nature, involving all of the subordinates who report to the interviewer.

When To Use Problem Solving

Favorable and Unfavorable Results. Since problem solving can lead to so many different approaches to job satisfaction, improvement seems possible for every employee. If no acceptable solutions come under discussion, the interviewer can ask questions to explore various possibilities and a selection can be made in terms of practicality and interest. If the goal of the interview is to experiment and to improve the job situation in line with the employee's wishes, then problem solving gives good assurance that a change in the desired direction will occur.

If the subordinate recommends changes that conflict with the goals of the company or the superior, the superior may respond by asking how the change can take place without being unfair to other employees or without violating company objectives. Invariably, such questions lead to further clarification. Superiors often turn down suggestions prematurely because they see obstacles in the path of the change, but if an obstacle is discussed, ways to avoid it may be discovered or the subordinate may realize that he has overlooked certain consequences of a new plan. Ideas that seem impractical can be tabled for future consideration and the exploration can be directed to other topics. An interview can give considerable satisfaction, even if only one of many new ideas can be implemented.

If a subordinate has no ideas and fails to respond to the Problem-Solving approach, it may be assumed that this method has failed, but this does not preclude use of one of the other two methods.

Underlying Organizational Philosophy. One of the unique advantages of the Problem-Solving approach is that it affords both participants a highly favorable opportunity to learn and communicate. Usually, training and developing others is a one-way process: the superior gives knowledge and know-how, and the subordinate receives them. The Problem-Solving approach, like the Tell and Listen method, offers the interviewer an opportunity to learn because it stimulates upward communication. Unlike Tell and Listen, Problem-Solving also creates a climate for high-quality decisions and changes because it pools the thinking of those most likely to have supplementary experiences. The Problem-Solving approach allows an interviewer not only to remove sources of frustration through *listening* skills, but to activate or stimulate change through discussion of a problem.

The interviewer is most likely to have the proper attitude for effective problem solving if he understands that effective plans, decisions, and ideas must be not only factually sound, but also acceptable to the persons who must implement them. This attitude encourages an interviewer to respect the problem-solving ability of each subordinate and to place mutual interests above personal interests. A favorable opportunity to explore a problem with an experienced and understanding superior can stimulate a subordinate's thinking and lead to increased job interest, as well as to a better utilization of a subordinate's talents.

The Problem-Solving method cuts across barriers created by rank and places the attention on mutual interests, rather than on prerogatives, status, and personality clashes. To use the method an interviewer assumes that change is an essential part of an organization and that participation in change is essential to healthy growth.

Figure 1 outlines the three types of appraisal interviews described on previous pages and compares them on ten different variables. Because the psychological assumptions vary considerably from one method to another, quite different outcomes may result from their use, as discussed previously.

As shown in the table, the underlying psychological assumptions differ for each type of interview and seem to be dependent on the desired objectives. The objectives an interviewer has determine the role he will play and the role he feels he must play determines the attitude he will have, as well as which skills he will use. The interviewer's attitudes and skills, in turn, influence the interviewee's reactions to the situation and his desire to change. How the latter reacts determines the possible gains and the probable results of a given interview situation. All these things also depend, in part, on the personalities of the participants. All aspects must be studied carefully before an interviewer decides which method to use in a given situation. His decision may also be influenced by whether he wishes to perpetuate existing organizational values or to stimulate initiative from below.

METHOD	TELL AND SELL	TELL AND LISTEN	PROBLEM-SOLVING
Objectives	To communicate evaluation To persuade employee to improve	To communicate evaluation To release defensive feelings	To stimulate growth and development in employee
Psychological Assumptions	Employee desires to correct weaknesses if he knows them Any person can improve if he so chooses A superior is qualified to evaluate a subordinate	People will change if defensive feelings are removed	Growth can occur without correcting faults Discussing job problems leads to improved performance
Role of Interviewer	Judge	Judge	Helper
Attitude of Interviewer	People profit from criticism and appreciate help	One can respect the feelings of others if one understands them	Discussion develops new ideas and mutual interests
Skills of Interviewer	Salesmanship Patience	Listening and reflecting feelings Summarizing	Listening and reflecting feelings Reflecting ideas Using exploratory questions Summarizing
Reactions of Employee	Suppresses defensive behavior Attempts to cover hostility	Expresses defensive behavior Feels accepted	Problem-solving behavior
Employee's Motivation for Change	Use of positive or negative incentives or both Extrinsic: motivation is added to the job itself	Resistance to change reduced Positive incentive Extrinsic and some intrinsic motivation	Increased freedom Increased responsibility Intrinsic motivation—interest is inherent in the task
Possible Gains	Success most probable when employee respects interviewer	Employee develops favorable attitude toward superior, which increases probability of success	Almost assured of improvement in some respect
Risks of Interviewer	Loss of loyalty Inhibition of independent judgment Face-saving problems created	Need for change may not be developed	Employee may lack ideas Change may be other than what superior had in mind
Probable Results	Perpetuates existing practices and values	Permits interviewer to change his views in light of employee's responses Some upward communication	Both learn, because experience and views are pooled Change is facilitated

Figure 1. Comparisons Among Three Types of Appraisal Interviews

CHAPTER TWO

Testing Three Methods in a Role-Play Situation

A Case for Role Play

To test the accuracy of the analysis of the three methods given in the first chapter and the overall effect of each method on the participants, a role-playing case previously used for developing skill in appraisal interviewing was selected because it had been found to raise issues and bring responses typical of those found in real-life appraisal interviews.

In role playing, compared with actual situations, there is a tendency for interviewers to be more patient, considerate, and conscious of human relations. In contrast, interviewees are inclined to be more outspoken and less concerned with human relations in role-playing situations. These differences mean that role-playing situations are more delicate and more difficult for an interviewer and make better training exercises than real-life situations. Skills that are only adequate for role playing are probably quite satisfactory for real-life interviews.

In general, role-playing interactions simulate those found in real life. For skill practice, demonstrations, and research, role playing is especially useful because the same case conditions can be used repeatedly for purposes of testing either methods or skills.

Role-Play Situation: The Evaluation Interview

The situation used for this study involved two persons: George Stanley, the interviewer, and his subordinate, a first-line supervisor named Tom Burke. Observers, as well as individuals selected to play these roles, studied the General Instructions, which set up background conditions and common knowledge about the job appraised and the situation. In addition, each participant was given some private information detailing his perceptions and personal feelings about the way things were going, which could conform or conflict with those of the other participant. The instructions entitled Role Sheet for George Stanley, Section Head, were studied by the persons acting as the interviewer, and the instructions entitled Role Sheet for Tom Burke, Supervisor, were studied by those playing the interviewee.

General Instructions

George Stanley is the electrical section head in the engineering department of the American Construction Company. The work in the department includes designing, drafting, making cost estimates, keeping maps up to date, checking standards and building codes, doing field inspection and follow-up, etc. Eight first-line supervisors report to Stanley. Their duties are partly technical and partly supervisory. The organizational chart for the section is shown in Figure 2.

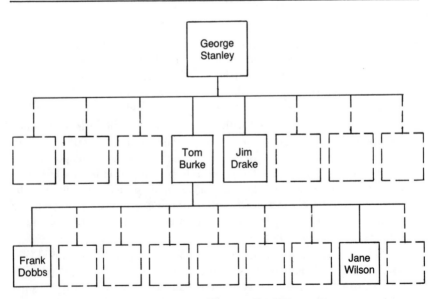

Figure 2. Organizational Chart for Electrical Section

Company policy requires that each section head interview the supervisors under him once a year. The purpose is to (a) evaluate each supervisor's performance during the year; (b) give recognition for jobs well done; and (c) correct weaknesses. The appraisal interviews were introduced because the company believes that employees should know how they stand and that everything possible should be done to develop management personnel.

Tom Burke, who reports to Stanley, has a B.S. degree in electrical engineering; in addition to his technical duties, which often take him to the field, he supervises the work of one junior designer, six draftsmen, and two clerks. He is highly paid, as are all of the supervisors in this department, because of the job's high requirements in technical knowledge. Burke has been with the company for twelve years and has been a supervisor for two years. He is married and has two children. He owns a home and is active in the civic affairs of the community.

Role Sheet for George Stanley, Section Head

You have evaluated all the supervisors who report to you and during the next two weeks will interview each of them, hoping to use the interviews constructively. Today you have arranged to interview *Tom Burke,* one of the eight first-line supervisors who report to you. Burke's file contains the following information and evaluation:

Tom Burke: twelve years with company, two years as supervisor, college degree, married, two children. Evaluation: highly creative and original, exceptionally competent technically. His unit is very productive and during the two years he has supervised the group there has been a steady improvement. Within the past six months, he has been given extra work and he has done this on schedule. As far as productivity and dependability are concerned, he is the section's top supervisor.

To your knowledge, however, Burke's cooperation with other supervisors in the section leaves much to be desired. Before you made him a supervisor, his originality and technical knowledge were available to your whole section. Gradually, he has withdrawn and now acts like a lone wolf. You have asked other supervisors to talk over certain problems with him, but they tell you he offers no suggestions. He tells them he is busy, listens with little interest to their problems, kids them, or makes sarcastic remarks, depending on his mood. On one occasion, he allowed *Jim Drake,* one of the supervisors in another unit, to make a mistake that could have been forestalled if he had let Drake know the status of certain design changes. You expect supervisors to cooperate on matters involving design changes that affect them.

Furthermore, during the past six months, Burke has been unwilling to take two assignments. He said they were routine and that he preferred more interesting work; he advised you to give the assignments to other supervisors. To prevent trouble, you followed his suggestion. However, you feel that you can not give him all the interesting work and that if he persists in this attitude there will be trouble. You can not play favorites and keep up morale in your unit.

Burke's failure to cooperate has you worried for another reason. Although his group is highly productive, there is more turnover among his draftsmen than in other groups. You have heard no complaints yet, but you suspect that he may be treating his employees in an arbitrary manner. Certainly if he is stubborn with you and other supervisors, he is likely to be even more so with his crew. Apparently, the high productivity in his group is not due to high morale, but to his ability to use his workers to do the things for which they are best suited. You feel this method will not develop good draftsmen and it may encourage them to leave. You hope to discuss these matters with Burke in a way that recognizes his good points and at the same time corrects some of his weaknesses.

Role Sheet for Tom Burke, Supervisor

One junior designer, six draftsmen, and two clerks report to you. You feel that you get along fine with your group. You have always been pretty much of an "idea" person and apparently have the knack of passing on your enthusiasm to others in your group. There is a lot of "we" feeling in your unit because it is obvious that your group is the most productive.

You believe in developing your employees and always give them strong recommendations. You think you have gained the reputation of doing this, because they frequently go out and find much better jobs. Since promotion is necessarily slow in a company such as yours, you feel that the best way to stimulate morale is to develop new personnel and demonstrate that a good worker can move up. The members of your unit are bright and efficient and there is a lot of good-natured kidding. Recently one of the clerks, *Jane Wilson*, turned down an outside offer that paid thirty-five dollars a month more, because she preferred to stay in your group. You are going to ask Stanley for a raise for her the first chance you have.

The other supervisors in Stanley's section do not have your enthusiasm. Some of them are dull and unimaginative. During your first year as supervisor, you helped them a lot, but you soon found that they leaned on you and before long you were doing their work. There is a lot of pressure to produce. You received your promotion by producing and you do not intend to let other supervisors interfere. Because you no longer help the other supervisors, your production has gone up, but a couple of them seem a bit sore at you. *Frank Dobbs,* your junior designer, is a better worker than most of the supervisors and you would like to see him made a supervisor. Stanley ought to recognize that the company has some deadwood and assign the more routine jobs to those units. Then they would not need your help and you could concentrate your efforts on jobs that suit your unit. At present, Stanley passes out work pretty much as he receives it. Because you are efficient, you receive more than your share of routine jobs, and you see no reason why the extra work should not be in the form of "plums." This would motivate units to turn out work. When you suggested to Stanley that he turn over some of the more routine jobs to other supervisors, he did it, but he was very reluctant.

You did one thing recently that has bothered you. There was a design change in a set of plans and you should have told *Jim Drake* (a fellow supervisor) about it, but it slipped your mind. Drake was out when you had it on your mind, and then you were involved in a hot idea that Dobbs (your junior designer) had and forgot all about Drake. As a result, Drake had to make a lot of unnecessary changes and he was quite sore about it. You told him you were sorry and offered to make the changes, but he turned down the offer.

Today you have an interview with Stanley, required by the company's management-development plan. It should not take very long, but it will be nice to have the boss tell you about the job you are turning out. Maybe there will be a raise in it; maybe he'll tell you something about what to expect in the future.

Background and Preparation of Participants

Tom Burke. Three advanced graduate students in psychology with role-play experience were asked to play Tom Burke at a demonstration of the three types of appraisal interviews given for management personnel. The students were not told that different interview styles were being tested. They were asked to play the role spontaneously and were not rehearsed.

George Stanley. The three interviewers (also advanced graduate students) were given preliminary practice sessions, each with a different method. An instructor played Tom Burke's part and the author served as critic. The interviewer who was to use Tell and Sell was asked to communicate the appraisal and to persuade the subordinate to accept it. He was told to use whatever ingenuity he had to achieve his objective but to stay within the framework of the assigned method. The purpose of the practice session was to train him to stay within the bounds of the method and to exploit techniques compatible with it. During the practice session, he was interrupted whenever he was not consistent with the Tell and Sell method.

The student who was to demonstrate the two Tell and Listen interviews was instructed to (a) communicate the appraisal as accurately as possible; (b) avoid arguing or selling; and (c) use nondirective counseling skills to allow the subordinate to express and clarify his feelings. He was told that he might avoid interruptions while communicating the appraisal if he told the subordinate that he would like to hear reactions to the evaluation but thought it best to first complete the appraisal.

The student who was to conduct the two Problem-Solving interviews was asked to dismiss any thought of communicating the appraisal. He was told to talk about any aspect of the job that interested the subordinate and to explore, from the subordinate's point of view, any new ideas to improve the job. He was told to be alert to any of the employee's statements that expressed a feeling about the interview, the job, or the supervisor himself, especially in the early part of the interview, when some time is usually spent in "small talk." He was told that an early response to the employee's feelings might be the best way to explore problems of vital concern to the employee.

If the subordinate asked how his performance had been appraised, the interviewer was told to avoid a direct answer. He could say, "Although the company asks us to make appraisals, I find I can get a better picture of what's going on in your job by having *you* tell *me* how things are going" or "Our real objective is not to appraise the employee but to appraise the job and to do what we can to gain a better understanding of the job and the employee's abilities and interests." Responses like this tend to turn the problem back to the employee and encourage him to talk.

During the practice period, the interviewer was interrupted several times when he missed opportunities to follow up on feelings or tended to follow a preconceived plan.

Each interviewer received preliminary instruction until he understood his particular interview style and felt comfortable using it. The interviewers had no opinions about which of the three methods would produce the best results. Each expected problems with his own method, but was motivated to accomplish his objective.

Demonstration and Recording of the Interviews

Each of the three interviews was demonstrated and recorded twice, on two successive days, in front of two different groups of about 250 supervisors each. The interviewers used the assigned method on both occasions, but the Tom Burkes were rotated so that they later could compare their experiences with two different methods.

Preceding the demonstration, the General Instructions were read to the whole audience; in addition, a copy of the Role Sheet for George Stanley was supplied to half the audience, and a copy of the Role Sheet for Tom Burke was supplied to the other half, so that half of the observers identified with the interviewer and the other half with the interviewee.

After each demonstration, the instructor made some general comments to set the stage for a general discussion of the participants' feelings. However, he could not supply the word count and other details given in the tables. Audience reactions were obtained from both groups of observers. Because the "Stanley identifiers" and the "Burke identifiers" were seated in different sections of the auditorium, it was possible to address questions to each group separately and to compare their opinions about the way the participants felt and about the objectives achieved by each interview. The questions were designed to discover trends in opinions, and responses were made largely by a show of hands. Contributions from the floor were welcomed, however, and sometimes requested. The questions were not designed to produce exact data, but to reveal the variety of reactions engendered. Each observer could then compare his personal reactions with those of other segments of the audience. After the observers' reactions were recorded and the feelings of both participants had been surmised, the questioning was directed to Burke and Stanley.

Role Play vs. "Real Life"

Although their reactions may not have been typical of "real life," the role players had certain genuine feelings and opinions about the experience and the role play was a valid opportunity for the observers to form judgments about the situation. Everyone had an opportunity to determine how well he could judge feelings from behavior. Members of the audience often had very different opinions about the feelings of the role players, a fact that demonstrates that observers often judge how others feel not so much by how others behave, but by how they themselves would feel in that situation.

Role playing is a useful technique to train observers to detect feelings. Both observers and participants in role-play situations soon realize how lifelike role playing can be. Although it may not be identical with real life, it allows cause-and-effect relationships to be accurately studied because the same appraisal condition can be repeated, using different interview styles. In the six interviews analyzed in the next chapters, the same background data were furnished and an employee with specified virtues and faults was interviewed using three different methods. No real-life situation can be duplicated and retested this way.

Use of Transcriptions and Analysis

The extent to which the role-play reactions conform to real-life behavior must be left to the judgment of the reader. The analyses accompanying these interviews should sharpen a reader's perceptions and make him more sensitive to feelings that are either unobserved or misjudged in real-life interviews.

The transcriptions of the recordings have been paired by interview style to emphasize the importance of the interviewer's assigned method and his skill in dealing with two different interviewees. The author's critical comments are supplied to permit the reader to draw his own conclusions about the merits of the methods and what was accomplished with each. Following each of the transcriptions, an evaluation section with an analysis of the interaction, reactions of the audience, and reactions of the participants gives readers a sense of being present for the interviews.

For the reader to most fully appreciate the dynamics of the interaction between Stanley and Burke, it is best to omit, during the first reading of the dialogue, the comments that follow each speech. The interview should be reread after an impression has been formed and each comment critically examined in connection with the speech that precedes it. The second reading should heighten the reader's critical ability so that he will be more sensitive to cause-and-effect sequences in situations of this type; it is evident that the role of a judge and the role of a helper are in conflict. Three transcriptions can be read identifying with Tom Burke and three identifying with George Stanley. The reader may wish to place a card over Stanley's actual responses to Burke's remarks and practice making responses of his own before reading Stanley's. This method is very effective for self-training in interviewing technique.

Skill, Personality, and Method Factors

The success of role-play interviews depends on (a) the situation described on the role sheets; (b) the personality of the interviewee; (c) the skill and personality of the interviewer; and (d) the method used by the interviewer. Because the situational factors and the interviewer's influence were the same for all three pairs of interviews, observable differences can be assumed to be the result of one of the other factors, and information about the interviewer's influence on the outcome can be collected. Differences in results obtained using the same method and the same interviewer are probably caused by personality differences between the interviewees and purely chance factors. It is possible, also, that the influence of the interviewee's personality on the outcome may vary from one method to another.

Skill and Personality. To isolate skill and personality factors completely from method factors, it would be necessary to use more than one interviewer to demonstrate each method, but that would require many more transcriptions. Comparisons between two interviews of the same type conducted by the same interviewer (on successive days) should reveal the skill and personality of each interviewer. In this case, the skills of the interviewer were in part equalized by their selection and training; the question of personality differences can be answered in part by the author's assurance that the interactions obtained are typical of the many he has witnessed with different personalities in the same parts. Whether a favorable or unfavorable reaction is caused by the interviewer's skill or by his method often can be determined by examining alternatives to selected statements the interviewer makes, without deviating from his method.

Method. The significance of the assigned method is most clear after a study and comparison of reactions obtained from participants during the three different types of interviews. The reader will see that the behavior of one participant influences that of the other and that certain cause-and-effect relationships are apparent. Understanding these relationships will help an interviewer develop the skills that will lead to the attainment of desired objectives. An interviewer's desired objectives, of course, are determined by the method he selects.

CHAPTER THREE

Tell and Sell Method: First Interview

Transcription of the Interview

[S1] GEORGE STANLEY: I've called you in because this is our annual report on your performance. I have your rating form right here and I thought I'd tell you just what we think of what you're doing. The first item is always, of course, production. I must say I've never seen a finer production record . . . than your department is turning out at very great speed; it's doing very well; the quality seems excellent. In the two years that you've been a supervisor, the group has been continually improving so that it's now one of our best producing units. I feel that I can turn anything I want to over to you; there's just no question whatsoever about the way you're doing this production. I hope and am quite sure that you're going to continue to do this in the future, because this is certainly a great asset to us. It's something we can rely on.

There's another side of the program, however; it seems that besides the production there is much concern nowadays for human relations. It seems in looking over the kinds of things that you've been doing that there is a great need for improvement, and I'd like to see you work on these things. I think that you could do a great deal to improve yourself and get ahead further in the company by changing some of the things that you've been doing—for example, this business of the routine work. As I recall, in the last three or four months, you've turned down a couple of routine jobs. We have a big outfit here; we have eight supervisors; we have a large crew; it seems only fair and only right that everyone do his share of all kinds of work. When one person turns down his share of the work, this seems to cause bad feelings; I don't think we should have that kind of bad feeling here in the organization . . .

A long introduction is characteristic of the Tell and Sell approach and follows naturally from the objectives implied in the name given to the method. The interviewer who tells and sells must talk to prevent the interviewee from expressing objections. Frequently, this type of interviewer engages in small talk in an attempt to indicate a personal interest, to distract, or to put the interviewee at ease. Small talk, however, seldom interests the interviewee, because he is anxious about the interview and knows full well that the interviewer is just passing time to warm up to the real purpose of the interview. If the interviewer spends a good deal of time on preliminaries, and if the interviewee is insecure, the latter may become anxious.

In this interview, however, Stanley goes directly to the point, clearly stating that Burke has been evaluated. As is customary, he takes up the good points first and does an excellent job of praising—he spells out specifics, using strong words to indicate the extent of his satisfaction with Burke's work. There is no question but that Stanley is the judge and that he is pleased.

During the discourse on Burke's good points, Stanley is not interrupted because any elaboration or spelling out of details must be initiated by him. (Apparently, Burke feels no desire to comment. He smiles uneasily—undoubtedly feeling that there is more to come. Despite the extensive vocabulary that an interviewer may possess, he soon runs out of words of praise and this portion of the interview comes to an abrupt end, as it does in this case. The remainder of an interview of this kind will usually center around the employee's deficiencies.)

Stanley approaches Burke's weaknesses with a sincere desire to be helpful. He implies that Burke has the capacity to improve and explains that it is in his own interest to improve. Next, he tries to motivate Burke by spelling out specific ways in which he might change in order to improve. Stanley explains how the situation looks from his own viewpoint and from that of other supervisors. (The request for change is not arbitrary but rational, because he does let Burke know "why.")

[B1] TOM BURKE [Interrupting]: But my feeling is since, as you've said yourself, the production of my unit is up—that means that we're doing extra work anyway—then it seems to me that we should get a little reward in the sense of getting some of the better jobs . . .

Burke's interruption indicates that he is not satisfied. As a matter of fact, he responds as one who has been treated unfairly. This is clear when he says that he feels entitled to some reward. The fact that he defends himself with Stanley's own words, however, shows a certain degree of respect.

[S2] GEORGE STANLEY [Interrupting]: I think the reward should be given, but I think that the decisions about the reward should be in my hands. I think the routine jobs should be distributed equally, and in terms of doing good work. Everyone likes to do the interesting jobs; I think they've got to be distributed fairly. From the larger picture, this is the way it looks—if we're going to have a smooth-running outfit, this is the way we're going to have to continue to do this.

> Stanley immediately detects the criticism and cuts Burke off before he can say more. He uses the "yes, but" counterattack, which is a polite form of letting a person know he does not have the full picture. When Stanley points out that he, the boss, should decide when to reward, he is highly defensive of his position as the judge. He proceeds to spell out his views on fairness, but completely misses the point Burke has been trying to make. (Actually, he repeats Burke's view of what constitutes fair assignments.)

[B2] TOM BURKE: I wouldn't argue that point . . . no.

> Burke recognizes the similarity and says he sees that Stanley's point is fair.

[S3] GEORGE STANLEY: Fine, that's what I thought—if once you knew about what was going on that this would be reasonable to you. There have been some bad feelings because of your turning down routine jobs and I think that we can improve on that to a great extent in the future—for our next report.

Another thing has been a concern to me, and it is something that I am quite sure you can improve. I think that if we see some changes on this we might be seeing you in my job someday, or jobs similar to it in the company. It's the business of helping out wherever it's needed on the line or when you see your fellow supervisors in difficulty. After all, in coordinating the jobs of group supervisors, it seems to me that if one of them has a special talent it is only reasonable that he should help out the others. I've had some feelings from what's going on around here that you're turning down the other supervisers when they're asking you for help. It seems to me that it's the cooperative spirit that you've got to have in order to be a good leader, in order to practice good human relations, which is very essential and something which you could work on.

> After obtaining apparent agreement from Burke on fairness, Stanley quickly moves to press his advantage to obtain an additional concession. Stanley again expounds his own views, as might a high priest, and explains to Burke that, by giving his all, he will become a good leader.
>
> (Stanley's response to Burke's partial agreement is especially interesting. He figuratively pounces on Burke's words and assumes that Burke has agreed to change. Actually, Burke has not agreed to accept routine assignments without protest, but only to accept his portion of them. Burke feels he has been given more than his share of routine jobs, but Stanley assumes that he will now

accept routine assignments, even though there may be no change in the method of allocating them.)

[This way of taking a conceding remark to mean more than the other person had in mind is common in debates and arguments when one speaker pays attention to the words of the other, rather than to inflection and meaning. It is a source of a great deal of misunderstanding when a person promises one thing to another who, in turn, feels he has been promised something else—usually what he wants.]

[B3] TOM BURKE: It seems to me that I've done my part on this; I don't think that anyone should be asked to do any more than his part.

Burke politely defends his past conduct and indicates that he feels too much is being asked of him.

[S4] GEORGE STANLEY: I hope that we're not asking anyone to do any more than his work. I think that everyone should do his fair share, but I think part of that fair share definitely should be working with others and working cooperatively with the ones who need help. If there is any problem of others taking a fair share, please let me know, but from my understanding of what's going on here there is a real problem of your refusing people assistance, and I think you should be more than willing. You see, before we made you a supervisor you were available to help everyone, and in the past few years there has been a little less of that cooperation.

Stanley defends himself from an implied charge of being unfair in his expectations and, in essence, says that what he is asking for is really part of Burke's job. He offers Burke the opportunity to complain, but goes on to attack him by pointing out that Burke is guilty of failure to cooperate when he helps others less than he formerly did.

[B4] TOM BURKE: Sir, I would like to take all the time I can with my own unit and I think that is . . .

Burke's use of "Sir" is significant. The distance between them has increased to the formal stage and Stanley is in reality a judge, and by no means a helper. Burke attempts to point out where he sees his own responsibility. (At this point, Burke is unlikely to expect understanding, but he may hope for leniency.)

[S5] GEORGE STANLEY [Interrupting]: That's fine. I don't want you to neglect your unit, but I don't think there's anything incompatible with working with your unit and also cooperating with the other supervisors. I think this is something you can certainly work on during the coming year.

Burke's explanation is cut short. Stanley wants Burke to continue the good he has been doing in his own unit and, in addition, to spend time with other units. (According to Stanley, it is very simple—one merely corrects one's faults without giving up virtues.)

[B5] TOM BURKE: I don't think that—well . . . O.K., I'll do my best.

That's all I can say.

> Burke begins to protest that this can not be done—then gives up trying to explain—although Stanley may take his capitulation as agreement rather than disgruntled resignation.

[S6] GEORGE STANLEY: That's all we're asking you for. If you just use these ideas, I'm quite sure you can do a fine job, continue that fine productivity, and make yourself helpful to others. Remember, you're part of a big team here. We've got eight groups and all of them can up their production if everyone is working together and pulling together as a unit. We can't have one foreman off by himself.

There is one other problem I would like to raise with you, and that's this business of the turnover among the draftsmen. As I said before, this again seems to be a problem not in terms of production—your production is fine down there—it's a problem in terms of human relations. You hire draftsmen (it's tough to get them) and as I look at your records and your draftsmen I find that they come in, they stay a few months, and they leave. Now, this seems to be a very surprising state of affairs. I think that if we concentrated on developing these draftsmen, working with them, and helping them to learn all parts of a particular job, we might have them stay with us a little more. After all, draftsmen are hard to find . . .

> Stanley is so anxious to win his point that he assumes that Burke has agreed with him, but no observer would be so misled. Assuming that Burke has given in, Stanley quickly moves to his next point, preventing Burke from modifying the position Stanley assumes he has taken. (Whether this is strategy on Stanley's part or insensitivity can not be known, but the behavior is characteristic of persons who follow the Tell and Sell approach.)
>
> Making his third criticism, Stanley has omitted some of the mildness with which he made his first criticisms and instead attacks rather ruthlessly. His concern for the feelings of draftsmen far exceeds his consideration for Burke's feelings. He speaks of a "surprising state of affairs" and does not hide the fact that he places all the blame on Burke.

[B6] TOM BURKE [Interrupting]: Well, sir, my feeling about any of the people in my unit, particularly a good draftsman like Frank Dobbs, is that I like to do everything I can to develop them. I think that if they get good and there's no place for them to go up in the company, it's more than natural that . . .

> Stanley is again addressed as "Sir"; Burke tries to explain that he is developing his crew and that part of the fault may lie with the company.

[S7] GEORGE STANLEY [Interrupting]: I don't want to object to your developing a draftsman; I think that you should develop them in a rounded way, so that they're good for the whole company. We have eight units; your unit seems to be the only one that has this turnover with draftsmen—there seems to be something going on down there that we ought to look into. Perhaps something isn't right on the relationship side and I think you ought to be very much aware of the . . .

> Stanley interrupts Burke before he can complete his point. Stanley concedes that Burke may be developing the draftsmen, but he still is not developing them in a "rounded" way. Then Stanley strikes at Burke's interpersonal relationships with the draftsmen. (The high turnover in Burke's group must be due to something Burke does, because that is the way Stanley sees the picture and it does not occur to him that he may be wrong. Stanley seems to see Burke as a bit dull—he does not seem to be aware of the obvious—so Stanley repeats his own analysis of the problem.)

[B7] TOM BURKE: I think that you're right and I would welcome the chance to prove . . .

> Burke agrees that something is wrong and he certainly can truthfully say that he would welcome a chance to prove himself, but Stanley does not give him a chance to say so.

[S8] GEORGE STANLEY [Interrupting]: You see what's happening with me right now is that I have the feeling that you are trying to argue with me, and you're trying to get defensive with me. This is perhaps the way you're acting with your draftsmen and you don't realize it, and that might be one of the reasons you've got this turnover. These are faults—they can be corrected—there's no reason that we can't do a better job on them. I'd sure like to see you get further.

> Stanley now uses the cruelest weapon that a judge has at his disposal. If Burke denies Stanley's claim, the denial is evidence of guilt. Burke's attempt to present his side is itself proof that his interpersonal relationships are poor. Burke must agree that he is guilty; a denial makes him even more guilty.

[B8] TOM BURKE: I'd like to give you just one example of what I'm getting at—there are two department clerks; one of them, Jane Wilson . . .

> Burke clearly is hurt and asks for an opportunity to cite one example. His manner is restrained, but he speaks quickly to put in his example before he is interrupted. (He can no longer hope for time to prepare an organized defense so he hurries, perhaps feeling that any defense is better than none.)

[S9] GEORGE STANLEY [Interrupting]: We're not really concerned with the clerks—they're doing fine; I don't have any concern with them—the problem is the turnover with the draftsmen.

> Stanley cuts him short with the implication that Burke's example is beside the point and not worth discussing.

[B9] TOM BURKE: I was just going to give you an example that she had a chance to go somewhere else for more money, thirty-five dollars a month to be exact, and she turned it down just to stay with our group—and the reason for that, I think, is that in our group we have a good group spirit. The people who work in that unit are proud to be members of it.

> Burke seems desperate—he overrides the interruption and quickly gives his example. (This persistence suggests that he is frustrated and becoming somewhat stubborn. He may be harder to change now.)

[S10] GEORGE STANLEY: Fine, and I think that this group spirit should be pushed more strongly; I think we should continue with it; I think we can even develop new ground in it, and at the same time keep these people with the company. It seems to me that what I've been reading lately about the human relations field is relevant. When you've got a high turnover, you've got human relations problems on your hands, and people will give you all kinds of alibis about why they want to leave or why they want to stay. This is a very serious problem here, having this big turnover, and it seems quite obvious what the difficulty is. It is apparent from what's going on here that we need a little more seasoning, a little more practicing, a little more thinking about how we are doing on the job in building good relationships with our people. You should ask yourself how you're doing with me in terms of this turning down the routines; how you're doing with these draftsmen in terms of giving them a well-rounded picture of the whole job; how you're doing with your subordinates so that they're going to want to stay; and finally, what you're doing to make them want to continue to grow and someday be able to hold your job. You see, they can grow into your job and you can grow into mine, and in this way there is going to be room for everyone to move up. We've got to always hold on to these people if they're good people—it's a real shame that we're losing them.

> Stanley accepts Burke's example as the kind of thing that is needed, but instead of giving Burke credit for what he has achieved, Stanley preaches about the need for Burke to do more. Burke is wrong if he failed to practice good human relations in his group and he is wrong if he has tried to practice good human relations, because it is obvious to Stanley that the attempt has not been successful enough. (Burke can not win because Stanley has judged him guilty before the interview; anything Burke says in his own defense is seen as incorrect. Stanley's own views are foremost because he has made the appraisal.)
>
> The fact that Stanley reiterates his charges and appears somewhat insensitive to Burke's feelings indicates that Burke's resistance and arguments are irritating Stanley. Burke's point was not too easy to refute and Stanley has had to show considerable ingenuity to hold his own. However, he becomes more generous after he regains his dominant position and suggests that Burke can work up and someday hold Stanley's job.

[B10] TOM BURKE: But if they have the chance to go somewhere else, I don't know . . . I'm not sure it's right to hold them under these conditions. If I develop a person into a good employee, he'll get a chance to get ahead somewhere else. I think that's all that's been happening—I don't think there's any dissatisfaction, and I'd be glad to know about it if there is, but . . .

> Burke seems frustrated and refuses to give up. He objects to Stanley's set of values if it justifies the company keeping an employee when he can do better elsewhere. Furthermore, Burke wants evidence to show that there is dissatisfaction in the unit.

[S11] GEORGE STANLEY: Are you aware, Tom, of what you're doing with me right now in terms of how you're handling a really serious problem with another person?

> Stanley appears to see Burke's response as pure stubbornness and gives proof—Burke's exhibition of poor human relations in this interview.

[B11] TOM BURKE: I'm just trying to explain things as I see them is all . . .

> Burke makes a feeble defense. He does not claim he is right; he wants to explain his side.

[S12] GEORGE STANLEY: I'm wondering if you have any discussions like this. This might be just the reason your draftsmen are saying they have better jobs and are moving out. You start to explain something to an employee, put him on a special job, and he feels on the spot. If an employee feels you're not really with him, that you only want him to turn out fast production on a particular job . . . well, the next thing you know you've lost a good worker by some kind of an alibi of a better job. Don't you realize what you're doing? I'd be glad to help you in any way I can by discussing these things with you. I think we could work on it.

> Stanley shows no mercy and presses his advantage. He seems sure of himself and concludes that because he has troubles with Burke it follows that Burke must be the cause of any trouble in his own unit. Even though an observer might think Stanley guilty of every fault he attributes to Burke, it is undoubtedly accurate to say that Stanley feels that Burke is unreasonable and blind to the obvious. He again offers to help Burke.

[B12] TOM BURKE: Well, now, I still say that these people are leaving because of better jobs and I've got one example that I'd like to ask you about right now while we're discussing the matter. What about an employee like Frank Dobbs? Now there's a good . . .

> Burke does not respond to the offer of help. He still defends himself from the charge of being the cause of the turnover and brings up the case of Frank Dobbs, who may be the next incident of turnover unless something better can be found for him in the company.

[S13] GEORGE STANLEY [Interrupting]: Well, this is why we're conducting these conferences right now. If we can find employees to move up from the supervisory level, because they're not only turning out the production but they're also doing a fine job with their human relations, there eventually is going to be a spot to move a person like Frank Dobbs up the line . . . but this is a matter that takes time. There are always openings and everyone has to work his way through the various steps as they come along. Now, he hasn't been with us so long that he should be impatient; anyway, that's not our problem today. Our problem is to talk about you and your relations with your group—how well you are doing down there on that job of yours. It seems to me that if you get at this thing, this report will read an awfully lot different next year from the way it's reading this year. There's a real possibility that you're going to be going places in this outfit, but these points I raised are really serious problems and, with the new developments in management these days, this handling of human relations may almost count more than the ability to get out production. I hate to say that kind of a thing to you, but I'm quite sure you're not going to hurt your production—that is going to stay real fine—all you have to do is work on these other things . . .

> Stanley interrupts Burke before he can make his point. In effect he says that Dobbs has no cause for dissatisfaction yet, and eventually he'll be taken care of—so there is no reason for concern. Anyway, preventing turnover seems not to be the purpose of the interview; the problem under consideration is Burke's handling of human relations problems. The assumption that Burke's inadequate human relations technique was responsible for the turnover in his unit is now being ignored. Burke's inadequacy is no longer an interpretation—it is now a fact for Stanley.

> After taking Dobbs out of the picture, Stanley tries again to motivate Burke by promising that Burke can move ahead in the company if he improves along suggested lines. (Perhaps Stanley will even notice improvement if there is no change, just because he wants Burke's promise.)

[B13] TOM BURKE: May I ask, did Jim Drake talk to you . . . was he one of the people who made any kind of complaint about . . .

> Unfortunately, Burke is not aware of Stanley's point of view. Because Stanley is so sure of himself, Burke suspects that someone has poisoned Stanley's mind. He wonders if it might be Jim Drake. (Burke takes a chance on the Drake story coming out unnecessarily by asking Stanley about Drake.)

[S14] GEORGE STANLEY [Interrupting]: Jim Drake didn't make a complaint. I think this is a very sad experience that you had down there when you didn't turn that information over to Drake. I wasn't going to bring that up; I was going to let that go and confine my remarks to talking in generalities, but now that you mention it, that was a very serious occurrence. I don't think that kind of thing should happen again because that's extremely bad. That's a perfect example of what I mean about this not cooperating with other people—turning away from them whenever you can help them.

Stanley concedes that Drake was in the picture but defends Drake by saying there was no complaint. He then proceeds to point out where Burke was wrong, clearly taking Drake's part.

[B14] TOM BURKE: It was a simple oversight though; I'd like to explain my part at least . . .

It is apparent from Burke's attempted defense that he feels Stanley is against him and for Drake. Burke's defense is to play down the difficulty by using the word "simple" and to indicate that he has a side, too. He attempts to present his side, but he is interrupted.

[S15] GEORGE STANLEY [Interrupting]: I think, also, we ought to learn to take responsibility for the mistakes we make, and that's the other side of this business of really having the leadership quality to stand up and take these things. Now I try to help you and you get defensive. I'm not trying to criticize you. I'm trying to get you to work better—to improve your job. Your work is just stupendous on the production side; there's no question about it at all, as I said before. But it's the other side of this issue that I want you to work on. This is not intended to hurt you. Oh, I know it hurts to be criticized, but all you've got to do is know about your difficulty and buckle down and do something about it, and the next thing you know you'll be getting along with those draftsmen; our turnover will be down; I can get these routine jobs done; and there will be no serious problem with this crew. We can really be a team together again, thanks to your improvement.

True to form, Stanley interrupts. He again shuts out all facts and any opinions that are not in line with his own. He, in essence, says that Burke need not defend himself—all he needs to do is reform. Stanley seems to be quite satisfied with his initial evaluation and points out that if Burke improves, all problems will be solved. (The success of the whole operation is in Burke's hands, it appears.)

[B15] TOM BURKE: Well, I want to tell you this. I think that you'd find if you come down and talk to them—and I sure would like you to do it—I think that you'd find that the members of my unit are . . .

Burke still wants Stanley to see his side—he just can not seem to overlook what he regards as an unjust charge. (He does not realize that he is expected to repent, promise to cooperate, and thank Stanley.)

[S16] GEORGE STANLEY [Interrupting]: I think that your evaluation of this crew is different from mine, and you're going to be . . . well, young man, you're going to have difficulties in this company—serious problems.

Stanley again interrupts Burke's attempts to explain and he now states the situation bluntly. He says that he (Stanley) has a different view of things and that if Burke persists in his views he is in for trouble.

[B16] TOM BURKE: My only suggestion is that I think I know how my people feel. I'm working with the people, and I think they're all happy in their work in my unit. I honestly and truly do think that, and I think that the turn-over is not because they've been disgruntled. I think it's because there's not enough opportunity to move up in this company, and I try to develop my group to be capable people, and it's natural that they get good jobs else-where. And if they go, I don't blame them.

> Burke, still attempting to win a point, repeats his former defense and bluntly blames lack of opportunity in the company for the trouble. His statement, "I don't blame them," is strong and reflects his own hostile feelings toward the company, for which Stanley, incidentally, may be primarily responsible.

[S17] GEORGE STANLEY: Well, all I can tell you are the kinds of things I have here in terms of your evaluation. This is the report that is going in on you. Of course, if you wish to go further up the line about this [shrugs], but I had hoped that as a result of this discussion we would be able to see quite a few changes in your human relations technique, because it seems these are the weak spots in the things you're doing—all this behavior today—I don't understand what's making you so defensive. After all, I was young once, too—but you've got to learn good human relations skills. On all levels of management, people are getting more interested in human relations nowadays—the human relations side to employment—and it's getting tougher and tougher to get good employees and to hold on to them. It's no longer possible to advance supervisors if they can't hold employees, if they can't work with others on their own level, and if they can't do their share of the job. It would be a shame not to see people like yourself get ahead, because your production skill and your inventive ability are just fantastically good, but putting someone who doesn't have the employees' side of things in the position of running a whole series of supervisors would be a very difficult thing for me to recommend. I just couldn't possibly recommend it for you this year; yet, no doubt you are an ambitious young man. I know about your affairs in the community; you're well respected outside the company, and you're well respected here too, but these things have just got to be changed; there's just got to be some development in the other direction.

> Stanley seems both irritated and hurt by Burke's failure to respond construc-tively. He has apparently reached the end of his resources and defends him-self by saying the points he has brought up were covered on the evaluation. His irritation is revealed when he says that he will send the appraisal in as it is and by his shrug, which should indicate to Burke the folly of protesting to higher authorities. Stanley's hurt feelings are apparent. He can not under-stand why his desire to be helpful has been met with defensiveness. Here is a potentially good employee (Burke) throwing away opportunity. Stanley almost begs him to see the light.

[B17] TOM BURKE: Well, to tell you the truth, this all comes as a kind of surprise to me, sir . . .

For the first time, Burke makes a concession. He blames his behavior on the surprise he had when he learned about Stanley's evaluation of his unit and consequently no longer questions Stanley's judgment. (Burke apparently realizes that Stanley will not change his views.)

[S18] GEORGE STANLEY: Of course it does, but that's all right, young man; this happens very often in these interviews. That's what we have them for—to help people to get on the right track. We avoid being aware of our weak points, because that helps us protect ourselves. Once we know about them, we're over the hump. There is no doubt in my mind that a person with your brightness and your ability can truly change and I'm sure we will see some differences around here within the next twelve months.

This concession is welcomed by Stanley. He forgives Burke, indicated by his calling Burke "young man," and points out that others also resist. (For the first time, Stanley has shown affection and warmth.)

[B18] TOM BURKE: Well, now I'm not sure that this is the right time to bring it up, but I have something I would really like to talk about if I could . . .

Burke responds to Stanley's warmth by attempting to discuss some of the problems in his unit. (He seems unaware of the fact, apparent to observers, that Stanley has had about all he can take and wants to terminate the interview.)

[S19] GEORGE STANLEY: If it relates to this evaluation of you, you may; otherwise we could probably take it up next week. That would be a good time to discuss other problems, because I want to get through with these other evaluations . . .

Of course, Stanley not only interrupts, but excludes the discussion of anything except what he regards as relevant to the interview. He does this politely, however.

[B19] TOM BURKE: I want to talk about a couple of people in my unit I think are doing well and I want to give them . . . well, I wonder if you can consider, for example, a raise for Jane Wilson and possibly the same for . . .

Burke perhaps feels cut off by his boss, but still feels obligated to do something about Jane Wilson. (He had this on his mind when he came into the interview and seems unable to realize that the subject is not appropriate for Stanley's mood. One of the difficulties of having a plan is that one tends to follow it even if the climate is unfavorable.)

[S20] GEORGE STANLEY [Interrupting]: Yes, why don't you submit those reports by the usual procedure, and I'll look them over and I'll call you in sometime during the week and we'll discuss them . . .

As might be expected, Stanley puts off the matter and makes a vague suggestion about a future date.

[B20] TOM BURKE: Well, I just thought we could talk about them now, but . . .

> Burke persists; his frustration seems to have made him very insensitive to problems other than his own.

[S21] GEORGE STANLEY: Well, this is an example of the point I was making today. Can't you see that if someone can't handle the thing at the time, a little more graciousness and acceptance of what the human relations side of the situation is would be appreciated? It's obvious that I'm pretty busy—all you've got to do is say, "O.K., see you next week." Now I'm going to have to make a little note to jog my memory about the fact that you weren't quite happy about having to wait until next week. I'll bet that's the kind of thing—in the way you relate with people—that is going on down there in your unit all the time. Just like that [snaps fingers] you can get hold of it; just keep working on it and you'll be surprised at your improvement.

> Stanley cuts Burke off and again accuses him of poor human relations skills. Stanley even intends to add a note to that effect so that Burke's evaluation will be more unfavorable than it was at the outset. Stanley terminates the interview by practically pushing Burke out of the room.

[B21] TOM BURKE: Well . . . O.K., I'll do my best.

> Burke capitulates with "O.K.," but the "Well" reveals doubt. His statement, "I'll do my best," indicates that his heart is not in it. There is no evidence of insight or motivation to act on the decision. To do one's best is, after all, only a vague promise.

[S22] GEORGE STANLEY: Thanks very much for coming in.

> Stanley's "thanks" reflects relief rather than pleasure. There is no warmth in his final remark.

Evaluation of the Interview

Because the interviewer is in a position to determine the style of the interview, he can either do most of the talking or he can have the interviewee talk. When he has the interviewee do most of the talking, it is probable that he listens, but when he does most of the talking it does not follow that the interviewee listens. The interviewer may talk a lot when he is teaching or giving information or when he is selling or persuading. In the first case, the interviewee may listen and accept; in the latter, his manner may be critical or even nonaccepting.

During this interview, Stanley spent a good deal of energy in persuasion, shown by the number of words spoken for the amount of information

Table 1. Words Spoken by Each Participant During First Tell and Sell Interview

Speech	Stanley		Burke	
1	322		46	
2	84		6	
3	216		26	
4	117		20	
5	43		15	
6	206		55	
7	82		13	
8	84		23	
9	24		71	
10	271		68	
11	25		12	
	1474	80.5%	355	= 1829
12	121		44	
13	245		22	
14	100		14	
15	170		41	
16	30		91	
17	294		17	
18	89		29	
19	39		42	
20	29		11	
21	138		6	
22	6			
Total	1261	79.9%	317	= 1578
Total	2735	+	672	= 3407
Percent	80.3		19.7	

contributed. Burke's nonacceptance was evident by his questions and protestations, which caused Stanley to spend more time on each point.

Analysis of Interaction

The number of words spoken by Stanley and by Burke differed greatly. Stanley completely dominated the conversation. Table 1 shows the length of the speeches for each during the complete interview. During the first eleven speeches of each, Stanley contributed 80.5 percent of the words; during the last eleven speeches, he contributed 79.9 percent. The pattern of domination was not relinquished by Stanley at any time.

A count of Stanley's first speech revealed 42 introductory words, 110 words praising Burke on the job, and 170 words about one unsatisfactory aspect of Burke's performance. From the outset, the weight of

Stanley's comments dealt with Burke's weaknesses. This alone tended to give Burke the feeling that he was more rejected than accepted. Because all of Stanley's remaining remarks had to do with correcting Burke, the balance was tilted toward the unfavorable side.

One favorable point does not balance an unfavorable one if equal time is not used to discuss each point. Even if the recipient of an unfavorable criticism actually forces the critic to elaborate on the unfavorable points, unpleasant feelings are still aroused in the recipient. The problem for the interviewer is to find ways to communicate the unfavorable and favorable points so that a more accurate balance is achieved. One way of doing this is through the use of a final summary, which was missing in this interview.

Reactions of Audience

The audience that observed the interview had an unfavorable reaction to Stanley. This was true for those who identified with Stanley as well as those who identified with Burke. They objected to Stanley's frequent interruptions and his dominant manner, although the objections were more to Stanley's manner than to the content of his comments. Many felt that he could have communicated the same information in a kinder way.

Those who identified with Burke were more hostile toward Stanley than those who identified with Stanley. Nearly all of those who identified with Burke thought Burke would quit his job; approximately half of those identifying with Stanley thought Burke would quit. Practically none of those identifying with Burke were sympathetic with Stanley's problem; some who identified with Stanley felt he had a difficult task to perform.

The audience felt that the appraisal objectives had been communicated. However, many thought that Burke did not appreciate how much Stanley thought of Burke's production. (The person who actually played Burke did evaluate this point accurately.)

Reactions of Participants

After the interview, the participants were questioned to determine the extent of communication and the feelings of each. In this case, Burke quite accurately understood Stanley's evaluation of him; he felt that Stanley thought well of his production, but was dissatisfied with his (Burke's) attitude toward Stanley, other supervisors, and his own employees. Burke realized Stanley wanted him to change by accepting all assignments, by helping fellow supervisors, and by reducing his turnover. Stanley agreed that what Burke had learned was what he had wanted him to learn.

Burke's estimation of Stanley went down during the interview and

Stanley's estimation of Burke also went down so that he no longer considered him promotable. Burke intended to look for another job and Stanley said that he hoped he would leave. It was not Stanley's initial intent to have Burke quit, so this development was a product of the interview rather than the evaluation.

Actually, Stanley's overall evaluation of Burke was favorable at the outset and only later became unfavorable. Communication of the evaluation was not accurate, as the final picture was more unfavorable than the evaluation with which the interview began.

From the point of view of development, nothing was accomplished. Stanley felt that Burke was untrainable because of his faulty attitude; Burke felt that Stanley really did not know what was going on, that he played favorites, and that he was very unreasonable. He indicated that until he found a new job he would accept assignments, watch out for Jim Drake, continue to treat his employees well, encourage them to leave, and have less job interest than before. He felt his production might suffer in certain ways; certainly, he would not inconvenience himself voluntarily in order to put a job out.

CHAPTER FOUR

Tell and Sell Method: Second Interview

Transcription of the Interview

[S1] GEORGE STANLEY: Come on in, Tom; have a chair. You may realize that this is the time of year that we go through our annual review of everyone's work, and I asked you in today because I've been going over your record, and everyone else's record, and I'd like to talk to you about it.

> Stanley's approach is friendly and he comes directly to the point, explaining the purpose of the interview so that Burke will not be anxious. He says that everyone's work is being reviewed, letting Burke know the routine nature of the interview. (Stanley uses "I" three times in one sentence, which might be a deficiency in skill, yet it seems to flow quite naturally from a judge. Because many interviewers see themselves as judges of an employee's performance, researchers believe that the expressed objective of the interview has a direct influence on the skills that an interviewer will use.)

[B1] TOM BURKE: Well, that's good.

> Burke lets Stanley know he approves of a review.

[S2] GEORGE STANLEY: I want to let you know how you stand around here. I have all the rating forms and everything else and we can just go down them point by point and let you know where you stand. Now to start with, I think that we ought to mention the first requirement of a company, obviously, is production. I don't know how I can tell you how fine I feel your production work is.

> Stanley seems too intent on his introduction to recognize Burke's response. (This is largely a slip-up in skill. A remark such as "I'm glad you welcome this opportunity, too," would not have disrupted his plan, but the telling type of interview causes an interviewer to plan his initial remarks rather carefully so an interruption is likely to be distracting. The phrase "I want to let you know" shows a personal orientation and a lack of appreciation for the fact that the interview might be of mutual interest.) Stanley proceeds to follow his interview plan; his manner, if anything, is somewhat less friendly than before. Burke's friendliness seems to have embarrassed Stanley. The use of the phrase "point by point" as he repeats the comment about letting Burke know where he stands emphasizes Stanley's role as a judge. He mentions Burke's production and is strong in his praise. (This may counteract any unpleasantness that his initial comments may have caused.)

[B2] TOM BURKE: Well, I'm glad you recognize that. It's something we've been working very hard on in our group.

> Burke seems friendly; he graciously accepts the praise from Stanley and gives his group a share of the recognition.

[S3] GEORGE STANLEY: You've been doing a splendid job producing down there. You turn out the work rapidly, it shows a very high quality, and since you've had this outfit the past two years the improvement has just been *marvelous* down there. When I have extra work, as I have in the past six months, I always turn it over to you and you produce and it's a real *pleasure* to put on this record for you that your production is just superb. I hope, of course, that in the future we're going to see more of this kind of thing from you.

> Stanley skillfully uses Burke's response as an opportunity to expand on his good points. He communicates exactly what he likes about the work Burke's unit turns out. (Stanley's hope that Burke will keep production up should make Burke feel secure because this is something Burke knows he can do.)
>
> [Specific praise for past performance is a constructive teaching method because it tells an employee what is wanted; reprimand teaches only what not to do. An employee may hesitate to change his behavior because he (a) has no clear knowledge of an approved alternative; (b) lacks skill to execute the desired alternative; or (c) disapproves of the alternative.]

[B3] TOM BURKE: Well, I have a good unit down there and I think we all work together pretty well.

> Burke graciously responds to the words of praise, showing no conceit or embarrassment at accepting Stanley's evaluation.

[S4] GEORGE STANLEY: Well, I completely agree with you. It seems that that is the situation; no doubt you deserve the major credit for this, and I think you ought to get it.

> Stanley reinforces his praise and agrees that Burke has a good unit.

[B4] TOM BURKE: Thank you.

> Burke seems pleased.

[S5] GEORGE STANLEY: However, as is always the case on these things and when a person is growing into a job (and you've only been on this job a couple of years), there are plenty of places for improvement—improvement we'd like to see made, and over the next year or so, I'm quite sure you can handle it all right. I'll let you know what those things are. It's a matter of quite a few issues of your cooperation—your working with people—and it seems to me there are two or three places where it is quite important that we see some changes over the next year or so. I'd like to itemize these for you and I'm quite sure that after I do you'll be able to go to work on them with no trouble at all. First of all, there's this business of cooperation in general with the whole crew.

> Stanley prepares an excuse for Burke—being new on the job—and makes it clear that he has confidence in Burke's ability to overcome his deficiencies. He mentions "plenty" of places for improvement.

[B5] TOM BURKE: You mean my own crew?

> Burke seems surprised at Stanley's implication.

[S6] GEORGE STANLEY: No, I mean with the whole crew on your own level—I'll get to your own crew in a moment. There have been at least four or five times in the past couple of months that I have asked other foremen—you know there are eight foremen here; this is a large team— and a person to get ahead has got to start to get a picture of the overall view in the company. I've asked these people to go down and get information from you and I've heard they're having difficulty doing that. You've been a little sarcastic, you've turned them away, you don't have time for them. Now a couple of years ago, before you were a supervisor, we had a real good chance to use this production ability of yours in the whole outfit, and it seems that now we've promoted you, this information isn't available to all of us any more and this is *very important* to the progress of the company.

> Stanley mentions specific instances so Burke will know exactly what he means by cooperation. He seems to exaggerate Burke's faults, but this may be to emphasize their importance. When he says that Burke has been a "little" sarcastic, he may be trying to avoid hurting Burke's feelings. Stanley shows concern over the loss of Burke's availability for the unit as a whole. (He uses a form of persuasion that is quite typical of an authoritarian leader—the kind of expression of disappointment that a loving father might both express and

feel. If Stanley fails to convert Burke, it would seem unjust to blame it on Stanley's lack of skill and ingenuity.)

[B6] TOM BURKE: Well, I try to cooperate with these other people, and I have been working with them quite . . . well. I don't know where you've been getting this information, but we have been working . . .

Burke says he is not aware of a problem and wants to know the source of Stanley's information. He makes a protective response without showing overt hostility or aggression. (To appreciate the lack of constructiveness in Burke's responses, imagine how inappropriate they would be in a problem-solving discussion.)

[S7] GEORGE STANLEY [Interrupting]: Well, the point is, I have heard from these people . . . it is *quite clear* that there has been a holdup of information, that you've felt that your own unit is too busy, and you've been focusing the energy on your own unit, *more* than is necessary because you've been neglecting these others. I think that a little consideration— remember, someday if, of course, we can improve these kinds of things, you'll be sitting in my job. Sitting in my job, we've got to look at these eight outfits, one, two, three, four, five, six, seven, and eight. All of them have to work together, and if we have an employee who's good on inventive ability and we send people to him for help, we expect him to give that help graciously, willingly, and cooperatively, and that's the kind of thing I'd like to see you do . . .

Stanley does not notice that Burke's expression of innocence is a protective response, but seems convinced that Burke really is not aware of his responsibilities. So, Stanley tells Burke what is expected of him and seems to talk down to him. Some impatience and hostility may have been in his final remark, which he is unable to complete because of Burke's interruption.

[B7] TOM BURKE [Interrupting]: Well, I started out that way [pause] . . .

Burke interrupts, which indicates that he feels Stanley's comments are inappropriate.

[S8] GEORGE STANLEY [Interrupting]: I'd like to see you *continue* that way . . .

Stanley sounds quite authoritarian.

[B8] TOM BURKE [Interrupting]: Well, I have been working that way really, but it got to a point where it was really interfering with anything I could do—I wasn't getting anything done at all.

Burke's reply shows aggression and defensive behavior. He criticizes his fellow supervisors for taking up too much of his time, implying their incompetence.

[S9] GEORGE STANLEY [Interrupting]: There's no reason here at all . . . I don't want you to neglect your own work, but there's *no reason* in the world why you shouldn't be able to do your work and have these other supervisors come down and get cooperation from you. That's one of the jobs of the supervisor. As I say, granted you've only been on the job a couple of years; it's a new position for you; it's reasonable that you will be having difficulty getting your own work done and at the same time helping others. The point is these are both part of the foreman's job. We'd like to see you work out on this thing and come up better on it. Now I've got another one to add to you that's even more in relationship to me than to the other people. In the last two (or maybe three) months I've asked you to do a routine job and you've said "uh-uh." Now let's face it. If I turn around to my boss when he tells me to do a routine job, I don't say "uh-uh"; that's no way to get ahead . . .

> Stanley, the judge, cuts through Burke's excuse with precision and says that Burke *must* help his fellow supervisors. He says Burke should learn how to do what is expected of him. Stanley does supply Burke with a face-saver by recognizing that he lacks experience. He names another of Burke's faults—a failure to cooperate with Stanley himself. (This may indicate Stanley's impatience with Burke's disinclination to admit the error of his ways.)

> In the final sentence, Stanley sets himself up as a model, simultaneously giving some encouragement by suggesting Burke can get ahead in the company by following in his footsteps.

> [Stanley's failure to listen to Burke's excuses conforms with the Tell and Sell method because it is Stanley's responsibility to develop Burke by informing him of his faults and by telling him how he should change. Using himself as an example also seems to be true to the assignment. It follows that if superiors are qualified to judge and recommend plans for improvement, then they must have superior wisdom and be willing to have their own conduct copied.]

[B9] TOM BURKE: [Interrupting]: I didn't say "uh-uh." I said I'd rather not do it and I think someone else ought to do it . . . isn't that right?

> Burke corrects Stanley in self-defense.

[S10] GEORGE STANLEY: Yes, but you see . . .

> Stanley accepts the correction and attempts to present his argument.

[B10] TOM BURKE [Interrupting]: Well, I didn't refuse it. I just said it would be better if some of the other guys did it.

> Burke continues to defend himself, distinguishing between refusing to do a job and making a suggestion that others should do it.

[S11] GEORGE STANLEY: The total situation was a refusal. In order to avoid controversy at the time—I was busy with other things—I waited for this occasion to let you know how I felt about that. It seems to me, again from the broader view, everyone's got to do his share of routine work. Everyone would like to have these nice, interesting jobs, but again you've got to start thinking in terms of your own advancement here. With that inventive ability you have, you can go ahead; you've got to take this broader cooperative view.

> Stanley refuses to make a concession and now defends himself. He resumes the judge's role and proceeds in a kind but firm way to let Burke know what is expected of him. He again compliments Burke for his superior workmanship and mentions advancement to persuade Burke to take a "broader cooperative" view of things.

> (Even though he is authoritarian, Stanley is both patient and kind. He does not take offense at Burke's resistance, but explains where Burke is wrong in thinking that his superior technical performance has earned him certain privileges. In a sense, he tells Burke that superiority can mean advancement, if Burke makes this superiority available to others.)

[B11] TOM BURKE: I'm interested very much in the cooperative view, because . . . [overriding Stanley's interruption] I think that in terms of the whole group the most inventive workers ought to have the most inventive jobs.

> Burke says he believes in being cooperative, but he also feels he should have privileges. (He seems to be developing a stubborn streak.)

[S12] GEORGE STANLEY: I think that *might* be the way you see it from *your* side and I felt that way a bit when I was down in your shoes, but let's face it, our jobs are different. The planning work is done on levels above and we're doing the planning level from up here. In order to maintain things fairly in the crew, to have harmony, to have everyone produce at his best, and to develop everyone as best we can, these assignments ought to be shared. No one ought to squawk about taking his—[Burke tries to interrupt]. You don't have to argue.

> Stanley continues to be patient. He tries to show understanding by saying he once felt as Burke does. He tells Burke what is fair and that he has his interests at heart. He tries to sell his views by showing Burke their wisdom and reasonableness.

> [When a superior argues that things look different from his position, he takes a stand that can not be refuted. Because the subordinate has a different vantage point, he must accept what his superior says on faith. This attitude is consistent with the Tell and Sell method and is paternalistic.]

[B12] TOM BURKE: I'm not arguing really, I just . . .

> Burke defends himself.

[S13] GEORGE STANLEY [Interrupting]: After all, I'm just trying to give you some ideas here to help you out a little bit.

> Stanley seems hurt that Burke is not appreciative.

[B13] TOM BURKE: I'm just looking at it the same way you are, that the whole crew has a certain production to meet, and the most inventive people should have the most inventive things and you give the other workers the things which are relevant to their level.

> Burke explains that he has the good of the whole unit at heart and says their difference of opinion is on how to achieve the best overall good. (Burke seems unaware that Stanley will not permit disagreement of any kind. Burke is so intent on protecting himself that he is unable to see that Stanley, the judge, is satisfied with the appraisal as it stands and has no wish to change it. His objective is to change Burke.)

[S14] GEORGE STANLEY: That raises other problems and that's exactly the point at which we need to have your views changed. Now if your productivity and your method of working are the kind that are going to keep you where you are in the company, that kind of attitude is a fine one, and you're right and you can keep working for your own crew to only get the better jobs, but if you are interested in moving higher in the organization, you've got to start taking a different kind of view, because the view from up here is that when you have eight people doing the same kind of work you have to be fair to all eight of them, and if these other people like to do the other kinds of jobs, you can't be unfair and give only one person the interesting work. That's the thing that I've got a hunch with your beginning in this outfit—I understand it's only been a couple years you've been doing this kind of a job—you've got to start getting out of the view of only you and your unit and see how it relates to the broader picture. That's the same business with aiding others, you see, and it's a matter of taking time and thinking about it and holding back a little bit and realizing that all these outfits have to work together. All I'm after here is a little change in these directions and in a few years I'll probably see you sitting in this chair because this production of yours is just superb, just fine, but people can't move beyond the production level unless they have the other kinds of things . . .

> Stanley attempts persuasion and dominates the interview, probably to overcome Burke's resistance. As he talks, he develops a rationale to justify his initial opinion. He says promotion is the reward for changing in the right way; he praises Burke's potential, and he takes a tolerant attitude toward Burke's limited perspective. (Stanley is very skillful at the selling approach and any failure he experiences in gaining acceptance seems to indicate a deficiency in the method rather than in the skill with which it is being used.)

[B14] TOM BURKE [Interrupting]: I agree these two things go together.

> Burke tries to interrupt Stanley.

[S15] GEORGE STANLEY [Talking at same time]: Fine . . .

> Stanley is not willing to let Burke talk.

[B15] TOM BURKE [Overriding]: And exactly what happens is that you give them the interesting jobs and they can't do them and so they come down and I'm doing them anyhow . . .

> Burke is not convinced. He exposes the inaccuracy in Stanley's thinking and denounces his fellow supervisors as inadequate with considerable hostility.

[S16] GEORGE STANLEY [Interrupting]: I have a feeling, Tom, that I'm a better judge of that situation than you are; I have had no complaints from above and I have had no complaints from the field of sales that any of the work turned out by any of my units is giving any trouble. The quality of ᵗhe work in all our outfits is high . . .

> Stanley continues to apply pressure. He takes the conversation from Burke and frankly tells him he is wrong. (Stanley's opinion and the facts seem to be one and the same.)

[B16] TOM BURKE [Interrupting]: They don't have as high as *my* outfit . . .

> Burke sounds frustrated and stubborn.

[S17] GEORGE STANLEY: The quality of your outfit is a bit higher in terms of productivity, that's true, but in the broader view there is this point that you've got to have a team working together; I can't have one person who is a favorite and the others who are not favorites. This is the thing that has to be worked out in higher echelons, and I'd like you in the future to start to get a feel for this. Start to think when you get in a situation and before you start to turn down an assignment from me, ask yourself, "What does he have in mind? How many employees does he have to deal with?" This kind of thinking on your part is going to really pay off for you in the long run, because this area—this cooperation area—these human relations skills that there's been so much writing about lately—these are things where we want to develop our foremen, and you in particular. Production—we have no complaints; you're going to be able to maintain that and work this other in as an additional skill. I'd really like to see you go places with this kind of stuff because it would be a shame . . .

> This clearly is an authoritarian approach. It is apparent that Stanley's patience is strained; although he has not made a cruel remark, he is extremely frank. For the first time, he clearly says that Burke lacks skills in human relations. However, he continues to express a desire to help Burke get ahead. (Stanley shows a surprising amount of patience and tolerance, considering the opposition Burke gives him. It is this kind of resistance that makes a superior resort to force, because a superior can not back down.)

[B17] TOM BURKE [Interrupting]: Are you suggesting that we're all equal in this group, that each one of these supervisors is as good as I am . . .

> Burke's hostility is quite apparent in this response and he obviously strains Stanley's patience.

[S18] GEORGE STANLEY [Interrupting]: Every person has certain abilities and other people have certain other abilities, but the question of fairness is the issue. You've got to start thinking of these other issues in order to function on a higher level than just a first-line supervisor. Our goal is to get employees like you to move up in the organization, but we can only do this if we have these employees thinking of the broader picture at all times. You're going to be having workers like yourself when you're in my shoes—*if you get to be in my shoes*—in a few years, and you're going to have to work with them on these problems; you're going to have to keep harmony between them and seven other supervisors and I think it's still a little early yet for you to feel the difference in responsibility, and how the job is different, and that's the sort of thing that I think you can work on well.

> Stanley continues to keep control of his emotions to a surprising degree. He patiently repeats the same arguments, using promotion as a selling point. His last comment is a polite, but firm, way of saying that Burke is in no position to judge others. [In discussions of this kind, the same arguments or points may be brought out several times. This repetition accounts for the unusually large number of words spoken by the interviewer.]

[B18] TOM BURKE: Well, isn't production the goal of the organization in this case?

> Burke still refutes Stanley and attempts to present a logical argument.

[S19] GEORGE STANLEY: Absolutely, in this case . . .

> Stanley agrees conditionally and starts to explain.

[B19] TOM BURKE [Interrupting]: The quality of production and speed of production?

> Burke tries to make his point.

[S20] GEORGE STANLEY [Talking at same time]: That's the point . . .

> Stanley is very impatient at Burke's persistence.

[B20] TOM BURKE: If you think of it in terms of your unit or in terms of my unit, the best worker has got to get the job that . . .

> Burke's argument is clear and to the point; the more convincing it is, the more trouble he causes Stanley. Neither of them seems to be aware of the feeling he engenders in the other.

[S21] GEORGE STANLEY [Interrupting]: Good production depends on good acceptance and good human relations among the different departments . . .

> Stanley interrupts before Burke can complete his argument. He does not seem interested in Burke's views. He repeats his point about the need for good human relations and successfully causes Burke to practice poor human relations skills, illustrating his own point about Burke's weakness.

[B21] TOM BURKE [Interrupting]: Also technical skill.

Burke interrupts again to add a point of his own.

[S22] GEORGE STANLEY: Right; we have a good skilled bunch up and down the line. This brings me to another point which I think I should bring up to you and it is another serious one. Out of these eight crews that we have—I'm quite sure that this relates to cooperation—just as you are arguing with me and have been giving a tough time to these other supervisors, your crew is the only one where we find turnover in the draftsmen. Month after month you've got a bunch of draftsmen who stay a few weeks and they disappear. In all the other groups we don't have this kind of problem. I'm wondering . . . My feeling is that you are pushing on these people—you are not developing these draftsmen all around in the same way that these other crews are. I'd like to see this whole notion of human relations and respecting the other person and thinking of everything in a team way . . .

> Stanley again dominates the discussion. He ignores Burke's implication and charges that Burke's behavior in the interview proves that he is not cooperative. He implies that because Burke's unit has high turnover he must lack the essential human relations skills for dealing with subordinates. (Burke, it now appears, fails to cooperate with superiors, peers, and subordinates. Stanley seems unaware that he demonstrates a lack of consideration for the feelings of subordinates while accusing Burke of the same weakness.)

[B22] TOM BURKE [Interrupting]: I don't think that's a fair criticism. I agree that some of these people have left, but they have left for different reasons.

> Burke's response is subdued; he may be somewhat intimidated.

[S23] GEORGE STANLEY: Now why are you arguing? You know, you're acting with me exactly the way you act with the rest of the crew. This is exactly the problem I'm talking about.

> Despite Burke's quiet defense, Stanley accuses him of arguing and being uncooperative. Stanley seems to feel more confident and may press his advantage.

[B23] TOM BURKE: Well, I don't know, I have people in my group who— in fact, I have one girl who just refused a job in another company because she wanted to remain in my unit. Did you know about that?

> Burke lacks assurance. His concise arguments have been replaced by signs that he is confused about where he stands. He asks Stanley if he knows about the employee who turned down an outside offer with higher pay. He seems to beg more than argue at this point.

[S24] GEORGE STANLEY: Workers give all kinds of reasons for leaving a position when they're not happy with it, you know.

Stanley brushes Burke's question aside. It is obvious he did not know about the employee in question.

[B24] TOM BURKE: No—she *stayed*.

Burke contradicts Stanley.

[S25] GEORGE STANLEY: Sometimes they say these kinds of things and they give all kinds of reasons to leave in order to not argue. Workers don't like to argue. Workers when they are unhappy will give you all kinds of rationalizations and it seems to me that you're falling for some of these. Apparently, some of your crew don't bother to give you these rationalizations; they just up and leave. Draftsmen are hard to get nowadays, as you very well know. And here we have eight outfits; seven of them manage to keep their draftsmen and turn out very good work. Their work isn't as fast as yours on many jobs, there is no doubt about that, but it still seems to me that there is no reason we should lose the draftsmen from your outfit. This is something that I think you've got to change and I am so impressed with this production record that I'm really quite surprised about this cooperative business—but it really makes sense, having only been in the supervisory job a couple of years—you'll have to learn to take a broader view. This broader view is the thing that we must have in our top management people. I'd like to be thinking of moving you ahead in the company, but it's going to take a year or so of seasoning and thinking about these kinds of things to get you ready. I'm quite sure that you could change . . .

> Stanley does not seem interested in the facts. He continues to sound like a patient father figure, but he leaves little doubt that Burke must mend his ways. He now compares Burke's ability unfavorably with the other supervisors' ability to keep their draftsmen. He repeats his point about the broader view (which originally was Burke's idea in B11) and expresses confidence in Burke's ability to improve.

> [Persistent pressure and repetition seem to come naturally from use of the Tell and Sell method. If one persuasive statement fails to yield results, it is common sense to supply more of them and also to increase their intensity. Stanley's patience is admirable.]

[B25] TOM BURKE: If I didn't have the cooperation of my crew, I don't see how I could get the production I turn out.

> Burke no longer contradicts Stanley. He seems genuinely puzzled but makes what is basically a loaded and hostile statement. (If Stanley has no answer ready, it may arouse his hostility, too.)

[S26] GEORGE STANLEY: I have a feeling that what is happening down there is that these people are doing jobs that they are very good at and they're not getting trained all around, and if a person isn't getting trained all around, of course he's going to be leaving the outfit. These draftsmen come in here fresh from school and they want to learn about all aspects of drafting. It's easy to turn out a good production job if you have one employee doing one part of the job and another employee doing a different part. Your job, just as mine, is to develop your employees to the maximum of their ability. Just as I am satisfied with your production and want you to continue it, now what I am trying to do is get you to work on this other side. On your crew if you've got a worker who can draft well on a particular kind of a job, it is your duty to see that he is also given other kinds of things to do.

> Stanley has an answer ready and explains how production can be high even without adequate job satisfaction. He avoids the point Burke previously made about Jane Wilson by confining his remarks to draftsmen. Without evidence, he makes a case against Burke for the inadequate training he gives his draftsmen and tells Burke how to correct his faults.

[B26] TOM BURKE: *I do*—once we get . . .

> Burke says he actually practices what Stanley has suggested.

[S27] GEORGE STANLEY [Interrupting]: Fine. I think that we ought to encourage this and increase this more because we ought to hold on to these people. I think that it would be real nice if we can end up this year with a real good set of draftsmen down there and not have to be retraining new ones all the time, paying extra money, wasting the cost of advertising for help, and putting an extra load on personnel. It's a real strain up and down the company when we have these employees leaving all the time.

> Burke's protest does not change Stanley's mind. He says "fine" and proceeds to tell Burke he has not done enough. (Stanley's discourse on the costs of training may be correct, but Burke can hardly be expected to accept the blame for the excessive training costs resulting from the labor turnover.)

[B27] TOM BURKE: Do you know why they're leaving? They're leaving because they can't move up in this organization. That's why they're leaving. And they're so good. It's not because they're so disappointed that they leave but because they are good and they don't have any place to go in this organization . . .

> Burke sounds annoyed and blames the turnover on lack of opportunity to advance in the company.

[S28] GEORGE STANLEY [Interrupting]: We don't have draftsmen leaving in seven other . . . We have seven other units the same size and these seven other units are not losing their people. Now these people are learning; they seem to be satisfied with the pension plan we have, with the fringe benefits, with the parking situation; the pay is excellent . . .

> Although Stanley shows his impatience, he is resourceful and points to the fact that Burke's unit has most of the turnover. [His reference to fringe benefits is purely fictitious, but this shows how people select, exaggerate, and

even make up facts when their opinions are undermined. This is why problem solving can not proceed when either participant is on the defensive.]

[B28] TOM BURKE [Interrupting]: For *their* kind of work, but my unit does better work—obviously, from the production I've got . . .

> Burke interrupts to point to the fallacy in Stanley's thinking. He seems to forget that he is talking to his superior. (This certainly is not problem-solving behavior.)

[S29] GEORGE STANLEY [Interrupting]: Yes, if they're being developed all around. The fact still remains that they're moving—and if they're leaving, it seems to me that there's dissatisfaction here. This dissatisfaction is something that I think you can handle and are very likely responsible for. All up and down the line, to summarize this, I think we can see this: this productivity we ought to keep up nice and high—I'd like to see this— I'd be willing to see a little of the productivity down in favor of the overall development of these draftsmen, so we can hold onto them. I think that this would be worthwhile, although I don't see that we would have to sacrifice too much of the productivity. I'd like to see this inventive ability that you have used for the whole organization. It is just a superb ability and it is a real shame that because of this breaking into your job you felt that you couldn't give the time to these other supervisors. I'm pretty sure that you are going to be able to change that over the next twelve months— six months—maybe we'll see an improvement right away. And the other side of it is the routine jobs; I think that you should start thinking, not only of taking them more graciously and willingly, but also start getting the mood of "What is it like being in Stanley's chair? What are the problems he has? When I start thinking of the job from his point of view, of course I must do my share of the routine work—I've got to maintain harmony in this outfit." And if that happens before I fill out this appraisal form next time, when we get together twelve months from now and talk about this, I'll have these categories checked high on the production side and I'll have them checked high on the human relations side, too.

> Stanley takes the conversation from Burke and makes turnover and dissatisfaction two sides of the same coin. He does not accept Burke's alternate interpretation. He remains unruffled and maintains his dignity, which indicates a high degree of skill. He summarizes the appraisal. (He must be commended for remembering to include and elaborate on Burke's productivity. His willingness to sacrifice some productivity to gain in other areas is an act of generosity that only a judge or father figure can grant. His praise of Burke's good points and display of confidence in Burke's ability to improve are well done.) Stanley brings up job assignments and almost promises Burke his own job if and when it becomes vacant. Stanley seems to have high hopes for Burke's future and offers rewards for loyalty and cooperation.
>
> [Usually such promises are considered bad practice, yet they are most com-

monly made by autocratic leaders. Stanley's desire for Burke's loyalty seems to be so great that he will pay a price for it.]

[B29] TOM BURKE: Well, I'd like to have you come down to my department and talk to some of the people, because I think that you are making the wrong assumptions about why these things have been happening. I really feel that we ought to get together *before* the twelve months are up and sort of check on the . . .

Burke stubbornly pursues a lost cause. He feels that he has been judged unfairly and does not seem to realize that what he is doing is equivalent to telling a judge he does not know his business.

[S30] GEORGE STANLEY: I think that this is an excellent idea. Why don't we get together and see about these things, and see as they change I can come down and help you change them some more.

Stanley goes along with Burke's ideas verbally, but does not seem to consider them seriously.

[B30] TOM BURKE: Well, I'd very much appreciate that.

Burke gives a polite response to Stanley's promise, which is really all he can do. Stanley seems too friendly and kind to provoke an openly aggressive act from Burke.

[S31] GEORGE STANLEY: O.K., fine.

Stanley closes the interview.

[B31] TOM BURKE: Thank you very much.

Burke thanks Stanley.

[S32] GEORGE STANLEY: You're very welcome.

Although the interviewer often expresses his thanks also, Stanley does not reciprocate, which indicates that he feels he has given help to Burke but has not benefited from the interview. (Stanley has accomplished his goals; he has told Burke where he stands and what he should do if he wants to move ahead in the company.)

Evaluation of the Interview

Stanley was more patient during this interview than during the first. The person playing Burke on this occasion seemed somewhat more receptive than the first Burke, but as the interview progressed he, too, became quite resistant to change. Stanley's increased patience and greater inclination to coax, if not to promise Burke a promotion, can not be accounted for by the different Burkes in the role because, with the exception of the introductory phases, the behavior of two Burkes was more alike than the behavior of the same Stanley on the two occasions. It is plausible to assume that the major change was in Stanley. During the first interview, he may have learned that bullying Burke did not accomplish his objective and he may have decided to avoid using intimidating tactics. This change required him to be especially patient and careful not to show defensive behavior.

To persuade Burke to accept his recommendations for improvement, Stanley was generous when praising for a job well done; gentle when referring to weaknesses; coaxing when persuading Burke to change his ways; liberal when giving Burke face-saving opportunities; reassuring when he showed confidence in Burke's ability and willingness to improve; and fatherly when he pointed out that Burke would make him happy by changing. He practically promised Burke a promotion as a reward for change along the suggested lines. These are the kinds of skills usually associated with the typical sales approach and Stanley showed both skill and resourcefulness in its use.

The change in Stanley's technique had very little effect on his dominance. Actually, he dominated Burke slightly more than previously (83.9 percent of words versus 80.3). Stanley may have taken more speaking time because Burke did not give up trying to communicate as soon when he was treated gently. As a matter of fact, Burke still had not capitulated or made any promises when this interview ended, and Stanley could only hope that Burke would come around to his way of thinking after he had a chance to think things over.

Stanley's patience did have one apparently desirable effect, however. The interview ended on a friendly note, and this certainly is important for both parties. An unpleasant interaction sets up a social distance that in turn becomes a barrier to subsequent contacts. This interview left no uncomfortable gap between Burke and Stanley and any residue of unfriendly feeling was of a subjective nature and would not necessarily be an obstacle to friendly conversation if they were to meet again.

Stanley did a good job of summarizing the discussion and avoided an argument or a reopening of a touchy topic at the end of the interview. His final speech made it clear that Burke had been told what was expected of him. Even though Stanley extracted no promises, he let Burke know he expected him to change his mind once he had time to think things over.

Analysis of Interaction

Stanley's pattern of domination for this interview was strikingly similar to the first interview. He was consistent with the Tell and Sell method, directed his efforts to informing Burke how he had been appraised, and tried to persuade him to change. Except for the favorable points on the appraisal, Stanley used Tell and Sell as each point was brought up in

**Table 2. Words Spoken by Each Participant
During Second Tell and Sell Interview**

Speech	Stanley		Burke	
1	53		3	
2	73		17	
3	100		17	
4	30		2	
5	151		5	
6	166		31	
7	146		6	
8	8		29	
9	189		23	
10	4		20	
11	93		29	
12	48		6	
13	18		45	
14	285		7	
15	1		27	
16	61		8	
	1426	83.8%	275	= 1701
17	206		22	
18	162		11	
19	4		8	
20	3		26	
21	14		3	
22	161		23	
23	30		38	
24	18		3	
25	242		21	
26	174		5	
27	92		49	
28	54		17	
29	321		56	
30	34		6	
31	2		4	
32	3			
	1520	83.8%	292	= 1812
Total	2946	+	567	= 3513
Percent	83.9		16.1	

the interview, so the interaction was very similar in the first and second halves. Stanley was responsible for 83.8 percent of the words spoken in the first half of the interview and for 83.8 percent of the words spoken in the last half (Table 2). Stanley's overall percentage was 83.9 percent, Burke's 16.1 percent.

Reactions of Audience

After this interview, Stanley had many admirers who felt he had been constructive and patient and that any unfavorable results were due to the unpleasant assignment he had to carry out. The group as a whole felt that Burke would show some improvement because he seemed to be convinced at the end of the interview.

As was to be expected, observers identifying with Stanley admired the patience he displayed and those identifying with Burke did not. Some of the former even thought that Stanley, at times, should have stood his ground somewhat better. However, they did feel that his summary wrapped things up and made him the master of the situation at the end of the interview. Of the "Stanley identifiers," more thought that Stanley had been too kind than thought he had been too inconsiderate. They thought Burke was a difficult person and several of them did not think Burke was an employee worth keeping unless he changed. Even though Burke was a good employee technically, many felt that he could not be developed. The majority, however, felt that once Burke was back on the job and thought things over he would correct at least some faults.

Most persons identifying with Stanley felt that Burke had lost in his estimation and most felt that Stanley also had lost in Burke's. But there was considerable difference of opinion.

The people identifying with Burke were somewhat unhappy with Stanley. They did not like his interruptions and thought he talked too much. They agreed, however, that Burke was quite stubborn and uncooperative and that he should have been more willing to cooperate. Some members of the audience were very irritated and said they would have quit their jobs if they had been in Burke's shoes; the majority said they would have been hurt at the time, but gradually would have recovered and profited by the experience. Many felt that the total effect would be for Burke's good and that he would show some improvement. A strong minority felt hostile toward Stanley. In general, those identifying with Burke felt Stanley had been more reasonable than most bosses.

More felt that Stanley had lost in Burke's estimation than felt he had gained. Most of those identifying with Burke felt that he had lost considerably in Stanley's estimation and none thought he had gained.

Reactions of Participants

Neither Stanley nor Burke was satisfied with the interview. Stanley was depressed because he felt that he had failed to persuade Burke; Burke felt unappreciated and bottled up and said he intended to look for a new job. When Burke said he had not felt appreciated, Stanley was very surprised and referred to all of the praise he had given. Actually, there was a surprising degree of failure to communicate Burke's evaluation because Stanley's post-interview expression of Burke's value was considerably higher than the impression Burke had gained from the interview. Therefore, the major purpose of the interview, to communicate the appraisal, had not been achieved.

The audience was surprised when Stanley said that his estimation of Burke had gone up somewhat during the interview. Most persons, including Burke, thought Burke had lost in Stanley's estimation. Had Stanley communicated this change during the interview, Burke would have felt much better. Stanley said that he might have jumped to conclusions in making the appraisal and that, in the future, he would be more generous in his evaluations. (This would be unfortunate, because a lowering of standards makes evaluations useless for promotional purposes.) He did agree that Burke would have to develop considerably and that it would take several interviews to persuade Burke to change as much as was necessary. Stanley understood Burke's defensiveness and did not let Burke's argumentative attitude interfere with his evaluation. Although Burke irritated him at times, he did not consider this grounds for discrediting Burke. He felt that Burke was a very good supervisor and he wanted him to be even better. The audience was quite surprised that such a fine attitude had not been communicated. Some even doubted that Stanley was sincere.

Stanley regarded the interview as an unpleasant chore and said there had been little satisfaction in it for him because his efforts were not appreciated. He was satisfied with his performance, however, and felt he had done better this time than on the first interview. He liked this Burke better, too.

Burke had a very bad feeling about the interview, not only because he felt unappreciated, but also because he had been treated in a condescending manner. He knew he was doing a good job and he had many ideas for improving things, but said he had no chance to tell Stanley. Burke felt that Stanley was a rigid person and said that even if Stanley had listened there was little reason to discuss the job with him because he had no imagination. Burke did not expect Stanley to visit his unit to check on the facts and he really did not care, he said, because he was quitting anyway.

Burke had not changed his attitude toward his fellow supervisors and felt that they were a bunch of unimaginative "yes men." However, he remained loyal to his own employees and hoped that when he had a new job he could hire them away from this company.

His estimation of Stanley dropped sharply as a result of the interview. He learned nothing constructive and realized how unaware Stanley was of conditions in the company. The secondary purpose of the interview, developing an employee, was not achieved. The results of the interview seem to have been unplanned and not intended, and to have been negative rather than positive.

Summary Notes on the Tell and Sell Interview

The Climate Created

In the last two chapters, the results of one specific approach to the appraisal interview have been presented. The climate created by both interactions between Stanley and Burke was formal and authoritarian. Early in each interview, Stanley established himself as a judge with superior wisdom and, consequently, superior insights into the situation. The process quickly led to feelings of frustration by both parties as Stanley assumed the role of a patient parent admonishing his child, thus promoting a win-lose situation.

Lack of genuine trust, rapport, and mutual caring contributed to this phenomenon and nonequal status was inferred from the outset. (In Transactional Analysis terms, the position was basically "I'm O.K., you're not O.K.") Most of the interview centered on correcting weaknesses that the interviewee chose not to acknowledge as valid. There was an overall feeling that little or no help was being given on either side.

Characteristics of the Interviewer

The interviewer who conducted the two Tell and Sell interviews spent significantly more time talking than did either interviewee (see Chapter 9). The former engaged in small talk, apparently to build some semblance of rapport, and then quickly implemented his plan for the interview. He gave praise for specific past performance. (This is part of a judge's role—to give praise where praise is due.) The approach Stanley used in each case was to point out deficiencies in Burke's performance and to specify areas for improvement. He left little or no room for interruptions or disagreement and assumed he had all the facts.

A "yes, but . . ." response set was evident throughout the exchanges and there was a lot of talking down to the interviewee. Many of Stanley's statements were "should" oriented. He decided when to correct and when to reward. Using a "carrot and stick" approach to motivating Burke, Stanley promised Burke possible advancement once problems were cleared up. Stanley assumed, sometimes erroneously, that Burke *wanted* to change.

Most of the energy of the interview was focused on words rather than on inflections and feelings. Stanley spent a lot of time attempting to win Burke over to his point of view. When Burke did not agree, Stanley's patience wore thin, which led to frustration and to his overlooking Burke's obvious feelings. Stanley thought Burke should retain his virtues and correct his faults, and he placed total responsibility on Burke for achieving this goal. To obtain instant reform, Stanley tried to make Burke feel guilty. When Burke did not "see the light" the result was irritation and hurt feelings for Stanley.

Characteristics of the Interviewee

Although two different interviewees were subjected to the Tell and Sell method, there was considerable overlap in their reactions.

Both were anxious and gave many protective responses. Considerable energy was expended defending past actions throughout each interview. Generally, each Burke showed respect for Stanley as a defendant does toward the judge—based on formal position rather than perceived help. After being neither heard nor genuinely responded to over a period of time, the Burkes became quite defensive. They were resistant to changing in the directions requested and demanded by Stanley, and they finally became locked into a rather stubborn position of self-righteousness. At times the Burkes expressed overt hostility; often it was present at a covert level.

The picture that evolved in each case was of a defensive, anxious, desperate person who could not make himself heard. Consequently, each Burke—in an attempt to terminate the interview—had a tendency to protect himself and to make promises that he did not intend to keep.

CHAPTER FIVE

Tell and Listen Method: First Interview

Transcription of the Interview

[S1] GEORGE STANLEY: Hi, Tom, how are you today?

> This friendly greeting could have been used for the Tell and Sell interview and would have served an equally good purpose. It requires Burke to respond.

[B1] TOM BURKE: Sir, fine, thanks—how are you?

> Burke's response is formal, indicated by the "Sir," but he responds to the tone Stanley sets.

[S2] GEORGE STANLEY: Come in and sit down for a minute.

> Stanley is standing and invites Burke to sit. He waits for Burke to seat himself.

[B2] TOM BURKE: Thank you.

> Burke's response is friendly.

[S3] GEORGE STANLEY: Well, Tom, as you know, we make appraisals of our employees every year. I've just completed your evaluation and I'd like to talk it over with you. As you also know, interviews regarding the evaluations are scheduled; the aim is to try to improve our people and to assist them in their development in the company. So I'd like to talk over some of the points on which you've been appraised and how you've been evaluated on them.

> Stanley comes directly to the point, stating the purpose of the interview. His use of the phrase "talk it over with you" implies that Burke is expected to participate. He mentions the company's desire to assist employees in their development, apparently attempting to appear as a helper rather than a judge. This role is stressed when he indicates that Burke's evaluation is a matter for discussion. (The method Stanley was requested to use is evident at this stage of the interview because Stanley makes an assumption that Burke will react.)

[B3] TOM BURKE: Well, that sounds like a good idea.

> Stanley's comments do not seem to have aroused anxiety, probably because Burke is quite satisfied with the job he has been doing.

[S4] GEORGE STANLEY: We are interested in helping every one of our employees to improve. First of all, I'd like to mention quite a few of the things that you're doing very well. You have creativity and originality, and your workmanship is excellent. You're to be commended on this.

> Stanley continues in his role as a helper. He seems to try to escape the difficulty of being a judge. As the previous Stanley did, he goes to the good points first. By mentioning quite a few good points, he amplifies Burke's merits, but he also suggests that there may be weaknesses. (This might serve to prepare Burke for critical comments or it might produce anxiety—an undesirable reaction.) Stanley hastens to praise several good points about Burke, as if to forestall any anxiety, but in so doing he assumes the role of a judge.

[B4] TOM BURKE: Well, I have a good crew working for me and we really turn out the work; I think a lot of the credit should go to these other people—like Frank, my junior designer. He does a good job and he's a good person to keep an eye on, I think.

> Burke shows no evidence of anxiety. He generously shares credit with his group and puts in a plug for Frank Dobbs. (An anxious person is too aware of his own situation to show consideration for others.)

[S5] GEORGE STANLEY: Yes, when you mention your whole unit being productive, I notice that, within the last two years especially, the unit itself has been able to handle bigger and better jobs and there has been steady improvement. And this latest example, when we've had to pile some extra work on you during the last six months (you know, we do have a new contract now) you were able to come through and get the work done on schedule. As far as I'm concerned, your productivity and dependability make you tops; that's all there is to it.

> Stanley shows skill when he does not move on to a different point, but elaborates on the good work, taking his cue from Burke and giving the whole unit credit. Toward the end of his speech, however, he points up the accomplishment in a way that gives Burke credit for the work of his group. He says that Burke is "tops."

[B5] TOM BURKE: Well, thank you very much. It's nice to know that you've done a good job.

> Burke now accepts the praise as a personal tribute. (After this buildup, he may not be prepared for unfavorable criticism.)

[S6] GEORGE STANLEY: Well, I'm sure that you know that you've done a good job, and I want to tell you that we're aware of it and we do appreciate good work like this. Now as you know, once again every story has at least two sides and I'd like to get you to aim toward improving yourself, so I'd like to bring up some things where I've had to rate you down a bit below your other exceptional performance. As you also know, we like to cite examples rather than just talk about something in the abstract when you're not doing something right; in other words, we like to sort of pinpoint the difficulty. Several things have come to mind; one of them, of course, is in the area of your cooperation with the other supervisors. Now, specifically, Jim Drake—now Jim has . . .

> Stanley responds to Burke's acceptance and summarizes the episode by expressing appreciation; then he takes on a somewhat superior air and assumes more definitely the role of a judge. He approaches the unfavorable issues, moving carefully and diplomatically, but not confining his remarks to generalities. He gives a specific reference so that Burke will understand. (Everything in this speech could have been said in a Tell and Sell interview. The methods are similar at this point; only the skills and styles are different.)

[B6] TOM BURKE [Interrupting]: Oh, I know about that—you're going to talk about this design change thing that happened? [Stanley nods.] Well, that was really something that got lost in the shuffle . . . it was something that I tried to straighten out with Jim. I didn't know that he had told you. I know it caused him some trouble, but I offered to correct everything. What happened was that I got caught up with some stuff I was doing and I had forgotten to tell him about it and I offered to correct it for him, but he sort of resented it; I don't know why. I've helped him out before—everyone is entitled to at least one mistake.

> Burke takes the discussion from Stanley. He seems to feel quite free with Stanley and confident that he can clarify the matter because it is a small thing. As he talks, however, he seems somewhat irritated with Jim Drake and shows no remorse for the trouble he caused Drake. (His final comment that everyone is entitled to at least one mistake is surprisingly defensive— the kind of remark that will irritate a judge or a superior.)

[S7] GEORGE STANLEY: Do you feel then that this was due to a misunderstanding?

> Stanley sharply deviates from the typical response. Instead of judging or showing hostility, he reflects Burke's feelings. (This is Stanley's first use of the nondirective procedure and it is designed to help Burke express his feelings at this point.)

[B7] TOM BURKE: It just got lost in the shuffle. It was written down on my calendar and when I tried to get to him he was out or something. Well, you know how these things happen. I was very busy and then when I got caught up on the rest of the work—well, I forgot to tell him about it. I don't know why he took it so hard, as if I'd knifed him or something. I don't understand it.

> Burke clarifies the matter further, but he obviously feels that Jim Drake has been at fault in behaving as he did. Stanley can now probe more deeply and help Burke to clarify his feelings or change the subject.

[S8] GEORGE STANLEY: Well, as you know, we're trying to develop good teamwork here; and, as you mentioned, your success is due partly to the success of the unit, so you can see why I feel the same way about the people working under me. We have to have teamwork among the supervisors, and I do like to decrease any friction that might arise. Now take the situation you mention here; Jim, of course, had one idea on it and as you present your views on it I can see that you had another. Since it was a mistake, there's a possibility that it won't happen again. This, of course, is what we hope because we want to make this a smooth-running outfit.

> Stanley lets the chance to further reflect Burke's feelings slip by. Instead, he does a little selling. It is difficult for an interviewer not to present another side of an issue when the other person persists in seeing only one side. However, Stanley is understanding and considerate and gives Burke an opportunity to save face by indicating that the incident was a mistake that might not happen again. He mentions his goal—a smooth-running outfit.

[B8] TOM BURKE: I'm very interested in that; in fact, I have some pretty strong ideas about how we could better it. For example, you could put some good workers in their units—I mean, I used to work right along with the other supervisors and I still do; I try to help out when I can and, as you say, I have been doing more work probably than any other unit, and I think that the other units could probably do this, too, if they would just buckle down to the job and have some good employees working for them.

> Burke's response is evidence of both problem solving and defensiveness. His initial sentence is a polite correction of Stanley's supposition that Burke must be "sold" on the idea of being part of a good team. (This is defensive.) He then describes a solution, which, although practical, reveals Burke's defensive feelings with (a) the several vague but unfavorable remarks about other units; (b) mention of his help for the other units in the past; (c) the claim that he still helps them, which is undoubtedly exaggerated, if not untrue; and (d) the reference to "good workers," meaning Dobbs, since this ties the discussion back to what Burke previously mentioned. In effect, Burke tells Stanley that the new topic is only a reflection of the problem that he (Burke) had been trying to solve a moment earlier.

[S9] GEORGE STANLEY: Well, you feel that it is partially the persons who are working in the unit and also the supervisor who is over them who are the big determining factors in how productive a unit is.

> Apparently, Stanley senses the feeling in Burke's response, but instead of reacting in the usual manner by counterattacking, defending himself, or using the force of his position, he reflects Burke's feelings. (This is a crucial point in the interview and Stanley, by his sensitivity and proper use of counseling skills, keeps it from deteriorating.)

[B9] TOM BURKE: It sure is. When you have an employee who just sort of gets along—one who just does passable work—and find there are other people in the organization who really know their business, it gets you down. Take Frank, for instance. He ought to be up there.

> Burke responds by clarifying his meaning. He specifically says that Frank Dobbs should have one of the supervisory jobs, and even implies that Dobbs should replace one of the other supervisors. Such an open remark indicates that Burke feels free to confide in Stanley.

[S10] GEORGE STANLEY: You feel that Frank then is a definite promotion possibility for the supervisory job.

> Stanley again reflects Burke's views about promoting Dobbs but leaves out the idea of replacing another supervisor. (This indicates Stanley's skill. Stanley's conservative interpretation permits Burke to reconsider.)

[B10] TOM BURKE: No question about that—you're really missing a bet if you miss him.

> Burke accepts Stanley's restatement as correct, emphasizing Dobbs' value without pushing him as a replacement.

[S11] GEORGE STANLEY: Well, I'm certainly glad to hear that; I'll put it down in my book here so I'll be sure to look into it to see if there are any possibilities. I'll certainly try to make sure that Frank does receive consideration for any future promotion.

> Stanley readily accepts the revised evaluation of Dobbs as something that should be followed up and he promises to do this. (If this acceptance is sincere and not a manipulative gesture, Stanley must let Burke know about any steps he takes.)

[B11] TOM BURKE: Well, I appreciate that because he's a good prospect and deserves a lot of breaks . . .

> Burke's response indicates that he wants and expects Stanley to look into something better for Dobbs, but he does not seem entirely satisfied. He continues to make a case for Dobbs.

[S12] GEORGE STANLEY [Interrupting]: O.K., let's talk about several other things that have come up. Along this line of teamwork—what we try to do here is not to show favoritism to people. We try to, and do, give the units job assignments that they're best fitted for and that, in the big picture, will carry out our function. Now twice in the last six months I've tried to give you several routine assignments and both of these times you suggested that you preferred to do the more interesting work—the more complicated work. You suggested that I possibly could give these assignments to other supervisors. Well, to prevent any difficulty at the time, I followed your suggestion; and it's true that when you were given the complicated jobs you were able to do them *quite* well. The thing is, I don't feel that I can give you *all* the interesting jobs. Some of them are going to have to go to other units, because I feel this is a share and share alike kind of situation. I feel that if you want to improve, and that's what I hope our talk will lead to, you will go along with the idea of accepting the routine assignments as well as the interesting ones. This will show that you have a high spirit of cooperation, which is one of the things that we prize highly around here.

> Although Stanley interrupts at this point, he apparently thinks Burke has finished. (Perhaps Stanley is being efficient by changing the subject after disposing of one matter. A safer way would have been to pause a bit. Stanley's approach to the new subject is artful. He does not find fault, but he describes a situation with which he is faced.)

> After describing the overall picture, Stanley mentions that Burke's behavior has caused him a problem. He plays down Burke's success by saying he's handled the job "quite well." The word "quite" seems to have slipped into the evaluation and Burke probably notices it. Stanley explains that he must be fair and can not give Burke "all the interesting jobs."

> (The use of the word "all" is unfair, because Burke does not want them all.) Stanley goes on to sell Burke on the virtues of cooperation; to the uncritical observer, Stanley's conduct might be seen as unusually kind and restrained. (Many observers who identified with Stanley thought that he should have spoken more forcefully, but the last part of the speech is clearly Tell and Sell.)

[B12] TOM BURKE: Well, that's one way of looking at it, but you can look at it another way, too—that we are working as a team and we've got to produce by doing the things that we can do best. And, as I say, some units can do mediocre work; they should get the mediocre jobs. But if you have a unit like mine that can do the better jobs—the stuff that requires a little thinking and ability—I think, for the benefit of the whole group, we ought to get the complicated jobs. As you say, we're doing the complex jobs well—why give them to a group that will do sloppy work on them. I don't see how it is uncooperative of me to want these jobs when I know that I can do them well, and I have doubts about some of the other groups.

> Burke clearly is hurt. He indicates that Stanley has not seen his side of the picture and implies that Stanley has not been giving recognition to his group. The desire for recognition is apparent—Burke now calls the work of other

units "mediocre" and even "sloppy," and praises his own work. (Though all of these statements may be true, Burke communicates that he feels unappreciated by making such claims under these circumstances. His defense is aggressive when he accuses Stanley of calling him "uncooperative.")

[S13] GEORGE STANLEY: You feel then that you have a superior unit and, as a consequence, you can handle these jobs better than some of the other groups?

> Stanley again avoids trouble and reflects Burke's feelings about the superiority of his own unit. (He could have denied the charge Burke made, as he had only talked about "a high spirit of cooperation" as an ideal condition.)

[B13] TOM BURKE: There is no question about it, and I think from the standpoint of productivity we ought to get those jobs. In other words, the more complicated and the more interesting job assignments should go to the better units—the ones that can really handle them as far as the company is concerned—and our unit is one of the better units.

> Burke now elaborates on his feelings and indicates how the assignments should be made. There is still a good deal of feeling behind his remarks.

[S14] GEORGE STANLEY: I see.

> Stanley continues to hear Burke out.

[B14] TOM BURKE: I don't agree with you that it is uncooperative of me not to want to take the routine jobs. I've had my share of them. I have shown you that I can do good work, so why shouldn't I get the interesting ones—the ones that we can do our best on?

> Burke goes on to justify himself and to attempt to prove that he is cooperative. Stanley's criticism, though carefully worded, seems to have hurt Burke a lot.

[S15] GEORGE STANLEY: Do you feel you should get all the interesting jobs and none of the routine jobs or . . .

> Stanley again reflects Burke's views of fairness, but he does it in a way that requires further elaboration. (Whether Burke wants all of or just more of the interesting jobs may show whether Burke is selfish, practical, or in need of recognition.)

[B15] TOM BURKE: No, but I think that, until the other groups can show that they can handle the jobs as well as I can—well, they'll have to prove themselves before they have the same right to claim them. I think that for the efficiency of the whole group we can do a better job if I get the good ones.

> Burke's response further clarifies his attitude. He feels that others must earn the right to the good jobs. (That this method of allocating jobs will be more efficient may be true, but this solution to the efficiency problem may be a rationalization. Burke feels entitled to some rights because he has earned them, so he is defensive about the question of cooperation.)

[S16] GEORGE STANLEY: Yes [pause]—again this taking a look at the big picture . . .

> Stanley apparently does not appreciate Burke's need for recognition and attempts to persuade Burke to see his side—the larger picture.

[B16] TOM BURKE: That's right—I mean this is the way you were looking at it and I figure that this is all right with me, because I think others have difficulties if they get the complex jobs in their units. You'll get a good job if you give them to my group and you'll make it easier for the other units.

> Burke interrupts to explain his view of the larger picture.

[S17] GEORGE STANLEY: I see. O.K., well, that's another suggestion along the lines of getting better productivity as a whole group. Now there's another thing I'd like to bring to your attention and I'm sure you're aware of it. It seems that a lot of time—perhaps your time—is spent in doing a training job on people and I notice we seem to have a big turnover problem in your particular department. This has come to my attention within the last six months. Even though your group is very productive, we seem to have a high turnover there. Some good people have been leaving your particular unit and have taken other jobs. Now, this isn't so true in any of the other groups. As I say, this is a problem for both of us. It's costing us money; as you know, high turnover takes up your time so that you can't devote your energies to the more interesting problems, because you have to take your time in training new employees. This is another thing that's on your appraisal because of [pause] well, it influences the way the company looks at you. Tom, you have realized that we're pretty cost conscious around here, and I want you to know that we're aware of this and so . . .

> Stanley realizes he is not making a point. He has not been convinced by Burke's views and he is not removing Burke's resistance. He does justice to the Tell and Listen method by avoiding an argument. He skillfully accepts Burke's views without evaluating them and without committing himself and proceeds to another point in the evaluation.
>
> (It may be too much to suppose that Burke will be receptive at this stage. Methods of letting a person know where he stands do not guard against a negative reaction. At any rate, Stanley seems to feel compelled to take up a third criticism. He brings it up kindly and seems to want to be helpful. However, he makes the assumptions that turnover reflects badly on a supervisor and that training given by Burke to new employees costs the company money.)

[B17] TOM BURKE [Interrupting]: Well, I agree the training we give is very good, and maybe that is the cause of what happens. However, I wasn't really aware of the magnitude of the turnover, but I noticed what's happening with Frank—he's looking for a supervisory job and I told you he's well qualified. If he can't get ahead faster in this company he'll go someplace else, and he can get a better job because he's a good employee. I don't think I neglected my training; it's just that when you train a person, well, he just expects to move up when he gets better. And some of these people get better and there's no place for them to go here so they leave. For instance, take my secretary. She just turned down a job to stay with my group. Although I've wanted to talk it over with you and see what we could do for her, I think she's satisfied. She's a real good worker and she enjoys working with me and vice versa, so she turned down an offer from another place, even though there was a big raise, too . . .

> Burke has a ready response. He admits his training is good and indicates that this may be the reason for the high turnover. (Stanley had made the turnover the reason for the training.) Burke gently but firmly contradicts Stanley. He shows appreciation for the importance of keeping turnover down by repeating the suggestion he made at the outset—promote Dobbs.

> He returns to the question of training and defends himself. He assumes that Stanley has charged him with neglecting training. He mentions that his secretary turned down a raise and new job, indicating that he feels Stanley is dissatisfied with his supervisory ability. (The tendency to defend against a charge that has not been made shows that communication took place without any words being said. Apparently, Stanley's specific dissatisfactions have become quite generalized in Burke's mind. Burke behaves as if he thinks Stanley considers him a poor supervisor.)

[S18] GEORGE STANLEY [Interrupting]: And she turned it down to stay here, huh? Well . . .

> Stanley reacts to Burke's point about the secretary, and shows surprise. (Apparently, he did not regard Burke as such a good supervisor after all.)

[B18] TOM BURKE: So, I don't really think that it's a training problem, but a matter of where they go after they're trained—especially if you stick them with a routine job. If they're good, they aren't even going to enjoy the job they've got here unless we do something. If they can't move up, well, they move out; that's the ways things go. I agree that there has been a fairly good turnover in my unit, but they haven't just been leaving for another job—they have been going to better jobs. I think it might be a matter of company policy—or maybe I don't know what it is. I guess I don't know how to solve the problem, but, as you say, our group has been producing well, yet they leave. I don't know exactly what your problem is for the department as a whole; it's true it takes some time to train new people, but it hasn't hurt my efficiency—certainly if considered with respect to the rest of the units in our department.

> Burke continues with the question of turnover. He, in effect, blames both Stanley and the company—Stanley because he expects good employees to be kept on routine jobs, and the company for not creating opportunities for advancement.

After he defends himself, he takes a look at the problem and finds he does not have an answer for keeping turnover down. He says he does feel he should continue to develop people, even if they do leave. His only new insight is that keeping employees satisfied isn't as simple as he once thought. However, he is firm in his belief that training should be continued.

[S19] GEORGE STANLEY: Well, it's the problem of turnover. It looks bad on our record as a department, and, as I said before, it is one of the things that you are evaluated on. We have to consider the cooperativeness of your unit and ask ourselves whether your people stay or do they go on? Do they go up in the organization, or, in this particular case, do they go out to other companies? I gather that you feel that you've trained these people, that the training has made them better, and that because there isn't any opportunity here they're leaving for better jobs, rather than because of dissatisfaction. Is that right?

> Stanley indicates that it is the turnover figure, rather than the training costs, that determines the evaluation. He tells Burke where he stands; summarizes Burke's defense without evaluating it; and asks Burke whether the summary is correct.

[B19] TOM BURKE: Don't you talk to them when they leave? Don't they tell you why they leave?

> Burke's response is quite defensive. Burke has assumed that he is right and apparently mistakes Stanley's question as an indication that his own interpretation has been doubted. His response indicates that he thinks Stanley should have the facts, and his manner is a polite expression of surprise.

[S20] GEORGE STANLEY: Well, yes, but frequently we must figure that they just want to get a good recommendation from us, so we have to be critical. They sometimes tell us things so that we can't put complete faith in what they say, because a lot of them are emotional when they leave, anyway.

> Stanley again avoids trouble by accepting Burke's response without being defensive. He gives a rationale for questioning information gained in exit interviews and implies he may know more than he is sharing by making a reference to the employees being "emotional." (The last remark seems to be an unguarded slap at Burke. It is doubtful that Stanley is aware of it.)

[B20] TOM BURKE: Well, they sure have a right to be. From what I hear in talking to those people before they leave, they express regret, but feel they can't overlook opportunities. That's the way the situation is. I agree that it looks bad on the record, but I don't know for sure whether it's my fault. Maybe it is—that's something I should think about.

> Burke does react to the word "emotional." He implies that he also has information about how employees feel about leaving his unit. Then, for the first time, he faces the turnover problem and gradually moves toward the question

of his involvement—he does not know whether it is his fault, but it is something to think about.

[S21] GEORGE STANLEY: Can you think of anything you might be doing that would make these people leave? You might be doing too good a job of training. . . . Well, we certainly don't want to discourage you from doing a good job for us, Tom; this is far from what we have in mind . . . [pause]

> Stanley feels that he has reached Burke. His initial question is a good one, assuming Burke is at fault. By implying that Burke is training the employees too well, he may be undermining one of Burke's greatest assets. (The value of this remark also hinges on what is assumed to be an improvement.)

[B21] TOM BURKE: Well, you know how it is—you train a person to do a good job and he expects you—well, [long pause] why have you been training me now? Suppose I can do your job as well as you can; why don't I have your job? If my people can do my job and I can't give it to them, well, [pause] it sometimes makes it pretty embarrassing to have to answer a question like that.

> Burke's response indicates that he is doing some thinking. His value system apparently has been disturbed.

[S22] GEORGE STANLEY: Well, the point of this discussion has been to try to get your ideas and also to do something in the direction of improvement. I do want you to keep in mind the idea of the team, and you working with other supervisors. This is important to us because I rely on your helping on my team, just as you rely on the people underneath you for helping your team show high productivity, dependability, and things like that.

> Stanley does not follow up. Either he does not have the answer or he wishes to stimulate Burke's thinking. Apparently, he wants Burke to take a new look at the whole operation, because he refers back to other negative points in the evaluation. He indicates approval of Burke by saying he "relies" on him for help and by referring to the good work of his unit.

[B22] TOM BURKE: I told you that my team, [pause] well, I feel it's a good team and shows a superior performance and, [pause] well, I don't know about the other people at my level, but I think you would do better if you put some other people in, but I don't know how you would do this. I don't like to see anyone get kicked out.

> Burke appears defensive again. Stanley's request for help for other supervisors does not set too well. Burke indicates his inability to respect some of his associates, but after saying it he is generous—he does not want them "kicked out."

[S23] GEORGE STANLEY: All right, I'll keep in mind what you've said here, but before you go let me just sort of put together some of the things we've talked about. We've pointed out the good points in your unit, then some of the things where we seem to have differences of opinion, and we've explored your ideas. As a result of some of the ideas that I have gotten from you, I gather that Frank down there is a very good worker and we should definitely consider him for promotion possibilities as a supervisor; another one of your feelings is that the best working groups should get the most interesting jobs, and, as far as you're concerned, you rate your unit as the tops.

> Stanley accepts Burke's opinions as something to "keep in mind" and summarizes the interview by referring to the plus items on the evaluation as "good points" and the negative items as "differences of opinion." His last sentence makes Burke seem something of a braggart and may embarrass Burke.

[B23] TOM BURKE: Well, you said that, too, Boss . . . it's not just my opinion—there are records to show it.

> Burke seems somewhat embarrassed, but handles it well.

[S24] GEORGE STANLEY: Yes, that's for sure, and the last thing that we mentioned here was that the turnover problem seems to be highly related to the opportunities the people have within the company—that people like Frank, and others who are highly trained, have gained a lot from working here, but they feel stymied if they . . .

> Stanley continues the summary to include the controversial turnover item, but he includes Burke's diagnosis and mentions Dobbs.

[B24] TOM BURKE [Interrupting]: I think it is a real shame that we're losing people like that.

> Burke interrupts to drive his point home. (That Burke continues to defend himself after Stanley has accepted and summarized his points indicates how much the criticism has disturbed him and his relations with Stanley.)

[S25] GEORGE STANLEY: Well, Tom, I sure do thank you for coming in and talking this over with me. I think we've both benefited from this discussion and I hope that the next time the evaluation comes up, I'll be able to rate you high in everything.

> Stanley's final statement is generous. He indicates that both benefited, but his hope that Burke can be rated high on everything on the next evaluation closes the interview with Stanley in the role of the judge.

[B25] TOM BURKE: Well, thank you very much.

> Burke responds with thanks, but it would be too much to suppose that the interview ended on a high note.

Evaluation of the Interview

An audit of the transcription revealed that the pace was more lei-surely in this interview than in the first two; each participant spoke more slowly and calmly and there were fewer interruptions.

Some of the differences between the two interview styles may be attributable to personality differences between the persons who played Stanley. The Stanley who conducted the two Tell and Sell interviews was a rapid and intense talker, but he was trained in counseling and was able to be a good listener. The Stanley who conducted the two Tell and Listen interviews had a strong voice and was by nature inclined to argue, although he was less verbose than the first. The interview methods assigned to these two interviewers seemed to suppress the listening aptitude of the first and the argumentative inclination of the second.

The two kinds of interviews showed a striking similarity in topics dis-cussed, which is to be expected when the methods have the common objec-tive of acquainting the employee with his appraisal. Both interviewers conformed with this objective and, although each presented the negative points in different ways, neither prevented Burke from becoming defen-sive. However, the last interviewer did avoid becoming defensive himself. This difference may be due to the methods practiced. The objective of "selling" makes the superior want *the subordinate to accept the appraisal* and the supervisor may have a mental set that causes him to suppress opposition, but the objective of "listening" predisposes *the interviewer to expect and encourage opposition*.

The interviewer using the Tell and Sell method revealed his set by not giving Burke opportunities to present his views, and the interviewer using the Tell and Listen method waited for Burke's reaction to each of the new points. The latter showed some excellent counseling skills in re-sponse to Burke's defensive behavior, but he also showed some oversights when he did not probe Burke's feelings deeply enough. His inclination to communicate the appraisal may have conflicted with his inclination to listen. (A training problem for this type of interview would be to increase the sensitivity of interviewers to mildly expressed defensive responses to prevent hurt feelings such as those that occurred during this interview.)

Analysis of Interaction

Analysis of the number of words spoken by the two participants revealed that for both halves of the interview the proportion was about equal; the percentage for Stanley was 56.7 for the first half and 49.4 for the second half. The decline in Stanley's dominance during this Tell and Listen interview was due both to Stanley talking less and to Burke talking

**Table 3. Words Spoken by Each Participant
During First Tell and Listen Interview**

Speech	Stanley		Burke	
1	6		6	
2	8		2	
3	78		7	
4	46		51	
5	95		15	
6	141		111	
7	11		78	
8	120		98	
9	35		48	
10	14		13	
11	45		15	
12	232		147	
13	25		61	
	856	56.7%	652	= 1508
14	2		52	
15	17		59	
16	10		59	
17	212		185	
18	10		175	
19	108		15	
20	51		62	
21	50		73	
22	78		61	
23	122		17	
24	54		13	
25	44		5	
	758	49.4%	776	= 1534
Total	1614	+	1428	= 3042
Percent	53.0		46.9	

more. Table 3 shows the amount spoken by each participant in each of his twenty-five speeches. Stanley's lack of domination was most apparent in the middle of the interview when Stanley was listening to Burke and was less concerned with introducing the evaluation or summarizing.

Reactions of Audience

The response of the audience was highly favorable, indicated by spontaneous applause at the termination of the interview. The general feeling was that this interview was a demonstration of the proper method for conducting appraisal interviews, and everyone was convinced of its basic merits. Most agreed that Burke knew where he stood and that he left feeling that he had profited from the experience.

Persons identifying with Stanley were almost unanimous in their praise of the way the interview was conducted and felt that he had shown a great deal of tolerance for Burke, whom they regarded as too "cocky." They thought that Burke had been made aware of his weaknesses, however, and that he would improve by being more cooperative with other supervisors and somewhat more willing to accept assignments, and that he had a greater appreciation of the importance of reducing turnover. They also felt that Stanley had learned something about Burke's problems and that he would try to find something better for Dobbs. They agreed that Burke had not gone down in Stanley's estimation, although he had gone down in the estimation of some of Stanley's identifiers.

Persons identifying with Burke felt that he could improve, but a small minority had doubts and reservations. Many felt that Stanley may have gone up in Burke's estimation and none felt he had lost. The general feeling was that, although Burke was disappointed in the appraisal, he would recover and be a better supervisor as a consequence.

Reactions of Participants

Questions directed to the participants added some interesting insights. Stanley was quite satisfied with the interviewing job he had done and had not found the task difficult or unpleasant. He said that he had become irritated at several points, but had remembered that he was supposed to listen. Burke had gone up in his estimation and he was inclined to think that Burke's ability to handle his unit was somewhat better than he had initially assumed. He felt that Burke had growth potential and that he (Stanley) was making progress with him in the interview. Stanley believed that Burke left the interview with a favorable feeling and would not question job assignments in the future.

Burke's response was also favorable and Stanley had gone up in his estimation. He felt that he had "gotten things off his chest" and that Stanley would do something for Dobbs. He knew that Stanley thought well of him and said that after the appraisals were over things would go on as before. Because he was obviously the best supervisor, he knew that Stanley could not get along without him. He indicated that he wanted to think about the turnover, but felt that he had discovered no ways in which he could do a better job. He asked how he could improve when no special ideas or plans had been discussed and said he felt the next move was up to Stanley.

CHAPTER SIX

Tell and Listen Method: Second Interview

Transcription of the Interview

[S1] GEORGE STANLEY: Hi, Tom, how are you today? Come on in and sit down.

Stanley sounds very friendly.

[B1] TOM BURKE: Fine, Mr. Stanley.

Burke seems relaxed but formal.

[S2] GEORGE STANLEY: Well, Tom, as you know, every year we conduct appraisals and our aim in conducting these is to try to help the employees to improve themselves and also to clear up any misunderstandings we have, but the primary aim is toward self-improvement. Now, in appraising you, I'd like to point out some of the things that you surely deserve credit for and I want to let you know that we recognize these things, too. According to our records on your evaluation, the things that are outstanding are your creativity and your originality. You're very competent technically—in fact you are *exceptional* in this way. Your unit here is very productive and during the last two years when you have been supervising them they have shown definite improvement. I want to let you know once again that we do appreciate things like this.

Stanley's introduction shows warmth and should put Burke at ease. Stanley brings out the purpose of the interview and quickly tries to remove any anxiety Burke may have. Although Stanley says that improvement is the primary objective of the interview, he makes it clear that an appraisal has been made. He assumes the role of a judge; his final sentence makes it clear that he decides which behavior is to be praised and should be continued. (Because Stanley's judgment is favorable at this stage, his conduct probably will not lead to conflict, and Burke seems to be at ease. A similar introduction could have been made in the Tell and Sell type of interview.)

[B2] TOM BURKE: I'm glad to hear about it, Mr. Stanley.

Burke expresses his appreciation for Stanley's compliments and seems to accept him as a judge.

[S3] GEORGE STANLEY: I certainly admire the way you have shouldered the load during the last six months—we've had to give you a lot of extra work and you've taken care of it. You've produced more than the other groups and we can always count on you to do an excellent job. These are some of the things I want you to understand: we do appreciate your efforts and we are aware of them and they are not just being ignored. Right?

After obtaining Burke's approval of the discussion up to this point, Stanley gives further praise. He implies praise for himself by telling Burke that his office keeps track of and appreciates good performance. When Stanley concludes with "Right?" he in effect asks Burke to endorse him as a competent and fair judge and creates an opportunity for Burke to respond. (Stanley has encouraged Burke to respond to each of his first two speeches. In this way he receives some feedback and gains some idea how Burke will respond to the interview. Seeking a response flows naturally from the Tell and Listen method.)

[B3] TOM BURKE: Well, thank you very much, Mr. Stanley.

Burke's response is most favorable. If he has reservations, he does not reveal them.

[S4] GEORGE STANLEY: Now, as I say, the aim here is to try to help develop you. I'd like to point out some of the things that you weren't as high on as you could have been; in other words, these are areas for improvement. One of the things that has come to my attention is the—well, the difficulty you had with Jim Drake. Now, he is a fellow supervisor and he made this mistake, which was a fairly serious one. The feeling was that possibly you could have forestalled this if you had given him the information ahead of time or in some way given him a hand.

Stanley frankly, but not unkindly, discusses an incident where he believes Burke was at fault. He does not say that he knows all the facts and his approach is more like asking for Burke's version. (It is apparent that he expects to listen to Burke's story.)

[B4] TOM BURKE: This was my mistake. I'll admit it, and I feel very badly about it, but it just happened on one occasion. There was this design change and I was involved in something else and I'll admit I did forget to let Jim know. When I remembered, I apologized to him, but there wasn't any more that I could do. It certainly wasn't intentional on my part. I'm sure it will never happen again. I can assure you of that.

> Burke accepts responsibility for the error and explains how it happened. He seems to have had no bad intentions toward Drake and he assures Stanley that it will not happen again. (Having an adequate opportunity to explain seems to prevent Burke from becoming defensive.)

[S5] GEORGE STANLEY: Well, this is one thing—anybody can make a mistake—but to make the same mistake several times . . .

> Stanley begins to accept Burke's explanation and gives him a face-saver by saying that anybody can make a mistake. However, some doubt seems to enter his mind and he talks about repeating a mistake. (This remark seems to be a slip-up in Stanley's skill.)

[B5] TOM BURKE [Interrupting]: But this has only happened once . . .

> Burke interrupts in his own defense, denying that there were "several times."

[S6] GEORGE STANLEY [Interrupting]: Well, *this* instance has only happened once . . .

> Stanley does not seem to sense Burke's defensive attitude. He concedes that the particular mistake has happened only once, but implies that there are others. (This vague type of charge is not required by the Tell and Listen method and is a deficiency in skill. Perhaps Stanley is attempting to use one incident as an entering wedge for a discussion of other faults.)

[B6] TOM BURKE [Interrupting]: Can you give me any other examples?

> Burke interrupts again and requests some other examples.

[S7] GEORGE STANLEY: No. As you know, what we try to do in making an appraisal here is not only to think of things in general—in other words, attitude and things like that—but actually to try and cite examples so that the person won't say, "Oh, you're just making a snap judgment" or something without any facts to back it up. . . . This incident was one of the things. Maybe it reflects a bigger picture and that is the cooperation between you and the other foremen. It seems to me that maybe you have drifted away from having contacts and helping the other foremen out.

> Stanley admits he has no specific example in mind, but avoids becoming defensive and justifies his approach. He says there is an attitude behind the mistake and it is this attitude that must be traced. He tries to make the Drake incident an opening to discuss Burke's relationships with his fellow supervisors. (Just because Burke admits an oversight that will not recur does not convince Stanley that Burke's attitude is good. He has prejudged Burke's

attitude and now is unable to accept Burke's description of the Drake affair as an honest mistake. He apparently *listened*, but did not *learn*.)

[B7] TOM BURKE: Well, my main responsibility is to my own group. I have to keep up my own production. [pause] But there are incidents in which I have gone out of my way to help other supervisors. I have had to neglect my own people and I think that my own production has gone down.

Although Burke might have said he regretted his drift away from his fellow supervisors under other circumstances, he is clearly defensive now. He mentions his responsibility to his own unit and he refers to other supervisors in a derogatory manner.

[S8] GEORGE STANLEY: You feel, then, the responsibility is primarily for your own unit, and as such if you take time away to . . .

Stanley seems to be aware of Burke's defensive reaction at this point and changes to a nondirective approach. He begins to reflect the feelings Burke has expressed, helping to clarify them.

[B8] TOM BURKE [Interrupting]: I have my job to do and they have their jobs to do. My responsibility is my own production and my own crew and I try to fulfill that responsibility.

Burke tells where he feels his major responsibility lies.

[S9] GEORGE STANLEY: Well, you are certainly doing a fine job and we don't want to discourage you from continuing to do the job.

Stanley's response is reassuring. He assumes the role of judge and takes a stand—this time on Burke's side. (It may have been better if Stanley had continued to reflect and draw out Burke's feelings.)

[B9] TOM BURKE: My job isn't to run the other departments; they're each under competent supervisors [pause] presumably.

Burke continues to defend his position. He has apparently been hurt by Stanley's generalization about his bad attitude. Burke's sarcastic remark about his fellow supervisors reveals his feelings toward them. The word "presumably" appears to have just slipped out.

[S10] GEORGE STANLEY: You say presumably. Do you have any ideas that the other departments aren't up to par?

Stanley picks up the key word and asks Burke to elaborate. (Burke may not feel free to express himself on this point, particularly after Stanley has questioned his cooperativeness with the other supervisors.)

[B10] TOM BURKE: Oh . . . I wouldn't like to say that exactly . . . no . . . [pause]

Burke reveals a reluctance to discuss the point.

[S11] GEORGE STANLEY: Well, as I say, the main thing is this: you have your unit and you have a team—you try to develop them and try to have it smooth-running and be highly productive and dependable. In my case, I have the same problem. I have to get my supervisors together and try to see that they work as a team, too. The team that we've got here is with supervisors and I like to get them to work together. You know we can't get anything really done around here unless there is a lot of teamwork. This is important.

> Stanley tries to draw Burke into a discussion of teamwork among the supervisors. (If Burke were not so defensive, this could be a problem of mutual interest. Here Stanley is taking his cue from the Problem-Solving method, but perhaps too late to be helpful.)

[B11] TOM BURKE: Well, it isn't only up to me; it is up to the other supervisors, too . . . I can't cooperate if they are going to be uncooperative. [pause] It's a matter of give and take. [pause] I don't want to take all the blame if there is any blame being handed out.

> Burke reveals his defensiveness. To avoid blame he places the fault elsewhere. He apparently assumes that Stanley is trying to determine innocence or guilt.

[S12] GEORGE STANLEY: Do you feel that you could possibly be contributing to this—this not having as much cooperation as we might have?

> Stanley's response indicates that Burke's suspicion is justified. Stanley reveals his belief that Burke is not doing all he should to cooperate with his fellow supervisors.

[B12] TOM BURKE: Outside of this one example that you gave, I can't think of anything else that I've done that I should feel sorry for. [pause] If you have any other examples, I'd be glad to hear about them, but this is the only one that comes to my mind and I've said that I'm sorry for it. There was nothing I could do—I forgot; it certainly wasn't intentional.

> (The interview is still where it was during Burke's fourth speech [B4] except that Burke now is defensive and feels somewhat hostile toward Stanley. Stanley's attempt to generalize from one case was a basic error.)

[S13] GEORGE STANLEY: As I say, we're all liable to make mistakes, and the big thing, of course, is, in the future, if we can cut down the number of mistakes, so much the better. Now several other things have come up, Tom, so that once again I had to mark you down a little bit below your other excellent performance. One of these has to do with the job assignments. As you know, in the last six months or so, I have been trying to give you your share of jobs and other people their share of jobs: the good, the routine, and the exceptional ones. In two instances in the last six months, you refused or said you'd rather do the more interesting jobs—the more exciting ones, if you want to call them that.

Stanley again goes only part way in accepting the Drake incident as a mistake that anyone could have made. Instead of dropping the subject, he mentions cutting down the number of mistakes in the future, despite Burke's initial assurance that the mistake would not recur. Then he introduces another of Burke's weaknesses, which he contrasts with Burke's otherwise excellent record.

(Stanley is surprisingly insensitive to Burke's feelings at this point in the interview. He seemed much more alert to Burke's feelings when he conducted the last interview. It may be that the present Burke did not express enough concern over the Drake incident. Had he told Stanley how very sorry he was and how he had tried to make up to Drake, Stanley might have been less critical. Instead, Burke only said that he had apologized and there was nothing more he could do [B4]. Actually, Burke tried to correct the error for Drake, but Drake refused to let him.)

[B13] TOM BURKE: Well, these are the type of jobs that I think we can do best. I'm just trying to do the best job I can in the company, and I think that my own production unit is ideal for jobs that are unusual—those that require imaginative thinking, creative thinking. I have one fellow that I wanted to talk about with you, Frank Dobbs, who is really an idea man, and I think my group really has some original ideas. When these routine jobs come along, they aren't too happy about them and I'm not too happy about them. I know we can do a better job on a job requiring some creative thinking.

> Burke defends himself on the job assignment question. He does a considerable amount of boasting—a sign that he does not feel appreciated. He appears uncomfortable when talking so highly about his own unit and shares the credit with Frank Dobbs. He praises Dobbs and points out why his unit is best suited for the nonroutine assignments.

[S14] GEORGE STANLEY: You feel, then, that you have an exceptional group . . .

> Stanley reflects Burke's feelings. (He is *listening* after engaging in some *telling*. So far in the interview, Stanley has been proceeding too fast with the *telling*.)

[B14] TOM BURKE: I think so. I think you have indicated that in terms of our production, which seems to be pretty good. I don't know whether the other departments have the same feeling about routine jobs that we do, but I think, perhaps, that routine jobs are more ideally suited for them.

> Burke responds to Stanley's counseling-type response by presenting more of his own views.

[S15] GEORGE STANLEY: In other words, I should more or less give the routine jobs to them, and give you the interesting assignments.

> Stanley continues the nondirective approach.

[B15] TOM BURKE: I don't think that they would object and certainly it would do wonders for my own group.

Burke expands his views further, hinting that perhaps all units would profit from a change in the method of giving assignments.

[S16] GEORGE STANLEY: So your feeling is that you do have an exceptional group and they should be rewarded by giving them the exceptional jobs.

Stanley seems to be trying to understand Burke's views. He reflects the idea that Burke's group is an exception and therefore should be given special treatment. (The desire to be rewarded for being an exceptional group has been in the background of Burke's speeches and Stanley has shown considerable insight to grasp it.)

[B16] TOM BURKE: If at all possible. I realize that we have to take certain routine jobs . . .

As soon as Stanley understands what he wants, Burke lowers his demands. He says he wants the exceptional jobs if possible; he recognizes that they are limited in number and expects to take a part of the routine jobs. (A meeting of minds seems possible because Burke's expectations are now within reason.)

[S17] GEORGE STANLEY: You do realize, then, that you do have to assume some routine jobs like . . .

Stanley reflects the idea that Burke expects to do some of the routine jobs, making it possible to settle this issue clearly.

[B17] TOM BURKE [Interrupting]: Of course, if the other units can't take them, we should take some, too . . .

Burke readily agrees to take routine jobs.

[S18] GEORGE STANLEY [Interrupting]: But your unit prefers, and you prefer, to take the more complex kind of job and you feel that your group can handle them.

Stanley further clarifies the point by reflecting Burke's preference for the complex jobs and the ability of his group to do them. (Stanley seems to have recovered from his errors and is now exploring Burke's ideas and avoiding conflicts.)

[B18] TOM BURKE: Oh, I'm sure . . . I'm reasonably confident of that. I'll match my unit against any other unit in the company.

Burke again accepts Stanley's interpretation and assures Stanley of the good job his unit will do.

[S19] GEORGE STANLEY: Well, we like to have people with pride in their units and you certainly have got the record to back it up. We don't want to discourage you at all in any of those ways. Now, one other thing that you may not be aware of, but I feel it should be brought to your attention and that is the area of turnover. As you know, I have the eight departments, and, as such, we do make some comparisions between departments, and your group seems to have more turnover than the other groups. You have about one employee a month leaving and the other groups seem to hold their people longer. Now, the pay seems to be about the same, working conditions and so on . . . [pause]

> After reaching an understanding on job assignments, Stanley resumes the role of a judge when he expresses his approval of the pride Burke has shown in his unit and with the record it has made. He then raises the issue of turnover. He is careful not to prejudge Burke, but presents him with the evidence and gives him a chance to reply.

[B19] TOM BURKE: I think that there is a perfectly logical explanation for this and it's the fact that I have got top people working for me . . . and as always happens with top people, I can't pay them any more than the top rate for the classification. It's the best I can do, and because they're so good they get attractive offers from outside and some can't turn them down.

> Burke does not seem to be defensive, but takes the issue in his stride, much as he did at the outset [B4]. He has a good explanation for the turnover in his unit and does not blame the company for failing to supply a greater number of opportunities for promotion.

[S20] GEORGE STANLEY: You feel then the people are leaving to take better jobs.

> Stanley reflects Burke's idea (and avoids making the mistake he made when he dealt with the Drake affair).

[B20] TOM BURKE: They have for sure. In fact, a few are staying when they could be making more money outside. One girl who works for me turned down a job that offered to pay thirty-five dollars a month more than she is getting from us, just because she likes the morale, the group feeling, the teamwork that we have in our group. Now, this is what always happens if you have top people. If you have top people, you lose them; if you have poor people, they stick around, but maybe you don't want them. I would rather take the top people and take the chance of losing them; although, if there is anything I can do to keep them, I would like to do my part. The morale is good, so that's not one reason for their leaving. If I could pay them a little more or if—and you brought this up before—I could give them more unusual and challenging jobs, I think that this would make them more inclined to stay.

> Burke responds with details. He seems to have a good attitude toward his employees and shows no defensiveness. He seems to think aloud about a

problem that concerns him. (Stanley needs to listen. If Burke's attitude is different from the one Stanley attributed to him, Stanley may have to re-examine his evaluation of Burke.)

[S21] GEORGE STANLEY: So, actually the way it looks to you is that turnover is due primarily to not having the promotional opportunities here because you have such an exceptional group. Is that right?

> Stanley continues to reflect Burke's thoughts and seems to be doing his best to understand rather than judge. (Stanley, at this stage of the interview, follows the Problem-Solving approach to a considerable degree. Once emotional behavior has been overcome, the technique of reflecting ideas brings results similar to those from a problem-solving discussion.)

[B21] TOM BURKE: There isn't anything I can do. If I could pay them more, I would, or if I could give them more intriguing jobs, I would, but this is out of my power. I do all I can in helping train and develop them.

> Burke continues to show problem-solving behavior and reveals a sense of responsibility toward his whole unit as well. Burke's attitude toward training seems quite clear from what he says.

[S22] GEORGE STANLEY: You feel, then, that everyone is very well trained in your group; that they know a lot of different jobs and can do them all well; and that part of this is due to your being able to give them more complex jobs.

> Stanley summarizes what Burke has said about his group and the way he has been handling his employees. (By integrating these ideas, Stanley checks Burke's general attitude against the previous impression he had of Burke's method of operation. The attitude Burke reveals is quite different from Stanley's original impression and he must either revise his own opinion or distrust the sincerity of Burke's speeches. The summary is excellent and shows that Stanley is now trying to understand Burke. He does more than let Burke blow off steam. Some problem solving takes place.)

[B22] TOM BURKE: This I regard as the supervisor's most important function: that of developing the people who work for him. All employees have abilities that are not developed and which we certainly could use. They just have to be brought out by a supervisor who is willing to stimulate each employee and help him to learn.

> Burke's response indicates that Stanley's summary is accurate. Burke discusses things in more depth and reveals his attitude more clearly.

[S23] GEORGE STANLEY: Now along this same line, just a couple of minutes ago you mentioned Frank Dobbs as one of the people here. Do you think there is a chance that we will lose him?

> Stanley seems convinced that Burke has a good attitude toward his employees. He goes along with Burke's opinion on the cause of turnover and

mentions Frank Dobbs, who might be a test case. (Stanley may be double-checking Burke's analysis, but it is more probable that he wishes to explore ways that he can be helpful.)

[B23] TOM BURKE: Well, I think that there is that possibility. As I say, Frank is really a top worker and I would like to see him get ahead in the company. Now, if there are any openings in supervisory positions, I think that Frank would be really topnotch for them. In fact, I think that he's probably as good as many of the supervisors we have working in the company right now. . . . There is a possibility that we might lose Frank.

> Burke thinks Dobbs is a potential turnover problem and he gives Stanley a clear idea of how to motivate Dobbs to stay. (He does not depreciate his fellow supervisors and is problem oriented rather than defensive.)

[S24] GEORGE STANLEY: I'm certainly glad to get that information because, as you know, having this many people to deal with, it's a little hard to keep in intimate contact with them, and an employee like Frank, who would be very valuable to the company, might go unnoticed if we hadn't had this conversation. Well, Tom, this is the general idea we tried to follow; we've tried to point out the good points, as you know here, and some of the other things that have come up, such as trying to get along with people. I want once again to stress the importance of teamwork. With your unit you're doing a good job, but all around teamwork is more than that— it's cooperating with the other supervisors, too. This working together is important for the good of the company. Also, as far as the area of taking the routine jobs, I can see your point that in getting the more complex jobs you can perhaps do a better job of training people; also, you can hold your people, which I didn't realize was one of the things—well, the way you were utilizing the jobs was as training jobs. Also in connection with this, you do understand the position of having to assume a certain amount of routine work. I mean this—I can't, once again, get in the position where I'm showing favoritism by giving all the dull work to some people and giving the other people the cream. I do want you to know that I'll consider this idea of trying to give your group as many complex jobs as we can. And, in the last instance, the area of turnover, with your view that many of the people who are leaving are doing so because they have promotional opportunities someplace else and the company can't give them anything. This is a serious problem. As you know, we only have so many jobs that people can go into, so I don't know what we can do about that part exactly. If we can work something out with the routine jobs and with the more complex jobs, this might give some people one reason to stay around. On the same subject, this Frank Dobbs, if he's as good as you say . . .

> Stanley accepts Burke's suggestion and shows his appreciation for the information. Because this is the time for evaluation and not for problem solving, he summarizes the interview as a whole. He briefly mentions that Burke has

good points and itemizes the less favorable ones. He has altered his initial opinion of Burke's ability to deal with his own unit, but says he still finds Burke's cooperation with fellow supervisors unsatisfactory. Stanley says he expects Burke to be more ready to accept routine jobs. Although he concedes Burke's points and is ready to give his group some consideration, he wants Burke to change. He seems to be satisfied that the turnover in Burke's unit may not be his fault. By mentioning Frank Dobbs, he indicates that he is aware of the recommendation Burke has given him. (This summary emphasizes Stanley's role as the final judge. He has listened and learned, and now he draws conclusions.)

[B24] TOM BURKE [Interrupting]: He is; I'll stand behind him . . .

> Dobbs seems to need no further endorsement and yet Burke feels the need to reinforce his point, which indicates that he is again defensive. (He may feel deflated by Stanley's summary and be using Dobbs to reassert himself.)

[S25] GEORGE STANLEY: Well, this is the situation then: the good points and perhaps the places where perhaps improvement can take place. I do want to give you a high rating, because I know that you are a good worker in a lot of ways. At the same time, there is this matter of cooperating and being willing to accept job assignments.

> Stanley treats the interruption as a distraction. He returns to his summary by briefly restating its conclusions. (His description of Burke as a good worker "in a lot of ways" amounts to damning with faint praise. His repetition of the need for cooperation and acceptance of job assignments indicates that he is aware of Burke's resistance. In this way, he applies pressure and may make things worse.)

[B25] TOM BURKE: As I've indicated, I don't think I can do anything about the turnover. It comes from the fact that my people are pretty good, and they get attractive jobs from outside. Now, if I could give them more interesting work, this might help to hold them, or if I could pay them a little more, this, too, would help to hold them. As far as the cooperation is concerned, I will certainly make a point of not forgetting to let Jim Drake know about any future design changes, but it's not all up to me.

> Burke clearly is defensive. He says that he can do nothing about turnover and that the remedy lies elsewhere. On the cooperation issue, he concedes only that in the future he will inform Drake of changes. (He had promised this at the outset. Stanley did try to extract more from him, but Burke has refused to yield.)

[S26] GEORGE STANLEY: Oh, no, I'm aware of that. It's a mutual affair, but as I say, we have to develop teamwork and we all have to shoulder our part of it. O.K., well, I sure do thank you for coming in, Tom, and I hope that in the future we will be able to give you higher ratings on these few things that I've mentioned and I hope you're able to maintain your high level in the other things.

Stanley avoids an argument, but he, too, refuses to yield. He calmly repeats his position. He says he hopes to give Burke a higher rating in the future, but it is clear that Burke must change if this is to occur. (If Stanley ever appreciated Burke's need for special treatment, his summary shows no evidence of it.)

[B26] TOM BURKE: I certainly hope so, too, Mr. Stanley.

Burke hopes for a higher rating and he obviously is not satisfied with the one he just received. He does not indicate what he will do to earn a higher rating.

Evaluation of the Interview

In general, the style of this interview conformed to the specifications of the Tell and Listen method. All aspects of the evaluation were directive; that is, they were introduced by Stanley. However, Stanley dealt with Burke's feelings in a nondirective manner and allowed and encouraged Burke to talk about the way he felt about each point on the appraisal. Stanley may be criticized, however, for not following through on the feelings Burke expressed on several occasions. The manner in which he avoided arguments was admirable. Sometimes an interviewer meets this requirement of the appraisal interview by avoiding touchy points in the evaluation, but Stanley did not shirk his duties with reference to *telling*.

Stanley followed a problem-solving pattern when he explored ideas with Burke. This is consistent with nondirective counseling practice, where ideas as well as feelings are explored. It differs from the use made of such exploration in the Problem-Solving method only because the problems were introduced by Stanley instead of Burke.

Stanley did not alter his evaluation greatly as a result of Burke's analysis, which seems to be a product of the method. Using the Tell and Listen method, Stanley was likely to interpret Burke's response to an unfavorable point as a defensive reaction—indeed, this usually was the case—and therefore listen with quite a different mental set than if he had been following a Problem-Solving approach. This may account for some of the times when Stanley seemed to be insensitive to Burke's suggestions.

By making some suggestions for Burke's improvement, Stanley also conformed to the Tell and Listen method, where the interviewer's responsibility is not only to appraise, but also to specify ways improvements can be made. Stanley fulfilled the latter responsibility without exerting pressure, which he might have used following the Tell and Sell method. Stanley's summary illustrates very clearly how the method he followed permitted him to make his criticism without becoming involved in an argument.

Stanley did alter his views about several points in the appraisal, which demonstrates how *listening* can be of value to upgrade appraisals, to prevent arguments, and to give relief from frustration. Listening is a way to hear feedback; although, in this interview, Stanley did not always probe for enough feeling, he did permit Burke to develop some ideas. Burke contributed some sound ideas, which shows that Stanley prevented a lot of defensive behavior and at several points made the interview a constructive experience. It is possible that with greater sensitivity he could have prevented more of Burke's defensiveness.

Stanley's failure to appreciate Burke's need for recognition and for some kind of deferential treatment in assignments to serve as a reward for the exceptional work his unit turned out was apparent at the end of the interview. Had Stanley been more concerned with understanding than with judging, this oversight might not have occurred. Judging and understanding tend to be incompatible mental functions.

Stanley's summary accurately revealed his understanding of the Tell and Listen method. He summarized the points on the appraisal and the points and areas of disagreement raised in discussion. He made it clear that he was the final judge, but he also let Burke know that he had been heard and that Burke's ideas had been taken under consideration. This seems to be an accurate reflection of the purpose of the Tell and Listen method.

Analysis of Interaction

Table 4 shows the number of words spoken during each speech. Stanley made almost the same number of speeches in this interview he did in the last, but he dominated somewhat more. For the interview as a whole, he spoke 60.3 percent of the words, compared with 52.2 percent in the other Tell and Listen interview. Comparison of the first and second halves of the interview shows that Stanley spoke 63.8 percent of the words in the first half and 57.4 percent in the second half. This decline in dominance from the first to the second half was similar to that of the other interview he conducted, but did not approach a fifty-fifty split as nearly. Thus Stanley's greater dominance with the second Burke seemed not to be due to a change in his own behavior, but more to personality differences between the two persons playing Burke. During his other interview, this Stanley spoke 1614 words and in this one he spoke 1630. The total number of words spoken by Burke in the other Tell and Listen interview was 1428, compared with 1073 for Burke in this interview. The second Burke seemed unusually perceptive of Stanley's role as a judge, perhaps because he was less frustrated and more problem oriented than the average person under comparable circumstances.

**Table 4. Words Spoken by Each Participant
During Second Tell and Listen Interview**

Speech	Stanley		Burke	
1	12		3	
2	142		8	
3	80		7	
4	107		79	
5	18		6	
6	7		7	
7	103		52	
8	20		30	
9	21		14	
10	16		9	
11	100		48	
12	21		67	
13	134		113	
	781	63.8%	443	= 1224
14	9		50	
15	20		17	
16	22		14	
17	14		14	
18	24		19	
19	126		67	
20	11		172	
21	31		37	
22	43		54	
23	33		78	
24	380		6	
25	59		95	
26	77		7	
	849	57.4%	630	= 1479
Total	1630	+	1073	= 2703
Percent	60.3		39.7	

Although Stanley spoke more words than Burke during both halves of this interview, his domination was not so obvious as that shown by the Stanley who used the Tell and Sell method. In those interviews, Burke's contributions were almost solely confined to protestations. In the two Tell and Listen demonstrations, it was not necessary for Burke to struggle for a hearing. Stanley's dominance was largely a result of the introduction in the first half and the summary in the second half.

Reactions of Audience

The general audience reaction to this interview was very favorable, particularly because it followed the second Tell and Sell interview, which left a somewhat unfavorable impression. It was generally agreed that Stanley had let Burke know where he stood and that Burke would cooperate with his fellow supervisors in the future.

Persons identifying with Stanley felt that he had done an excellent job. Although some felt he had let Burke influence him too much, there was a majority agreement that the final summary proved Stanley to be less gullible than he at times appeared. A minority felt that Stanley had been too firm in his final summary and that the issue of cooperation should not have been reopened.

The majority of the Stanley identifiers also felt that both participants were satisfied with the interview and that each had gone up in the other's estimation. The general opinion was that Stanley (a) had increased his appreciation of Burke's ability to supervise; (b) was not sure how he felt about the turnover problem; (c) still felt the same about Burke's need to cooperate with other supervisors; and (d) thought Burke should not question assignments. Most of the observers felt that Burke was aware of the need to show more cooperation and that he would improve. There was a difference of opinion about whether Burke realized that he was expected to accept all assignments in the future. Some believed that there was a misunderstanding on this point and that there would be trouble in the future; others believed the matter would be dropped, both because Burke had a better understanding of the problem and because Stanley would be more careful and considerate in the future.

Persons identifying with Burke agreed in most respects with those identifying with Stanley. The major difference was that fewer of them expected a change in either Burke or Stanley. In general, they thought the interview was successful, but a fairly large number disliked Stanley's summary. More felt they would have been hurt by Stanley's summary than felt that Burke had been hurt by it, however. Burke's last comment about his ratings next year caused almost half of Burke's identifiers to feel that he had not been hurt, but that he expected to be more cooperative with his fellow supervisors in the future. There was disagreement on whether Burke would be less critical of job assignments, but most felt that Burke expected Stanley to work out a better arrangement. They felt that Stanley had promised to give Burke better assignments and that Stanley would appreciate Burke more when he took another look at the turnover problem. If Stanley did his part, there was little doubt in the minds of the observers that Burke would do his.

Reactions of Participants

Stanley was satisfied with his conduct during the interview. He felt that (a) he had come to know Burke's side of things and consequently had learned from the interview; (b) he had communicated the evaluation and accomplished his assignment; and (c) Burke would improve his relations with other supervisors, be more willing to accept routine assignments, and be more concerned with turnover.

Stanley said that Burke had gone up in his estimation and that he now realized Burke was practicing human relations skills with subordinates, but that there was considerable room for improvement in his cooperation with other supervisors. If anything, he was more convinced than ever that Burke tended to concentrate on his own group. He felt that Burke had a point about the cause of turnover and hoped he could promote Dobbs in the near future. However, he was not convinced that Burke should receive special consideration on assignments; he said he had to consider turnover as a problem for all groups and could not give Burke's group preferential treatment.

Stanley considered Burke's faults to be small in comparison with his virtues and felt that he would go a long way in the company if he matured. He felt that he had let Burke know how highly he was regarded and that Burke had been able to accept the criticism in the spirit in which it was given. He granted that Burke's feelings may have been hurt somewhat, but thought this would serve more to motivate than to discourage him.

Burke revealed that he had been confused and hurt by the interview, but that he was not angry with Stanley. He neither lowered nor raised his estimation of Stanley, because he had derived both satisfaction and disappointment from the interview.

The parts that hurt Burke were Stanley's (a) failure to appreciate the superior job he was doing, shown by Stanley's inability to understand why the superior performance of his group should entitle the members to some kind of special treatment; (b) inclination to take sides with Drake; and (c) lack of constructive ideas.

Burke's satisfaction stemmed from several sources. He felt that he had (a) brought Dobbs to Stanley's attention; (b) convinced Stanley that there were several sides to the turnover matter; and (c) made Stanley more ready to give his unit the better job assignments.

Burke said he doubted that his own behavior would change, because he had not learned any ways to improve. He felt that he had cooperated with fellow supervisors too much already and he still had no desire to help them in their work. Burke said the Drake incident was an accident he had tried his best to correct, but Drake had failed to cooperate by refusing the help offered and by going to Stanley. He said he would be careful to avoid incidents and appear to cooperate, but he was more convinced than ever that Stanley was being deceived by incompetent supervisors. His anger, therefore, was directed toward Drake rather than Stanley.

Burke did not say that his productivity would change. (However, if Stanley did fail to live up to the agreement about giving his unit the more complex jobs, Burke could lose interest and production might suffer.) Although he had lost some of his enthusiasm because of the interview, Burke said his job interest and productivity would remain high because of the inspiration he received from his group.

Summary Notes on the Tell and Listen Interview

The Climate Created

The climate established during the two Tell and Listen interviews enabled the stated objectives to be met: communicating the evaluation and releasing defensive feelings. The interviewer tended to hear what the interviewees had to say and the structure was not as rigid as for the Tell and Sell interviews. Interruptions were permitted—even encouraged—and an atmosphere of "give-and-take" was created. Each had an opportunity to influence the other. Generally, Stanley adopted a non-faultfinding posture and set the stage for effective listening. The fact that each participant spoke approximately the same amount implies a sense of equality.

During each interview, Stanley seemed to be patiently waiting for Burke to accept the appraisal evaluation and to respond. Because he did listen, Stanley was able to establish a climate in which Burke's perceptions and feelings were accepted as valid. However, a judgmental atmosphere was present to a significant degree, in that Burke was expected to accept Stanley's evaluation.

Characteristics of the Interviewer

The interviewer was friendly and quickly established the agenda for the meeting and proceeded to the evaluation. He seemed to have a mental set of "talking things over" with his subordinate and an implicit assumption that Burke would have some reactions to the evaluation. This was reinforced when Stanley heard and reflected Burke's feelings. Stanley tried to establish himself as a willing helper, open to what Burke might think or feel. Stanley's praise of positive aspects of Burke's performance seemed to reduce Burke's anxiety, and the appraisal started on a positive note.

However, there was no doubt that Stanley was in a judgmental position—the appraisal had been made and was now being communicated. Stanley seemed to seek endorsement of his role as a competent and fair person—to want Burke to be on his side—although there are indications that his mind was already made up and that his objective was to persuade Burke to come around to his point of view. Stanley did listen, but did not essentially change his pre-interview position. There was a pattern of tell-listen-tell, with overemphasis on telling.

There is some evidence that Stanley was paving the way for problem-solving behavior when he encouraged Burke to go deeper into his feelings and reactions. Rather than counterattacking or defending his own position, Stanley fairly consistently reflected Burke's feelings to make issues less emotion laden, but he did close the interview in a judgmental fashion.

Characteristics of the Interviewee

Both interviewees seemed to be responsive people. Each of the Burkes clarified issues and became involved in the interview. Some defensiveness was evident when Stanley took on the air of a judge, but each Burke apparently could see that Stanley was willing to hear what he had to say. The Burkes did seem to feel the need to justify themselves, but apparently sensed their freedom to confide in Stanley. Each Burke, because he was heard, did ultimately arrive at a point where he could examine his own behavior and look at its implications. Each accepted Stanley as a judge, but resisted when he felt he was not understood.

CHAPTER SEVEN

Problem-Solving Method: First Interview

Transcription of the Interview

[S1] GEORGE STANLEY: Well, I guess it's about that time of year. I think that these interviews are good things; it seems that without them we get awfully involved in day-to-day problems and don't take time to talk about where we're going, how we're getting there, what kind of progress we're making.

Stanley's greeting is friendly, and he goes directly to the purpose of the interview—discussing progress, rather than evaluating Burke or his job. This seems to put Stanley at ease, as well as Burke.

[B1] TOM BURKE: I agree, George; I think that development is certainly an important thing—one real facet of every supervisor's responsibilities. I certainly have been trying my level best to develop my people . . .

Burke's response indicates no feeling of rank difference; he accepts development as everyone's problem.

[S2] GEORGE STANLEY: Yes, I think I've noticed that. You think that part of your job is training your people, is that it?

Stanley makes capital use of Burke's initial response. (He follows one of the specific instructions for the Problem-Solving method—to follow up leads from the interviewee. Opportunities to respond to important feelings are frequently overlooked in the early stages of an interview because the interviewer usually begins with a carefully laid plan. For this reason, planning too carefully is inadvisable.)

[B2] TOM BURKE: I do the best I can . . . yes, I believe that everyone has certain hidden talents and interests and that it's important nowadays, perhaps, for the supervisor to try and develop those special abilities and talents. Naturally, it pays off, too, in terms of productivity. I think I have a really effective group and, perhaps because of the fact that people who work for me realize that they have a chance to improve themselves, they try to learn and produce as much as they can. When they find that they get the best of results, that makes for morale. I think good morale is an important asset to any group's productivity.

> Burke's response shows a willingness to share his ideas with Stanley. He reveals a good deal of initiative and enthusiasm and shows his attitude toward his subordinates, which happens to be one of Stanley's concerns. (Without introducing the subject, Stanley has an opportunity to explore Burke's methods of handling people.)

[S3] GEORGE STANLEY: You think they're happy, is that it?

> Stanley reflects Burke's feelings about his employees and how they feel about their jobs.

[B3] TOM BURKE: Well, I think so—as far as I know, anyway.

> Although Stanley's question could have been answered with yes or no, Burke reveals a bit more. He is not sure of the accuracy of his answer, and further thought has been stimulated.

[S4] GEORGE STANLEY: How do you accomplish this? How do you go about getting this productivity?

> Stanley's question stimulates Burke to share his methods; Stanley indicates a desire to understand, rather than to judge.

[B4] TOM BURKE: Well, you just have an interest in people, I think, and realize that they have certain abilities and try to help them develop their ideas. An interest in their ideas should stimulate them.

> Burke reveals what seems to be a healthy attitude toward his subordinates. (This is in conflict with the attitude implied on Burke's evaluation and indicates that either the evaluation is inaccurate or that Burke's present remarks are misleading. Because Burke's attitude toward his subordinates was inferred from the turnover, it is important for Stanley to discover Burke's views when he is not defensive.)

[S5] GEORGE STANLEY: Do you feel that they give any trouble at all?

> Stanley explores the turnover problem. (If Burke is at all defensive, he may

think Stanley is checking up on him, but if he has not been made defensive, he is likely to see the question as a quest for information.)

[B5] TOM BURKE: No, on the contrary, I think I've got an effective unit; you can probably see that. I hope so at least.

Burke seems a bit surprised by the question about "trouble," but he apparently does not feel called upon to prove his point. He dispels any thought that he is covering up any facts.

[S6] GEORGE STANLEY: Yes, there's been real progress—we've even given you a couple of extra jobs to do in order to keep you busy. Do you feel you have any problems? Is there anything that's troubling you?

Stanley seems to be satisfied; he accepts Burke's remark, but at the same time explores for trouble spots. (It would have been better to explore ways of improving the job, rather than asking about trouble. Had Stanley been less familiar with the evaluation, he might have done a better job of exploring Burke's views; even so, he is not too obvious in his exploration.)

[B6] TOM BURKE: No, [pause] except that I'd like to be able to care for my people a little more, perhaps. [pause] You see, they've had attractive offers from outside, but I realize that there are limitations and I'm restricted to the top rates of the classifications, for example . . . [pause]

Burke pauses and, fortunately, Stanley waits; then Burke mentions the lack of opportunity for good people. It is the same point that was made during the other interviews, but on those occasions it was made as a criticism of the company.

[S7] GEORGE STANLEY: Do you mean the people are leaving for better jobs?

Stanley's response shows interest and stimulates further comment on the point.

[B7] TOM BURKE: Oh, that has happened—of course, that always happens when you have really topflight people, such as I think I've got working for me. If you have poor people you have them for a long time; if you have topflight people they're attracted outside. You can't win.

(Burke's response is a more moderate statement of the problem of people leaving the company for better jobs than was made by the Burkes in the other interviews. Stanley expresses concern that employees leave the company without placing blame, and consequently Burke seems to feel no need to compensate by overstating the situation from his point of view.)

[S8] GEORGE STANLEY: I wonder if there is anything we can do to attract these people inside. Do you think it's money alone that they want, or . . .

(This response is a good example of the kind of interaction that is conducive to stimulating problem-solving behavior. Stanley's willingness to help makes the problem one of mutual interest; this attitude is essential to cooperative interaction.)

[B8] TOM BURKE: No, I don't think so. I have one girl, Jane Wilson, who is working for me who was given an offer of thirty-five dollars more per month than she was actually getting working for us and she turned it down, which I think illustrates the fact that she's happy with us. Being a member of a good group, such as I think we have, [pause] is important—a more important factor than money. Of course, you can't blame some people for going someplace that offers them more, naturally. The only thing I can think of, that we should act on, has to do with one of my crew. I've been meaning to speak to you about this for some time now. He's my junior designer. I think that I've spoken to you about his ability before; he's a topflight worker. In case you have any opportunities for promotion, I think that Frank Dobbs is really the one. He's really got ideas and is the type of person I like to see get ahead.

(Burke's response indicates that he is thinking about the problem rather than jumping to conclusions. He does not seem to feel that he needs a ready answer, because the climate is conducive to discussing rather than convincing Stanley of something. He uses Jane Wilson's decision and his desire to promote Dobbs to weigh the relative merits of financial incentives and morale in reducing turnover. It is also interesting that Burke does not criticize his fellow supervisors to make a case for Dobbs. Apparently, because Burke does not feel that he has been criticized, he is able to discuss these questions without running down his fellow supervisors and without extolling his own virtues.)

[S9] GEORGE STANLEY: Do you think there's any danger of dissatisfaction right now with Frank?

(Stanley continues to ask questions that stimulate problem solving; he explores various aspects of the situation without suggesting answers or remedies.)

[B9] TOM BURKE: Oh, I haven't seen any. I think he's very happy in his work—as far as I know he hasn't sought any outside offers.

Burke's response indicates that keeping Dobbs is not a problem requiring immediate action. (During some of the other interviews, Burke gave the impression that Dobbs was an emergency problem.)

[S10] GEORGE STANLEY: Is there some way we could use these exceptional people to build up talents elsewhere? Do you feel that there's some way we can use a person like Frank to develop our other people? It would pay off if we could make these people more productive in that way. Do you feel, for example, that your group is better than some of the other groups?

Stanley accepts Burke's disposition of Dobbs, but instead of changing the subject, he pursues the matter, restating the problem as finding a way to make better use of exceptional people. A solution to the problem could give needed recognition and justify pay raises. (However, Stanley does not give Burke a chance to answer the question because he asks another. The last question requires Burke to give a "yes" or a "no" answer, rather than elaborate or explore further. Here is Stanley's first example of a mistake that is commonly made—continuing to question when the subordinate needs time for thought. A better question would have been to ask Burke why his group was so productive.)

[B10] TOM BURKE: I'm sure of it. I know that may sound as though I'm bragging a bit, but you can consider the results as a tribute to my department, and if you come down sometime I'm sure that you'll never find a higher degree of morale than we have.

Burke says he does not want to brag. Stanley's question implies his ignorance about Burke's productivity, so Burke is forced to take a defensive position. He invites Stanley to visit his unit and see for himself.

[S11] GEORGE STANLEY: I wonder if there's some way that we can make use of these extra talents in people like Frank Dobbs for training elsewhere?

Stanley apparently does not hear Burke's response. He seems preoccupied with an idea and suggests it to Burke.

[B11] TOM BURKE: Outside of my department?

Burke seems to be surprised. He asks a question to explore Stanley's idea.

[S12] GEORGE STANLEY: Yes. Is there some way we could work that out—do you have any ideas? We have all these special talents, you see, and we want to try to make the best use of them.

Stanley clarifies his idea further and seems to want Burke to agree that Dobbs should assist other supervisors. (This kind of participation approaches manipulation and is not what is meant by cooperative problem solving, although it is a common error. Burke does not have much of a problem-solving opportunity because Stanley, in effect, has suggested a solution and seems to want Burke to concur.)

[Stanley could have been more direct by asking such questions as (a) What are the advantages and disadvantages of loaning Frank to other units? (b) Could we create a special job for Frank to assist other units? (c) How would you feel about sharing an employee like Frank with other units and what kind of recognition should you get for developing employees like him?]

[B12] TOM BURKE: Well, as I said before, I think that Frank could certainly help out in a supervisor's job; he could do a lot in holding down a supervisor's job. I think that he would be as good or better than some of the people we have as supervisors now. I may be prejudiced, of course, but this fellow Frank is loaded with ideas and enthusiasm; he's got good potential.

Burke does not agree with Stanley. He presents his own beliefs that Dobbs should be a supervisor and that he would be superior to some of the people who are now supervisors. (This is the first time Burke has felt the need to make an unfavorable comment about his fellow supervisors, probably because Stanley has implied that Dobbs should be used to assist the weaker supervisors—an idea Burke opposes, perhaps because it was suggested by Stanley.)

[S13] GEORGE STANLEY: I think we'd better have another talk about Frank; it sounds like a very important . . . [pause]

Stanley seems sensitive to what is happening. He abandons the discussion about using Dobbs as a troubleshooter and places Dobbs on the agenda for future consideration.

[B13] TOM BURKE: I'd really appreciate it, because there is always the possibility that we might lose him, as we've lost other good people.

Burke does not wait to hear all Stanley has to say. He uses Stanley's hesitation as an opportunity to reinforce his own idea of promoting Dobbs and implies that turnover is due to company neglect. (Earlier in the interview he was not this aggressive.)

[S14] GEORGE STANLEY: You feel that these other people have left because they have learned to do the job and were looking for greater challenges, is that it? They were looking for a bigger thing to do?

Stanley continues to be sensitive to Burke's feelings and reflects the degree of concern Burke has expressed. By using different words to restate Burke's point of view, he demonstrates that he understands what Burke has said.

[B14] TOM BURKE: Well, yes, they're able to do more complicated jobs than I can give them. The more routine jobs we have aren't particularly challenging, you know. We need to give the really good people the more challenging work.

Burke comes up with a constructive solution to the problem of finding challenging work for well-trained people. He wants Stanley to reduce the amount of routine work his unit is given. (It is clear that shifting Dobbs to other units would not solve the problem.)

[S15] GEORGE STANLEY: And you do feel that you have an unfair proportion of the routine jobs to do, is that it?

Stanley ties Burke's idea about routine jobs in with fairness. (Because Stanley wants to make assignments in a way that is fair to all of his supervisors and Burke wants to be treated fairly, this introduces a problem of mutual interest. Although fairness is a relative matter, it is possible that Burke has not seen the problem with a broad enough perspective. Thus, Stanley's question may help him see more sides to the issue.)

[B15] TOM BURKE: Yes, I guess so—I know that there are these routine jobs to be done, and we have to pull our load as well as the next person, but I think that in terms of my own group, they really appreciate something challenging. If there is any dissatisfaction, perhaps it's due to the fact that the work is routine, but I don't think that dissatisfaction is the main problem in our turnover.

> Burke indicates he has no solution in mind. His ideas are unclear and seem incompatible. He says he feels he should do his share of the routine work, but he would appreciate more of the challenging kind, and dissatisfaction, if present, is related to routine work, but dissatisfaction is not serious. (Problem-solving discussions often resolve conflicts of this kind.)

[S16] GEORGE STANLEY: Do you think that we could do a better job of distributing the routine and nonroutine jobs?

> Stanley's question states the problem without implying that the present method of job distribution is right or wrong. He suggests searching for a better way.

[B16] TOM BURKE: Well, I've spoken to you about that before, George, and I'd just like to ask you if there's a possibility that some of the routine jobs be given to the other supervisors. I think these jobs would be a little more along their lines.

> Burke expresses the idea that differences in ability could be used as a basis for assignments. He does not ask for favored treatment, but for the application of an objective criterion—assignment of jobs according to the ability to do them.

[S17] GEORGE STANLEY: How do you suppose they would feel about it?

> Stanley again takes a broader view. He asks whether the feelings of other supervisors should be considered, too.

[B17] TOM BURKE: I never thought about it, but I've never heard any complaints from them about routine jobs—it's the kind of work that's more in their line, I think.

> (Burke's perspective has been changed without his becoming defensive.) [Stanley might have asked: (a) "Aren't you ignoring the feelings of others?" (b) "Don't you think other supervisors have as much claim to these assignments as you?" (c) "Do you think this would be fair to other supervisors?" Questions of this type would probably have lead to defensive behavior.]

[S18] GEORGE STANLEY: Do you think that they're not as capable, or . . .

> (If completed, this question would require a "yes" or a "no" answer. At this point, Stanley is not exhibiting skill and his manner is approaching cross-examination. Although his attitude is friendly, any type of question that requires a choice between alternatives that are supplied tends to put a person on guard.)

[B18] TOM BURKE [Interrupting]: Oh, I don't want to say that exactly . . .

Burke does not wait for Stanley to set up the alternatives and backs away
from a commitment. He seems to feel that Stanley does not understand.

[S19] GEORGE STANLEY: Do they have any idea that you feel that
these routine jobs would be more appropriate for them?

[The same question could have been worded more effectively as "Have you
ever talked to the others about ways for improving job assignments?"]

[B19] TOM BURKE: Oh, I don't think so, no . . . I have no basis for
saying anything about that one way or the other.

Burke gives an evasive answer.

[S20] GEORGE STANLEY: How do you feel about the relations with
other people?

Stanley continues his pointed questioning. (He again seems preoccupied
with an idea of his own and unaware of Burke's failure to participate.)

[B20] TOM BURKE: Why do you ask that?

Burke's defensiveness is now apparent, although there is no evidence of
hostility in his voice.

[S21] GEORGE STANLEY: Well, there are matters of coordination on
some of these jobs, you know. Some jobs require that two or three units
look at them because people in one unit may have something to say or
may know something in particular—and I'm interested to know if you
think we have anything like a team here.

Stanley respects Burke's question, but he does not see that it is defensive;
he takes it as a request for information and explains why he is interested
in Burke's relations with the other supervisors. (In this speech, Stanley
sounds more like a judge than a helper.)

[B21] TOM BURKE: Well, I have a team, but as for the other departments, I have my work to do and they have their work to do.

Burke's response is protective and unfriendly toward the other units, although
some of this unfriendliness could be due to certain aspects of Burke's work
relationships. (It appears that Stanley is aggravating rather than reducing any
bad feeling about fellow supervisors that Burke may have brought to the
interview.)

[S22] GEORGE STANLEY: Do you think that that's the way it should
be? That these departments should be fairly independent?

(Stanley could either be exploring Burke's feelings or be somewhat critical
of his being "independent.")

[B22] TOM BURKE: No, [pause] I guess it would be better, perhaps,
if we all could work together effectively as a team, but I don't know . . .
[pause]

Burke agrees that cooperation is a good thing, but the "I don't know" shows doubt.

[S23] GEORGE STANLEY: Yes, I think I see what you mean. It's something you can't do by yourself because it's my problem. I haven't done the job of getting these people together to talk about these things. If the team spirit isn't as much as it could be, it's a group problem. But this is a thing that I'm interested in talking over and doing something about, and I'd appreciate your ideas on the values to be gained by working more closely with each other.

Stanley clears Burke of any blame by taking it himself. He says the difficulty is a group problem and requests Burke's assistance. (He has made a good recovery.)

[B23] TOM BURKE: I guess I can see the need for it—certainly I'd like to be able to work more effectively with some of the other supervisors, but, of course, my first responsibilities are to my own unit.

Although Burke warms up to the problem and indicates a desire to work with the other supervisors, he explains that he sees his own unit as his first responsibility. (This last may be a hangover from his earlier defensive feeling.)

[S24] GEORGE STANLEY: I wonder if this assignment of jobs, such as the problem of who should be given special jobs and what not, as compared to the standard routine type of job, isn't something that we ought to discuss.

Stanley seems to be thinking aloud about the problem, not imposing a solution on Burke. (This type of situation is nonthreatening and, at the same time, is a stimulant for problem-solving behavior.)

[B24] TOM BURKE: Sure, perhaps allocate the jobs in some sort of way—and I'd be happy to get together with you and the other supervisors to see if there is some better way we could work out what would be mutually satisfactory to all. There might be something in it for all of us.

Burke's response shows a strong willingness to cooperate. He shows a concern for the views of other supervisors and recognizes a possible gain for all. There is no evidence of competitiveness or defensiveness in his response.

[S25] GEORGE STANLEY: Well, that certainly calls for a group meeting. Are there any other things that you feel are either helping or hindering progress—do you feel that you're getting all the satisfaction that you want out of this job of yours?

Stanley changes the subject to explore some other points. (He may have changed the subject too abruptly and have failed to test Burke's feelings about some of the supervisors.)

[B25] TOM BURKE: Very much so—yes, I think so. I can't emphasize what I've said much more, although . . . [drifts off]

> Burke gives a strong yes, followed by an "I think so." (Apparently Burke feels that the point has been covered and wonders what Stanley has in mind. Suspicion of the interviewer's motive is one of the difficulties encountered when an attempt is made to stimulate discussion with questions, especially when the questions are designed to explore specific feelings after the other person has shown defensive behavior. The nondirective method is better under such circumstances. Questions are much more effective when the discussion is directly about the job and the participants are problem solving.)

[S26] GEORGE STANLEY: We've talked about these routine jobs that have to be done—the effect of that on progress. We've talked about the possibility of losing good people for want of something better for them to do—something that they really want to do. Are there any other things that we ought to go over?

> Stanley probably senses that Burke is a little defensive and unable to leave the previous topic. He skillfully summarizes the discussion up to this point, showing that he has understood and accepted for consideration the contributions Burke has made. He asks a general question that leaves Burke free to discuss anything about the job he wishes. (Summarizing is a skill that can be used effectively to pull an interview out of a rut and to clear up misunderstandings. Here, Stanley did not recognize Burke's sensitivity about cooperation soon enough, but he can recover lost ground if he is able to interest Burke in problem solving again.)

[B26] TOM BURKE: No, I can't think of anything else. We've talked about the fact that we have turnover, and I realize now that we have it to a considerable degree. Is there anything we can do about it? Have you any suggestions that might not have occurred to me as to how we can keep these good people that we have?

> Burke has no new problems—at least none that he can think of at the moment. He returns to the turnover situation and asks Stanley for ideas. Apparently, Burke has picked up Stanley's concern about turnover. (Stanley apparently moved too quickly to new topics in this interview and now Burke returns to old ones. Burke may be testing Stanley to see if he has more in mind; if he wishes to stimulate problem solving, Stanley must avoid giving pat answers.)

[S27] GEORGE STANLEY: I think that there's a possibility that somewhere in the company there may be opportunities for them.

> Stanley's reply is too vague to be seen as a solution. He implies that an answer to the problem may be found.

[B27] TOM BURKE: I'd like to be able to pay them a little more, but I guess that's impossible.

Burke seems to be testing Stanley's feelings about more money for his employees; he does not seem sure how receptive Stanley will be to his ideas, but feels free to suggest something. (An observer may wonder why Burke did not make his suggestion earlier. Perhaps he would have done so, but was not able to prepare the ground at the time. More pay may not be the most important incentive for the workers, but may substitute for promotion within the company.)

[S28] GEORGE STANLEY: I think that's something that should be considered. I don't think by any means that we should regard pay as a static proposition. . . . It's pretty clear that a lot of other people in the company are involved in this, but I'd be happy to set up a meeting with personnel people. We could at least ask for a job description to be made again and then make a comparison with other jobs at the same level to make sure that our job classifications haven't gotten out of line.

> Stanley accepts the idea of pay increases and talks about relevant procedures. (His response is an excellent one for a helper rather than a judge. He accepts without agreeing or disagreeing.)

[B28] TOM BURKE: Well, I'd certainly go along with that, but I doubt that the job description is off very much. Some of the employees are just able to do more than the job requires.

> Burke states his views on the need for better job descriptions and says he feels certain individuals, rather than certain job categories, are in need of pay adjustments.

[S29] GEORGE STANLEY: You don't feel that a new job description will be the answer to the problem. Where do you think the solution lies?

> Stanley reflects Burke's views and asks Burke to go a step further.

[B29] TOM BURKE: Up to a certain point we've been successful in keeping them here, even though they could be getting more money outside. And if they have challenging interests in work assignments they're more inclined to stay. Well, I've done what I could as far as the morale is concerned and my hands are tied with respect to pay—I can't go beyond the top rate in the job classification and I can only assign the jobs that I have to give to them.

> Burke continues to explore the pay question and points out the uses he has made of nonfinancial incentives. He pinpoints the problem and again brings up job assignments. (If Stanley had thought Burke was too work oriented, Burke's responses to this point have not supported his belief. In situations of this kind, a supervisor may wish to revise his preliminary evaluation, which was formed after limited observation and was usually made from one particular point of view.)

[S30] GEORGE STANLEY: I certainly can understand your feelings there.

Stanley sympathizes with Burke's situation and his feelings on the matter and does not make suggestions.

[B30] TOM BURKE: I wish that there was something that I could do because, as I told you, they are topnotch people and I would like to do everything I can for them.

Burke continues to register his concern for his employees, probably to emphasize his previous points.

[S31] GEORGE STANLEY: Do you feel that perhaps some separate categories might help? What are some extra skills or demands on technical competence that we can require of certain individuals so that we can create some additional job categories? Would that propose a morale problem for people who are not put in those categories?

Stanley's response indicates his belief in payment according to job classification. He seems willing to create new job categories if there is a need and morale problems are not created. Stanley foresees complaints of favoritism from other supervisors if he gives merit increases to some persons in Burke's unit, but if he puts them in new categories he feels the pay question would not be raised. (Managers at higher levels usually do try to take a broader view of all problems.)

[B31] TOM BURKE: That's conceivable but, as you say, it might develop new problems. You know that as things stand we haven't had much status differential in our unit; we're sort of all one big happy family. I don't know what would happen if we started formalizing things with new classifications—perhaps Clerk Grade A and Clerk Grade B; I don't know what this would do to us.

Burke appreciates Stanley's position and seems to fear that additional morale problems would be created by the formation of new job grades. He registers discomfort with the idea of job categories. (This is the second time Burke has failed to accept Stanley's contributions toward a solution.)

[S32] GEORGE STANLEY: You think then that it's better to try to raise the overall level somehow. Is that right?

Stanley recognizes Burke's reluctance to go along with the plan and restates Burke's idea about raises for talented people in a more general way—some kind of overall raise in the level of pay.

[B32] TOM BURKE: Yes, if it were possible.

Burke accepts Stanley's version of his idea, but implies that it may not be possible.

[S33] GEORGE STANLEY: Of course, this would involve all the other supervisors in the section, too, wouldn't it?

Stanley continues to show reluctance and raises the problem of other supervisors. (Bringing up other points for discussion is consistent with the Problem-

Solving approach. However, Stanley seems to be reluctant.)

[B33] TOM BURKE: That's true, you just can't do something for my exceptional employees and not do anything for the others. This might really present a problem for our section as a whole.

> Burke's response is both generous and sympathetic with Stanley's position—indicating a problem-solving attitude.

[S34] GEORGE STANLEY: Well, I think that these are important matters that we have thought about today. There's a question of pay for these people comparable to what they can get on the outside, and there's a question of making work challenging in the form of new and interesting work—something that's not routine. These things we should try to do something about. Then, there is the question of distribution of the routine jobs, which, I believe, you feel sure we should do something about.

> Stanley takes this opportunity to summarize the interview, first covering the point just discussed. (This gives the summary good continuity with Burke's last remark. The next two points concern job interest. Stanley demonstrates respect for Burke's views. He includes only the points Burke raised—those on which Burke is willing to work for improvement. Stanley's restatement not only mentions the items, but accurately reflects the strength of Burke's feelings.)

[B34] TOM BURKE: Yes, that's one that I'm particularly interested in, and perhaps if we got together with the other supervisors they might be content with the routine jobs. I don't know, but it's my estimation that they would be—although I may be wrong about it.

> Burke says that his major interest is job assignments. He shows an appreciation and concern for the feelings of the other supervisors when he expresses a willingness to have a group meeting. He says he believes the other supervisors might agree to take a greater proportion of routine assignments and that a group discussion meeting might be of mutual interest. Burke seems to feel quite friendly toward his fellow supervisors.

[S35] GEORGE STANLEY: Then we talked a little, too, about the extent to which you supervisors are teamed up—the extent to which you are working together and coordinating jobs—and we raised the question of whether I'm doing a good job in promoting the kind of working relationships that seem desirable.

> After gaining Burke's acceptance of the summary up to this point, Stanley restates the problem of Burke's relations with fellow supervisors. (This is the issue on which Burke previously became somewhat defensive [B20]. By making himself responsible for the problem, Stanley avoids making any criticism of Burke and instead requests assistance. Stanley again shows skill in accurately summarizing not only facts, but Burke's attitudes as well.)

[B35] TOM BURKE: I think that that's probably quite important. As a matter of fact, I might be able to improve my relationships with some of the others—Jim Drake, for example—oh, that's unimportant.

> Burke shows interest in the problem Stanley has raised and indicates where he (Burke) can improve and help attain Stanley's objective. He starts to mention the Drake incident, but calls it "unimportant." (The two previous Stanleys introduced the Drake incident themselves and caused the Burkes to become defensive. On this occasion, Burke brings up the Drake incident as the interview draws to a close. The closing moments of an interview often bring out some of the most important items for discussion.)

[S36] GEORGE STANLEY: Do you feel, though, that there might be some difficulties there?

> Stanley probes Burke's feelings. [A better question might have been, "Is there anything I should have known about?" and a good reflective statement might have been, "You feel you may have caused Jim Drake some kind of problem."]

[B36] TOM BURKE: Oh, slightly, you know—perhaps I've been paying attention more to my own department and not doing what I could do to cultivate relationships with the other departments.

> Burke admits he may have been too concerned with his own unit. (His response is insightful and shows that Stanley's question was adequate. Burke's awareness of a personal fault exceeds any gained during either of the other two types of interview and shows what can be accomplished by encouraging self-evaluation.)

[S37] GEORGE STANLEY: Well, Tom, I think this has been a very valuable interview; I think we've brought up a lot of important problems that have to be dealt with. I'm certainly going to make a note of these and you'll hear more about them—either I'll be talking to you or I'll try to get the group together.

> Stanley lets the matter drop and seems satisfied that Burke has made a discovery; he proceeds to close the interview. By saying that he himself has profited, he reduces the social distance between them. He also promises a follow-up of the items discussed and refers to a group meeting. (Stanley remains true to the Problem-Solving approach to the end and avoids making an issue of the Drake affair. This is a distinct achievement because people making closing remarks often are unable to resist giving a bit of advice.)

[B37] TOM BURKE: Well, thanks, George; I certainly have been helped to become aware of some problems, too, and I'll see what I'll be able to do about them.

> Burke's warm response indicates that he not only has had a pleasant and profitable experience, but that he intends to take action on certain things.

[S38] GEORGE STANLEY: Thank you.

> Stanley can honestly thank Burke for the worthwhile experience he has had.

Evaluation of the Interview

This interview accurately revealed the style of the Problem-Solving approach to appraisal interviewing. At no time did Stanley actually tell Burke how he had been appraised, and Stanley implied his opinion only on a few occasions. In general, Stanley remained in the role of helper with a high degree of consistency and seemed to be free of the conflict between a tendency to help and a tendency to judge.

The Stanley in this interview seemed to have a much easier task than the other Stanleys sometimes did because this Burke seemed to be more cooperative and reasonable than some Burkes. The question of whether personality differences among the Burkes or differences among the approaches were responsible for Burke's "reasonable" behavior in this interview can best be answered when all six interviews have been studied.

Misunderstandings often are due to communication failures because people are inclined to think reasonably about the opinions of others only when they are in a generous state of mind. When people are on the defensive, they assume differences in viewpoint to be caused by the faults of other people.

Analysis of Interaction

An analysis of the length of speeches made by the two participants revealed the usual pattern of a Problem-Solving interview. Table 5 shows the number of words spoken by each participant in his successive speeches. It took thirty-eight exchanges to complete the interview, even though a smaller total number of words was spoken in this interview than in the others. The large number of speeches meant that an exceptionally high degree of interaction occurred during the interview. (The degree of interaction, as such, is not a virtue because a great deal of interaction also occurs in quarrels. Because the Problem-Solving method presupposes a lot of interaction, other criteria must be used to distinguish between quarreling and cooperative problem solving. For this interview, quarreling can not be an alternative interpretation of the high degree of interaction.)

The percentage of words spoken by Stanley during this interview was somewhat lower than for either Tell and Listen interview, and the pattern for the two halves was reversed. During this interview, Stanley contributed 33.5 percent of the words in the first half of the interview and 54.1 percent in the second half. Stanley's small contribution during the first part of the interview suggests that he used this period to prompt Burke to talk, whereas the other two interview styles required Stanley to use the initial period to communicate part or all of the evaluation.

The Appraisal Interview

**Table 5. Words Spoken by Each Participant
During First Problem-Solving Interview**

Speech	Stanley		Burke	
1	49		31	
2	20		110	
3	7		10	
4	13		35	
5	10		21	
6	37		44	
7	10		47	
8	24		172	
9	12		24	
10	65		47	
11	23		4	
12	35		68	
13	15		21	
14	34		37	
15	19		72	
16	17		44	
17	9		28	
18	9		8	
19	18		20	
	426	33.5%	843	= 1269
20	10		5	
21	55		24	
22	17		22	
23	82		36	
24	37		52	
25	40		16	
26	53		59	
27	18		16	
28	88		32	
29	22		82	
30	7		30	
31	51		65	
32	17		5	
33	15		30	
34	82		44	
35	49		32	
36	11		28	
37	56		26	
38	2			
	712	54.1%	604	= 1316
Total	1138	+	1447	= 2585
Percent	44.0		56.0	

The Problem-Solving style is in contrast to the other two styles because Burke, rather than Stanley, introduced the topics for discussion. Nevertheless, the topics discussed in all the interviews were about the same. It might have been expected that the Problem-Solving approach would require many words to cover Stanley's evaluation because the approach was nondirective, but the total number of words spoken in this interview was only 2585, compared to 3407, 3513, 3042, and 2703 for the other interviews, respectively. During the first two interviews, many words were used for the selling process, and during the second two, the listening process caused Burke to express a good deal of feeling. The argument that a supervisor does not have time to listen was not supported by the interviews so far recorded.

Reactions of Audience

In general, the reactions of the observers to this interview were favorable because of the friendly tone that was maintained throughout the interaction. The ease with which the interview progressed also left a very good impression. Many observers attributed the success of the interaction to Stanley's skill, others thought it was due to Burke's cooperative nature, but most thought a combination of both was responsible.

There was general agreement that Burke rose in Stanley's estimation. Those who identified with Burke agreed that this was as it should be, but many who identified with Stanley felt that the person role playing Stanley had been "taken in" by Burke's "smoothness." Several suggested that Stanley should have been more critical; others thought Stanley should have presented his side of the evaluation.

There was general agreement that Stanley had learned from the interview and that he had increased his understanding of Burke as a result. Those identifying with Burke felt that Stanley should change in some ways, but those identifying with Stanley were inclined to feel that Stanley should change only if Burke improved or if additional facts indicated that Stanley was wrong.

It was generally agreed that Stanley had risen in Burke's estimation, but those who identified with Stanley said that he bought Burke's good will for a price. They criticized Stanley for failure to hold up his end of the interview.

When they were asked whether Burke knew where he stood, the Stanley identifiers were convinced that Burke either did not know or that he had gained an exaggerated good opinion of himself. On the whole, those identifying with Burke did not feel that he had gained an inflated impression of himself; most felt that Burke had no way of knowing where he stood because Stanley had not told him.

When the audience was asked whether or not Burke would improve, considerable doubt was registered, more from the persons identifying with Stanley than with Burke. Those who felt Burke would improve thought that his increased good feeling for Stanley would be responsible for improvement. There was no agreement on the form that any of Burke's improvement would take.

In general, the audience was favorable to the good will and friendly interaction shown by the participants, but was skeptical of the method's value as a way to develop employees because Burke had not been told where he stood. However, a strong minority felt that the interview was a great success and that the approach was good.

Reactions of Participants

Both participants reported a high degree of satisfaction with the interview and each reported that the other had definitely gained in his estimation.

Stanley reported that he had revised his evaluation of Burke. As a result of the interview he was satisfied that (a) Burke was doing a good job supervising his employees; (b) the incident with Drake was not as serious as he had thought; (c) some revisions should be made in assigning the complex jobs; (d) something should be done for Frank Dobbs; and (e) turnover in Burke's group was as much his problem as Burke's. He believed Burke would cooperate in the future, at least as well as he had in the past, and he did not expect Burke to be unreasonable at a group meeting with supervisors on how to make the section more of a team. It was his intention to hold group meetings with his supervisors regularly, and it was his understanding that job assignments would be one of the first items on the agenda.

Burke reported that he wanted to take a new look at turnover to see if there were angles he had overlooked. He felt he had not been as helpful to other supervisors as he should have been, and he looked forward to the group meetings with Stanley. In his opinion, such meetings would lead to friendlier relationships with his associates, provide opportunities for him to be helpful, and perhaps even help him to gain ideas himself. He expected to take up the question of Frank Dobbs with Stanley in the future and felt that something might be worked out. He felt he had made Dobbs a supervisory possibility for the next vacancy and derived satisfaction from this. He also hoped to provide a small raise for Jane Wilson. He did not feel that Stanley had criticized him, and he had found the discussion stimulating.

When he was asked how he thought Stanley had evaluated him, Burke reported that from an overall viewpoint Stanley regarded him very highly. His feelings about specific aspects of the job were that (a) his best points were quality and quantity of production; (b) there was room for improvement with respect to team spirit; and (c) finding a way to reduce turnover was important to Stanley.

These opinions checked with Stanley's revised evaluation, except that Stanley was less concerned with turnover than Burke thought. Stanley now was closer to Burke's opinion, expressed during the interview, that high turnover is good if people move to better jobs. "Competition with other companies will keep a company on its toes," Stanley said.

CHAPTER EIGHT

Problem-Solving Method: Second Interview

Transcription of the Interview

[S1] GEORGE STANLEY: It's that time of year again and we're in the midst of our annual interviews. I think that these interviews are quite worthwhile. In our day-to-day press of problems, we frequently never take time to ask ourselves where we're going, how fast we're getting there, and what sort of progress we make. I like to have the opportunity to talk about how you feel about the progress that you're making. Maybe that's a good point to start with. How do you feel about the way things are going?

> Stanley suggests that the appraisal interviews serve as an opportunity to discuss matters of mutual interest. There is little indication that he will appraise Burke. Instead, he expresses an interest in Burke's job satisfaction.

[B1] TOM BURKE: Well, I feel fine about them. I'm sure pleased with my own unit; I think they're turning things out well, they seem happy, and I enjoy working with them. As far as I'm concerned, things couldn't be any better.

> Burke freely shares his sources of satisfaction in his work with Stanley.

[S2] GEORGE STANLEY: You feel that your employees are happy and that the morale is good. Is that it?

Stanley reflects the attitude Burke has revealed and gives Burke an opportunity to elaborate. Stanley's response also shows his interest in understanding Burke's feelings and ideas.

[B2] TOM BURKE: I sure do! For example, maybe this is not the time to mention it, but one of my clerks—I don't know whether you know Jane Wilson or not, but she has been with us awhile—had a job offer from another place. The name is not important, but it was a better salary than she is getting here by some appreciable amount and she turned it down in order to stay with the unit, and that pleased me, of course. As far as I'm concerned the people in the unit look happy to me.

Burke shares a specific incident with Stanley. (This lets Stanley know why Burke thinks morale is good. From this example, Stanley may gain an appreciation of the way Burke thinks and of the conclusion he has drawn.)

[S3] GEORGE STANLEY: Have you had other people like this who were offered . . . ?

Stanley's question explores whether or not the example is typical. (Such a question can lead in a number of directions. If improperly expressed, it could communicate doubt and reveal an evaluative judgment, but if properly expressed it indicates curiosity and interest in implications.)

[B3] TOM BURKE: We have had some of the others who under similar circumstances took outside jobs, but they were people with families to support and they got better job offers, and I think they got them because they are good workers. I think they deserved it.

Burke's response obviously is not defensive. He reveals more about the turnover in his unit by telling Stanley about employees who left when they had better offers. He shows a sympathetic understanding of their reasons for accepting outside job offers with increased pay. (Burke introduced the turnover problem into the discussion as a result of Stanley's exploratory questions on job satisfaction. In this interview, the turnover in Burke's group did not become something Burke needed to defend, and therefore he did not blame the company for failing to offer more opportunities for advancement.)

[The manner in which turnover among draftsmen entered the conversation in this interview is a good example of how problems can be made the subject of conversation with a nondirective approach. The appraiser often fears that essential points will not be covered unless he introduces them. However, if he follows through on what is expressed, he will be able to cover many, if not all, of the points he wishes to include. Furthermore, points that he overlooked or problems that may never have occurred to him may be brought out. The reason the same problems are likely to be brought up by either party in a job discussion of this kind is that anything that is really serious in a situation is likely to be noticed by both.]

[S4] GEORGE STANLEY: In other words, these people are good, they're learning, and they're looking for bigger things to do.

Stanley briefly summarizes the implications of Burke's remarks.

[B4] TOM BURKE: You can't blame anybody for that.

> Burke seems to be defending the employees who left for other companies.
> (Apparently, he feels that Stanley's summary showed an unfavorable reaction
> to some employees leaving. Perhaps Burke is correct in his interpretation of
> Stanley's reaction; if it is negative, this undoubtedly is because the turnover
> appears as an unfavorable point on the evaluation.)

[S5] GEORGE STANLEY: Sure, if that's what they want to do. Do you
think this poses a problem for us at all? Is there any problem in keeping
these people interested?

> Stanley accepts Burke's defensiveness and goes along with the way Burke
> protects the employees who left. He converts the question of the people quit-
> ting the company into a statement of a problem. (Stanley handled this situa-
> tion very well and clearly shows that his mental set was problem solving rather
> than judging.)

[B5] TOM BURKE: I think that the company would be wise to watch for
the better workers and try to make it worth their while to stay. I do think
that—because I know I've had some people come along through my unit
and I like to take special pains in helping them develop. I believe that if
you look back over the people I have had in my unit you'd see they came
along that way. Those who have ability and really get good, if they get
another job offer, I think that we ought to be in a position to try to match
that offer if we want to keep them or else we can't be angry if they leave;
that's my point of view. I'd like to mention Frank Dobbs, my designer;
he's doing a bang-up job. That guy has more ideas than a barrel of monkeys,
as the saying goes. He is really coming and I think that if we don't do something about him, he is one of the kind that we might lose. And I would hate
to see that happen, because he is a good employee.

> Burke explores the problem of why employees leave and indicates that devel-
> oping good employees and having them receive good job offers go together.
> He says a solution is for the company to take steps to meet outside offers.
> He mentions Frank Dobbs, who may receive a better offer soon, and says he
> would like to prevent Dobbs from being the next to leave. (Stanley has stimu-
> lated Burke's thinking. Burke discusses ways to prevent the turnover, which
> indicates a realistic and constructive attitude.)

[S6] GEORGE STANLEY: Well, we're in the position then of having more
productive capacity than we need. Is that right? That's a very enviable
position for an organization.

> Stanley says that Burke's analysis indicates that employees outgrow their
> jobs before the company can find a way to use their full capabilities. He inter-
> prets the situation from the point of view of supply and demand. (Stanley is
> right to regard an excess of talent as a desirable condition; certainly it is

preferable to a shortage of talent. However, this is not the choice with which the company is faced. The problem is to make the most effective use of available talent.)

[B6] TOM BURKE: In my unit anyway, yes.

> Burke concedes that Stanley's summary is accurate only in a limited sense. (Stanley implied an excess in capacity to produce; Burke concedes an excess of talented manpower in his unit. Even this much of a concession could terminate the problem-solving interaction, because the problem has disappeared.)

[S7] GEORGE STANLEY: We need to figure out something to do to keep these people. We'd like to keep them in the organization, wouldn't we?

> Stanley brings up the problem of keeping talent in the company and checks with Burke to determine whether this is desirable. (He speaks of keeping people in the organization and does not specifically mention Burke's unit, which indicates that the problem concerns everyone. If Burke agrees, the problem will become one of mutual interest. The problem as stated by Stanley is an extension of the initial one stated by Burke, but the new statement broadens the scope of possible solutions. Taking time to restate problems is one of the skills associated with the Problem-Solving approach.)

[B7] TOM BURKE: I sure would, and I'd like to see the company do what it could in that respect.

> Burke enthusiastically accepts Stanley's statement of the problem and agrees with the objective of keeping good employees.

[S8] GEORGE STANLEY: I wonder if there is anything else that we could do? Can we use these superior individuals to develop other people elsewhere in the organization?

> Stanley expresses the desire to find solutions. (The term "anything else" apparently refers to solutions beyond those previously suggested by Burke.) He goes a step further and suggests a new position—developing or training others—that apparently occurred to him as a result of his own question. (This statement of a solution may be premature, particularly because it comes from Stanley and has to do with Frank Dobbs.)

[B8] TOM BURKE: I hate to lose Frank, but I'd rather see him go out of my unit into another part of the company than lose him entirely. I think that he is at the point now where he could be used in some sort of supervisory position.

> Burke resists Stanley's idea by indicating that he would hate to lose Dobbs, but he also indicates that he would rather have Dobbs in the company than have him quit. He suggests a solution of his own—promoting Dobbs to a supervisory position. (If Dobbs became a supervisor, Burke would also lose him, but he does not seem to resist this plan. Such ready acceptance is the chief value of having ideas initiated from below.)

[S9] GEORGE STANLEY: I see. You feel that he is ready for a supervisory job?

> Stanley responds to Burke's suggestion by asking a good exploratory question.

[B9] TOM BURKE: That's my feeling, and I'm tickled to have the chance to recommend him, because he's good.

> Burke assures Stanley of his confidence in Dobbs. He does not use strong adjectives to support his position, apparently because he does not feel he must defend his suggestion. He reveals his satisfaction at having a chance to help Dobbs receive a promotion and apparently no longer feels that Dobbs' promotion will be a loss for his unit.

[S10] GEORGE STANLEY:You say you develop these people. How do you do that; how do you go about it?

> Stanley turns the discussion to the question of employee development. (Although Burke had discussed this previously, Stanley takes the liberty of reintroducing it into the conversation. Stanley may be following a lead that was sidetracked, or he may be using Burke's earlier mention of this topic as an excuse to discuss one of the items on the appraisal.)

> [If Stanley is using the appraisal as an agenda for the interview and is watching for openings, his motivation may be open to question because he may be manipulating Burke. Manipulation implies that one person is taking advantage of another, not just influencing him for his own good. If an interviewer makes an employee think he has one objective when he has another, he may be judged insincere. An interviewer may verge on manipulation, but his motive may be to help. These questions are ever present in human relations discussions and it seems that both manipulation and insincerity can be avoided if the interviewer respects and tries to understand the employee's views. The author feels that Stanley was manipulating at this point, but that his attitude was, in general, so problem-solving oriented that suspicion ordinarily would not be aroused. Interviewers sometimes strive to achieve this type of manipulation and consider it to be a nondirective skill, but it is really an *indirect* approach rather than a *nondirective* one.]

[B10] TOM BURKE: I didn't mean anything in particular by it. It's just that I take an interest in them, I think. I think they know I do, and we work together and whenever I can give them any benefit of my experience, such as it is, I do so. I have the feeling that we work together as a team, and I think in that way I am giving them information that they can use, and I think that this plus the general enthusiasm in our unit helps bring them along—keeps them interested in their work—that's my feeling.

> Burke freely discusses his method of operation. (He apparently was not offended by Stanley's direct questioning.)

[S11] GEORGE STANLEY: How about this enthusiasm? Where does it come from? Does it come from this personal interest, is that it?

Stanley asks some exploratory questions. (A desire to understand Burke's methods was needed to select questions.)

[B11] TOM BURKE: I wouldn't want to say that it's just me, no; I'd say it's the feeling of the whole group—you know when you feel proud to be in an outfit. Why, it sort of spreads around through the group. That's my feeling about it.

Burke clarifies his feelings. (He has been stimulated to think about some human relations issues.)

[S12] GEORGE STANLEY: Do you feel that your group is better than the other groups? The other parallel groups in the section?

Stanley continues to question Burke, but the things he asks about seem to be more and more specific. (Specific questions can clarify issues, but they can also channel the subject of conversation and fail to lead to matters that are of concern to the interviewee. The motive behind this question is not clear, but it may be Stanley's attempt to persuade Burke to talk about the total operation.)

[Perhaps Stanley is again using manipulative tactics to bring out Burke's relations with other supervisors. A more direct approach to this topic would have been a question such as "How much do you enjoy your associations with the other supervisors?"]

[B12] TOM BURKE: Well, now that you ask about it, yes, I do. I think that we have the hottest group in the bunch, as a unit. That gives me a chance to say one other thing if you don't mind. Since Jane Wilson, the one I told you about, turned down the outside job—she is doing well, she's happy here, and we're all happy with her—that may be another case in point. I would like to suggest that she be considered at least for a raise, if such a thing would be possible. She deserves it and she has showed that she is loyal to the company. I think that kind of reward would be well in line for her.

Burke uses Stanley's question as an opportunity to praise his group and to prepare the ground to obtain a pay increase for Jane Wilson. (The request is reasonable and probably could have been the subject of a memorandum to Stanley at a later date. The request, therefore, is somewhat beside the point of the interview and may be Burke's way of avoiding a pointed question from Stanley. Specific questions may be "hits" if they happen to be well chosen. However, the chance of "misses" is also present.)

[S13] GEORGE STANLEY: I think that we ought to do two things then, shouldn't we? We ought to see personnel about what kinds of raises are possible for Jane—what kinds of inequities it might create, if any—and we have to see personnel about what supervisory positions might be opening up. I wouldn't like to take Frank Dobbs away from you, either. Maybe there is some way we can use him in the section, but I think perhaps we should write some action paragraphs on those two people.

Stanley summarizes and demonstrates a good method of changing the subject while disposing of the topics of Dobbs and Wilson. He says that action will be taken and that details and routine matters will be considered later. (The fact that Stanley accepts the need for action should please Burke, but Stanley's reluctance to take Dobbs from him may make Burke think Stanley is hesitant about making Dobbs a supervisor.)

[B13] TOM BURKE: That would be fine; I'd be tickled to death with that.

Burke seems very pleased to have his recommendations considered. He does not appear to be bothered by Stanley's reluctance to take Dobbs out of his unit.

[S14] GEORGE STANLEY: Do you feel that we have any other things that we ought to talk about? Is there anything else that could go smoother than it has?

Stanley now explores with a very general question that permits Burke to discuss anything about the job that may be bothering him. (General exploratory questions of this type are of a nondirective nature. They are useful in the early stages of an interview, but they also may be used at other stages to determine whether some problems have been overlooked.)

[B14] TOM BURKE: There is one thing that has kind of bothered me. [pause] I might as well mention it now . . . as later . . . because you've probably heard of it anyway. I had a little run-in with Jim Drake about two months back. The way it happened was this: you may remember that we made some changes on these plans and I was supposed to tell him about them. I would have been glad to and I had every intention of doing it, but when I went down to his office he wasn't there. I went back to my place and Frank had come up with a tremendous idea and we got to talking about that and the first thing I knew the day had slipped by and the next day I forgot about it. It's my fault; there's no question about that. I made a mistake. Then when it came to my attention it was a little too late—that is, things had already started into production. He had to make a lot of changes that he wouldn't have had to make if I had told him on time. I apologized about it; I told him I was sorry; in fact I even said I would make the changes myself, since I knew it was my fault. I'm afraid he was a little angry; in fact he had a right to be. I apologized and that's all I could do. I don't know if he's still mad or not, but that is one thing that is still kind of bothering me, but I think I did what I could about it. It was an honest mistake.

Burke takes this opportunity to tell Stanley about something that has bothered him for some time—the Drake incident. (Stanley always introduced this into the discussion with the other two types of interview.) Burke takes full responsibility for the incident, shows no evidence of defensive feelings, and exhibits concern for Drake's feelings, rather than hostility.

[If Burke had not mentioned the incident, it probably would have been best for Stanley to let it pass, too. Burke probably would wonder if Stanley knew about it, which would have caused him to think through the affair again even if it were not mentioned during the interview.]

[S15] GEORGE STANLEY: Well, as we all make mistakes like that, I think that's quite understandable. I'm glad to know about it. I'm glad you told me about it.

Stanley assures Burke that his explanation has been accepted and uses Burke's confession as an opportunity to develop a relationship where Burke can feel free to talk about his mistakes. (Stanley had little reason to believe that there was more to the incident than Burke covered and this may explain why he did not explore the matter further.)

[Giving reassurance may be regarded as the province of a judge, and Stanley's statements may seem inconsistent with the Problem-Solving approach. However, a person can also reassure in the role of a helper and this seems to be the spirit in which Stanley behaved.]

[B15] TOM BURKE: Better I should tell you than you hear it someplace else. That's the truth of it, though.

Burke's response indicates that at this moment he views Stanley more as a judge than as a helper. (Stanley's reassuring remarks may be responsible for this, but it seems more likely that Burke is responding to the rank difference in the job situation. The most that Stanley can hope is to decrease rather than increase the extent to which he is seen as a judge.)

[S16] GEORGE STANLEY: Well, it raises a question, perhaps. This indicates some sort of . . . It could happen again, I suppose—maybe to Jim Drake next time. It indicates something in coordination is missing, doesn't it? I wonder if the supervisors with me need to be a team. Is it important that we coordinate the thing? And if it is important, are we doing the things we ought to do to try and build the team? Am I doing the things I ought to do to build the team?

Stanley again reassures Burke and states the problem in terms of coordination within the whole section. (Now the problem no longer is Burke's behavior, but a work situation.) Stanley raises the question of what can be done to build a team and implies that he himself might be at fault.

[By stating the problem in situational terms, Stanley moves from placing blame toward objective problem solving. His last question, however, brings personalities back into the picture, this time by referring to his own behavior. This is the kind of error a person might make in an attempt to relieve another person's guilt feelings.]

[B16] TOM BURKE: I think you're doing a good job. It's not my intention to complain about this. But now that you mention it, it has occurred to me on a couple of occasions that if during certain planning sessions that involved work for all units we would get in the habit of having all the supervisors present, then people who were concerned could hear it first hand.

This is no excuse for my mistake regarding Drake; I should have told him—there's no doubt about that—but in light of the general thing that you are talking about now, I think there have been other times when inefficiencies, at least, have come about because all the people involved in a particular project weren't present at our early planning meeting. I think that's a good idea. I think that would be beneficial. I sure do.

> Burke seems to feel the need to reassure Stanley (clearly revealing how Stanley's attempt to share the blame has served as a distraction). He comes up with the idea of having group meetings to discuss jobs that involve all units. (This is a constructive suggestion and is relevant to the problems of improving communications and building a team. Apparently Burke developed his idea while talking and does not want Stanley to think he is making excuses for his own mistake. He seems to feel that the Drake incident was entirely his fault and does not want Stanley to take part of the blame.) Burke talks more about the idea of group meetings, clearly quite enthusiastic about the plan.

[S17] GEORGE STANLEY: We should have more meetings over the planning of production . . .

> Stanley reflects Burke's idea.

[B17] TOM BURKE [Interrupting]: With all the supervisors who are going to be involved there . . .

> Burke injects another point.

[S18] GEORGE STANLEY [Interrupting]: With all the supervisors.

> Stanley reflects Burke's idea.

[B18] TOM BURKE: That's just a suggestion—well, it was your idea really—I think it's a good one.

> Burke seems careful not to impose his thinking on Stanley. He calls his idea a suggestion and gives Stanley credit for it. (Perhaps Stanley actually deserves credit because he caused Burke to think of the idea.)

[S19] GEORGE STANLEY: Are there any things that you think make it tough for the supervisors to cooperate here? Is there anything going on that could keep them from . . . ? Is there any competitive feeling here?

> Stanley changes the subject. (Perhaps he has accepted the idea of group meetings, but it may be that he is not quite satisfied at this point. His question is rather specific and seems to be intended to explore Burke's feelings about his relationships with the other supervisors. When he asks about competitive conditions, Stanley appears to be somewhat manipulative. He seems to be trying to maneuver Burke into talking about his fellow supervisors. Although this kind of questioning is successful if not pushed too far, the same objective probably could have been accomplished with the first question alone.)

[B19] TOM BURKE: I've had the feeling that . . . It seems to me that there is a tendency sometimes for some of the supervisors to try to get excess help from other units, when these units already have their own work load. That is one thing I have noticed. I'm not pointing to any one person here. It's a general thing.

> Burke takes the opportunity to bring up something unfavorable about his fellow supervisors. He reveals that some supervisors are taking advantage of others. (It is obvious that he feels other supervisors are taking advantage of him, but he is careful not to say who is the abused person.)

[S20] GEORGE STANLEY: Sure . . . In other words, one section can be called upon to do the work of another section, and nobody knows who did it . . .

> Stanley reflects his understanding of the feeling Burke has shared and keeps the criticism on an impersonal level. He apparently believes that loss of credit may be bothering Burke.

[B20] TOM BURKE [Interrupting]: It's not the knowing so much, it's just that . . .

> Burke denies that receiving credit is his main consideration.

[S21] GEORGE STANLEY [Interrupting]: It isn't fair . . .

> Stanley brings up the question of fairness.

[B21] TOM BURKE [Interrupting]: Well, in a way it's just not fair. A person likes to think that his own unit's work is getting done; nobody minds helping somebody—when there is some need for it—or even if there seems to be a need for it occasionally—but to have the situation where other supervisors are expecting me, for example, to help them through some of their problems when I have my own work to do, I'm not sure that this is the fair thing all the way around. I wanted to tell you about it anyway—now that you've asked.

> Burke interrupts to agree and explains why he is bothered by the unfairness of the arrangement. (This answer shows how reflecting feelings can lead to clarification and improved communication. Burke reveals that he is the one who has been treated unfairly when he slips from the third person to the first. His last sentence indicates that he has noticed the slip.)

[S22] GEORGE STANLEY: Now, how does it happen that these people need help? Do you have any ideas why it is that these people are around looking for help? Does it mean that they haven't got enough people to do the work? What kind of help are they looking for?

> Stanley asks Burke a battery of related questions. (He seems more concerned with the "why" than with Burke's feelings. However, his questions reveal that he is interested in correcting the cause of Burke's difficulty.)

[B22] TOM BURKE: I'd hardly be in a position to say why.

> Burke seems a bit defensive and denies that he had anything specific in mind.

[S23] GEORGE STANLEY: I realize that. I'm just trying to see what we can figure out . . . [pause]

Stanley reassures Burke and implies that he was just thinking aloud about the problem.

[B23] TOM BURKE: Well, maybe if they had my unit, they wouldn't have the same kind of trouble. [pause] The kind of help that I get from my unit —it would be hard to think that any of them were getting that much support from their crews, but maybe I'm wrong—I don't know their units as well as I know mine. That could be part of the problem, I guess. I don't know why it is; it happens, though, and it doesn't seem quite fair to me.

Burke seems either unable or unwilling to answer Stanley's questions. (As a matter of fact, there probably is no simple, ready answer available, because the problem has not been isolated.) Burke responds by praising his own unit and saying that other units could produce better if they had his employees.

[S24] GEORGE STANLEY: Well, now you have accepted some extra work, I believe, and have gotten that out. This suggests that there's something . . .

Stanley mentions Burke's extra work load. (Stanley again fails to respond to Burke's feelings. He appears to be refuting Burke when he points out that Burke has had time to do extra work. Stanley appears to have slipped into the role of a judge.)

[B24] TOM BURKE [Interrupting]: I don't mind doing extra work. Maybe you are thinking about this thing we talked about awhile back. In fact, I have been wondering about it. I wanted to make sure that you didn't misunderstand my point of view at that time. Do you remember when I made a suggestion a month or two ago about giving certain of the routine jobs to the other units? I've been concerned about one part of that thing; I didn't want you to misunderstand me. I don't want you to think for a minute I think everyone else should get the dirty work. What I really think is that if my unit is doing more extra work than any of the others are (I think that that is probably a fact) then it seems to me that the work we do extra should not always be the routine stuff. It seems to me that if we turn out more work, we should be given a chance to pick some of the jobs that will give the unit more kicks—some special work that keeps interest up. I have worried that you might have misunderstood my intent, but that's the sense in which I meant that suggestion. [pause] I still think that something along that line is not unreasonable.

Burke interrupts and does not give Stanley an opportunity to clinch his point. He hastens to correct any impression Stanley may have that he is unwilling to do the extra work. He seems to sense Stanley's dissatisfaction about something and tries to locate the reason. He says Stanley may have the wrong impression from his suggestion recently that a particular routine job assignment be given to other units.

(The proposal he now makes seems reasonable because it incorporates motivation for doing work beyond the call of duty. Burke's defensive behavior seems to be somewhat greater than Stanley's single action as a judge would warrant. Undoubtedly, Burke's own sense of guilt and the fact that this is an appraisal situation contributed to his sensitivity. Stanley should respond in an understanding manner to this proposal to help Burke overcome the feeling that he has been criticized.)

[S25] GEORGE STANLEY: Then it is possible that this is sort of a circular business—that getting of extra work makes these people happy and makes them want to do extra work. Is that right?

Stanley picks up the constructive aspect of Burke's remark and reflects the idea that the employees are motivated to do extra work.

[B25] TOM BURKE: That's the way with my group. They're proud of the fact that they get extra work. I think there would be less—there would be *no* chance for any concern on their part if the extra work didn't tend always to be the routine jobs. By making the extra jobs the special or difficult ones, they would be kind of plums, something worth working for.

Burke responds with further details. He points out that employees are motivated to do extra jobs and that special or challenging jobs add to this motivation, whereas routine jobs detract from it.

[S26] GEORGE STANLEY: I see. They're really working for these extra jobs? They're really working for the group, among other things . . . [pause]

Stanley's response reveals that he begins to accept Burke's analysis. He seems to be gaining an insight into Burke's problem.

[B26] TOM BURKE: Well, they take pride in these extra jobs and I think that it wouldn't be unreasonable if they didn't have to take routine jobs all of the time when they get these extra jobs.

As soon as Stanley accepts Burke's problem as worthy of consideration, Burke reduces his expectations of what constitutes fair treatment. He points out that only *some* of the extra jobs should be of a nonroutine nature.

[S27] GEORGE STANLEY: This makes me wonder a little bit if [pause] how the other supervisors feel about this; I wonder if they want the extra jobs, too, for their people. . . . Maybe we ought to investigate this, too, along with a planning of technical matters. Maybe we ought to discuss in a meeting how these extra jobs should be distributed. I'm just throwing this out as an idea. How does this . . . [drifts off]

Stanley now becomes involved in problem solving himself. He says he wonders whether other units will object and whether special jobs are attractive generally. (He seems to be thinking aloud and comes up with an idea, group meetings, which he and Burke have already agreed [B16] might be used to solve problems.)

[B27] TOM BURKE: It's O.K. with me . . . sure.

Burke accepts this idea. (The addition of "sure" may indicate that he likes the idea better as he thinks about it.)

[S28] GEORGE STANLEY: I wonder if it is possible that they don't want them?

Stanley is still problem solving. He speculates on the possibility that other units will not want the challenging jobs. (Obviously, this would be the ideal situation because everyone then could profit from the change. The thought that a group meeting might lead to a plan for differential treatment seems to be an insightful experience for Stanley. It perhaps is new to Burke, too.)

[B28] TOM BURKE: They may not. I mean, I don't know if they do; it all depends on how the units look at it, and of course I wouldn't know that. I have my own unit and I know how they feel. The others may not be interested; I don't know. I know that our group likes unusual jobs and I think a little reward, a little bonus, the good problems, you know, stuff that really takes a little thought and a little work, gives you a little satisfaction. I would rather have these extra jobs than take the routine ones, since they're extra ones anyway. That's the way I feel and I don't think that some of the other supervisors particularly go along with my point of view. [pause]

Burke expands his theory. (He apparently has been set off on this train of thought by Stanley's last remark. He begins not knowing how other supervisors feel and ends by entertaining the possibility that they may see things differently than he does.)

[S29] GEORGE STANLEY: On the routine versus the extra.

Stanley reflects one of Burke's thoughts.

[B29] TOM BURKE: I just don't think they understand my point. I have the impression that some of them may think that I am all for giving them the dirty work, but you can see that that is not my point.

Burke suggests that the other supervisors may misunderstand him and he apparently wants to make sure that Stanley does not.

[S30] GEORGE STANLEY: But we don't want them to feel that there is favoritism here, either . . . so maybe this is something we ought to take up together as a group. . . . Some way of allocating these extra jobs so we don't get people feeling that they are getting stuck with something.

Stanley restates the problem and says it would have to be considered at a group meeting. He seems to appreciate Burke's problem and indicates that he is interested in being fair with everyone.

[B30] TOM BURKE: Right, some equitable way of distributing jobs would be fine with me. If we want to have a general meeting on it—get the supervisors together—good, and get this thing settled. I wasn't going to bring it up, but I think there have been some hard feelings. I feel that some of the supervisors are down on me because they just don't understand my point of view. I think that this is all there is to it. They know that I helped them in the past—maybe they worry about that.

> Burke accepts the new statement of the problem and reveals another problem that concerns him. He says that his relationship with his fellow supervisors has been strained because he has withheld his help. He seems to want to be friendly with them, but he does not want to do their work. (The problem with fellow supervisors might have been revealed earlier had Stanley responded more to Burke's feelings. That it came out anyway demonstrates that oversights are not serious if the interviewer has an overall constructive and understanding attitude.)

[S31] GEORGE STANLEY: Well, these are all very interesting points. We've said now that we have a problem to deal with in connection with keeping people interested and getting them the money that they need, in the form of promotion or otherwise.

> Stanley begins his summary.

[B31] TOM BURKE: When they deserve it.

> Burke agrees, but adds a thought.

[S32] GEORGE STANLEY: When they deserve it and earn it. This is a matter that we want to take up again in detail. We have a problem of [pause] coordination among the supervisors—technical coordination. We have a problem also of an understanding on the distribution of extra jobs; that involves some human relations problems, I guess. It is not clear who should get them. These are very important things and are definitely influencing our progress. [pause] Let's plan, then, to try to get together. I'll talk to the other supervisors about it, too. Try and get together and talk over these matters. I certainly feel that this has been worthwhile. I've learned a lot in this session. I'm glad you talked so frankly with me.

> Stanley summarizes the meeting. He says the next step is to have a group meeting. It is apparent that he has learned some things from the discussion, and he makes it clear to Burke that this is true. (Thanking Burke for his frankness may avert guilt feelings Burke might develop later for thinking he has talked too freely. This summary is good, not only because of what is included but also because of what is excluded. No further mention has been made of the Drake incident, but each step for action has been mentioned. All of the questions Stanley had on his mind have been discussed and clarified, apparently to his satisfaction.)

[B32] TOM BURKE: I'm glad to say what's on my mind—any time.

> Burke mentions his willingness to confide in Stanley. (He apparently appreciates the opportunity to talk freely.)

[S33] GEORGE STANLEY: Thanks a lot, Tom.

> Stanley closes the interview on a high note and sounds truly thankful.

Evaluation of the Interview

Although things did not progress too smoothly at times and there was one incident of defensive behavior [B4], the general impression left by this interview was of cooperation and friendliness. The person playing Stanley made problem solving his major objective and rarely gave the impression that he was concerned with appraising Burke, although he may have been too concerned with solving a situational problem and probing for the facts. He was sometimes slow to detect the nature of Burke's feelings.

The permissive nature of the interview was apparent because (a) the number of exchanges was quite large; (b) the speeches in general were quite short; and (c) there were few interruptions.

All of the critical issues that Stanley discussed in the two *telling* types of interviews came up for discussion during this interview, but they were introduced by Burke, as was also the case in the other Problem-Solving interview. This is not surprising. Problems that disturb the smooth flow of an operation can be experienced in different ways and can come into the conversation by a number of routes. It is unlikely that many problems a superior thinks are troublesome are so unimportant to an employee that some aspect of the problem will not come up for discussion without probing by the superior. In this interview, once a problem was introduced, it was not difficult for Stanley to bring in related matters that concerned him. Stanley at times was a bit overanxious to have his topic of interest discussed (see S8, 10, 12, and 19), so the question of manipulation was raised. On one occasion, he put Burke on the defensive with his approach, and on no occasion did his effort to direct the discussion seem necessary.

Analysis of Interaction

Table 6 shows the number of words spoken by each participant in his successive speeches. Stanley's two longest speeches were at the beginning and the end of the interview and were concerned with introduction and summary, respectively. Burke made four speeches that were at least as long as Stanley's most lengthy discourse.

In all, 3055 words were spoken, and only 33.6 percent of the words were contributed by Stanley. His proportion remained fairly constant throughout the interview—30.9 percent for the first half and 36.3 percent for the second half. Only the other Problem-Solving interview showed Stanley's contribution increasing from the first to the second half, and only that interview compared with this one because Stanley's contribution was less than Burke's for the interview as a whole and distinctly less (approximately a third) for the first part of the interview. The differences among methods were apparent quite early in the interview.

**Table 6. Words Spoken by Each Participant
During Second Problem-Solving Interview**

Speech	Stanley		Burke	
1	88		39	
2	16		95	
3	10		44	
4	17		6	
5	29		191	
6	25		5	
7	22		17	
8	25		45	
9	12		16	
10	17		98	
11	19		44	
12	19		120	
13	86		11	
14	26		273	
15	26		17	
16	85		142	
	522	30.9%	1163	= 1685
17	10		11	
18	4		16	
19	32		57	
20	23		9	
21	3		98	
22	47		9	
23	13		84	
24	20		215	
25	32		65	
26	18		34	
27	67		5	
28	11		126	
29	6		38	
30	47		92	
31	39		4	
32	121		10	
33	4			
	497	36.3%	873	= 1370
Total	1019	+	2036	= 3055
Percent	33.6		66.4	

Although the total number of words spoken was low, as was the case in the other Problem-Solving interview, it exceeded the number spoken in one of the Tell and Listen interviews, but it was distinctly less than the number of words spoken for either of the Tell and Sell interviews.

Reactions of Audience

As they had after the other Problem-Solving interview, the audience reacted favorably to the friendly spirit of the interview, but felt that Stanley rather than Burke was making all of the concessions. The feeling that Stanley had made too many concessions was more marked among his identifiers than among Burke's, but the opinion was present in both groups.

Almost everyone believed that Stanley would start holding group meetings, and the majority agreed that this would be a good idea. The majority opinion was that Stanley would change his evaluation, overlook the Drake affair, be less concerned with turnover, and be disinclined to be critical of Burke's relations with other supervisors. There was a general feeling that Burke had risen in Stanley's estimation. Those identifying with Burke clearly favored this change in Stanley, but a good segment (perhaps half) of the Stanley identifiers felt he either had been naïve or was just trying to avoid trouble. Many of the Stanley identifiers felt that Stanley had failed to conduct an appraisal interview.

The general opinion was that Burke had revised his estimation of Stanley upward; both halves of the audience expressed this opinion. The audience thought that Burke had had a successful experience and would therefore feel that Stanley was a good supervisor, especially because Burke had received practically everything he wanted.

All agreed that Burke would continue his good work, but most felt that he would not improve because no improvement plan had been discussed. A minority felt that Burke would show some general development because he would see problems in relation to a larger picture and become more friendly with fellow supervisors. Those holding this opinion were largely members of the group that identified with Burke.

In general, those identifying with Burke felt that he was such a good supervisor that he did not need to improve, while those identifying with Stanley continued to feel that Burke was selfish and conceited and should have been deflated a bit.

When asked what had been achieved, members of the audience listed such things as (a) improved communication; (b) improved respect and liking for each other; (c) heightened motivation on Burke's part; (d) a start on reducing turnover by having Frank Dobbs promoted; (e) better understanding of each other's jobs; (f) better understanding of their own jobs; (g) a fair trial with group meetings; and (h) a raise for Jane Wilson. That Burke would change his ways or feel that he should was not mentioned. When specifically questioned on Stanley's communication of the appraisal, the audience said that Burke realized that Stanley thought highly of him, but no one was sure of any faults that had been communicated to Burke. A few thought that Burke had reason to expect a raise after this interview.

No one seemed to be aware of Burke's defensive feelings [B4 and 22]. The audience also was unaware of the times that Stanley's questioning verged on manipulation [S10, 12, and 19].

Reactions of Participants

The person playing Stanley experienced considerable success and satisfaction with what had been accomplished. His specific reasons for these favorable reactions were that (a) Burke's human relations were better than he had been led to believe; (b) all aspects of the appraisal that he thought should be discussed had been covered; (c) the idea of having group meetings with his supervisors impressed him very much and he expected to upgrade the performance of his whole unit as a result; and (d) the interview was far more interesting and pleasant than he had anticipated.

He thought that Burke would accept the group's solution to the problem of assignments, and consequently this problem, as well as some of the differences between his supervisors, would be settled. He was no longer concerned with the problem of turnover and felt that Burke's analysis had merit. He intended to accept Burke's interpretation of the cause of the turnover unless subsequent events failed to support it.

Stanley thought that it was appropriate for Burke to bring up a promotion for Dobbs and a raise for Wilson. It indicated to him that Burke had the interests of his employees in mind and that he was willing to do what he could to build and keep a good team. Stanley intended to do what he could to assist Burke in these advancements. He said if these employees were as good as Burke indicated, he certainly appreciated knowing about them and rewarding them appropriately.

When asked whether Burke learned indirectly about his appraisal from this interview, Stanley said he was not sure but he felt that Burke must realize that he was very much appreciated and that he had an influence on improving conditions. The weaknesses mentioned in Burke's appraisal had not been communicated, but Stanley felt that this was fortunate because he had changed his mind about them. Stanley now saw the criticisms in the appraisal largely as misinterpretations.

The person playing Stanley was impressed with the ease with which all aspects of the appraisal came into the conversation. He did not know whether or not the role instructions helped bring this about, but he felt that because of this experience he would be more relaxed in interview situations and would not be anxious about the need to cover all topics.

The person playing Burke was happy with the way the interview ended and said that Stanley had risen in his estimation. He was somewhat worried at times because he felt that Stanley had something in mind, but felt that Stanley had treated him very generously, particularly with respect to the Drake incident.

Burke admitted that he had acted quite selfishly at times, perhaps because he felt that his unit had not been appreciated. He now realized that Stanley did recognize his good work, and he no longer felt that other supervisors were "getting away with things." He was very pleased because Stanley agreed to take steps to upgrade Dobbs and Wilson.

The discussion had given him a number of insights. He was more aware of the overall objective; he appreciated the need for more coordination among the units; and he felt that the group meetings would solve a number of problems, as well as give him an opportunity to become more friendly with other supervisors. He definitely wanted a chance to do something for Drake. He now felt that the turnover problem was a complex one and he wanted to give it more thought. He said he would be glad to have his well-trained employees transferred to other units if it meant a promotion for them.

Although he felt that he was appreciated, he had learned that his greatest weakness was being unable "to see the forest for the trees." He felt that Stanley was aware of his limited perspective as well as the fact that the interview had developed and broadened him.

Observer Reactions Compared to Those of Role Players

After each of the Problem-Solving interviews, the audience seemed somewhat insensitive to the constructive accomplishments of the Problem-Solving approach, although the participants reported much satisfaction with the method. During both of the Problem-Solving interviews, Stanley communicated to Burke the need for better relations with fellow supervisors, and in both cases Burke reported that he intended to do his part to achieve this objective. Other objectives, such as reduced turnover and a better distribution of assignments, seemed to be attainable by solutions that were satisfactory to both Stanley and Burke. This left only the initial goal of improving Burke's interpersonal skills. In each case, however, the problem disappeared when Stanley realized that it was the result of a false conclusion on his part. It therefore appears that the overall goal of employee development was achieved quite well in the last two interviews, especially when compared to the other four interviews in which some unintended, undesirable goals were attained (e.g., loss of Burke's morale, Burke's leaving the company, poorer relations with other supervisors, and poorer relations between Stanley and Burke).

The last two interviews accomplished the objective of "letting the employee know where he stands" better than the other four interviews because the earlier Burkes usually felt less appreciated than their Stanleys tried to convey. Despite Stanley's strong praise in the first four interviews, his criticism more than neutralized it.

Why, then, were the observers so insensitive to the constructive accomplishments of the Problem-Solving interviews? First, the observers were probably influenced by what they expected from an appraisal interview. This expectation, of course, was based on their own experiences. Generally speaking, superiors pass judgment and we expect them to be good judges. Because Stanley did not supply the remedies for Burke's improvement during the Problem-Solving interviews, he apparently seemed somewhat weak and uninformed to an observer. Those identifying with Stanley tended to be most sympathetic with him in this role. And although persons identifying with Burke perceived Stanley as being unfair at times, they were more willing to submit to his authority than were the actual role players. However, the Burke identifiers' perceptions did make them more insightful than the Stanley identifiers.

A second possibility is that it is generally assumed that something must be spelled out in detail in order to be communicated. In both of the last two interviews, Burke surprised the observers by his report of the changes he intended to make that had not been mentioned during the interview.

Burke's worth to the company was perhaps better communicated by his feelings of contributing to a solution for some of Stanley's problems (e.g., better relations between supervisors) than by his being praised. A great deal of spoken praise (as in the first four interviews) can be neutralized by the mention of one fault, but influencing a decision and discovering one's own negligence can have an important constructive influence on future behavior.

Finally, these studies were made before supervisors received the degree of training in interpersonal relations that now exists. Many readers will find the reports of the role players to be in line with their own reactions to the interviews. As a matter of fact, the unexpected negative reactions to criticism during the appraisal interview have caused much research effort to be directed at solving the problem.

Because criticism has such a negative impact, many supervisors avoid criticism and become permissive. Such permissiveness is not a substitute for either the Tell and Listen or the Problem-Solving method but represents a lowering of standards.

Summary Notes on the Problem-Solving Interview

The Climate Created

The pervasive feelings of these interviews were cooperation, friendliness, and mutual concern. There was a general absence of defensiveness, although such feelings did surface occasionally. The interviews were used as an opportunity to discuss topics of mutual interest. Burke's work was evaluated within the framework of a fairly nondirective development session, although Stanley did attempt to raise some topics in a manipulative fashion.

The interviews centered on issues, progressing to joint problem solving. Each Burke, apparently as a result of Stanley's attitude, did some self-evaluation. Although neither Burke was ever told directly where he stood, most of the areas of concern that Stanley wanted to cover did come up during the interviews. There appeared to be a commitment by both participants to follow through on solutions discussed.

Characteristics of the Interviewer

Stanley set the tone for the interviews by focusing on progress and on how things were going for Burke. He seemed to have a flexible plan of procedure.

Stanley reflected and clarified Burke's ideas and feelings; he tested out ideas with Burke and sometimes asked leading questions. Stanley did not place blame; his position was basically "I'm O.K., you're O.K. . . . we're in this together." Consequently, there was an effort on Stanley's part to engage in the problem-solving process. He came across as a concerned helper who had Burke's interest at heart. There were occasions when Stanley stepped into the role of a judge, but this happened infrequently.

At key places in the interview, Stanley effectively functioned as a summarizer and facilitated moving the interview to other levels. There was a willingness on Stanley's part to be influenced by Burke—to change his mind based on new information. By often avoiding giving advice and by focusing on problem-solving activity, Stanley was able to learn from Burke.

Characteristics of the Interviewee

It appeared that each Burke gradually sensed the situation as a meeting of two equals and accepted Stanley's word that they were there to discuss matters of mutual interest rather than to evaluate Burke's performance.

Each Burke was open and willing to share his ideas and feelings rather freely. Each took initiative and showed enthusiasm for the conversation. The relatively free and open climate established enabled the Burkes to think about problems that were opened up, rather than coming to premature conclusions. They discovered constructive solutions, with Stanley's active involvement, and took responsibility for the interview's direction. Occasionally, Burke became defensive, guarded, and withdrawn, but, generally, each showed a strong willingness to cooperate with Stanley.

A hallmark of the Problem-Solving approach was evident in each Burke's behavior—each discovered his own solutions to problems that he owned and took responsibility for.

CHAPTER NINE

Problems Associated with Interview Styles

Comparison of Interaction Patterns

Although this book is not intended to be a report of research findings, a number of comparisons have been made of the six interviews. Some of the results show basic trends and clear up questions, even if they do not supply specific solutions to problems. The author's industrial experience with appraisal interviews and knowledge of psychological principles made possible a selection of interactions typical of real-life occurrences.

Because each of the three types of interviews was conducted twice, pairs of interviews of the same type can be compared with interviews of a different type on the basis of the number of words spoken. Table 7 shows the combined number of words spoken by both participants during each interview.

The Tell and Sell method yielded many more words than the other two methods. Given the same topics to discuss, it took 6920 words, using the Tell and Sell method, to cover the two interviews; the other two pairs of interviews required only 5745 and 5640, respectively. The matched interview styles show surprising similarities despite the fact that different persons played the part of Tom Burke.

Table 7. Total Number of Words Spoken During Each Interview

Day Recorded	Tell and Sell Method	Tell and Listen Method	Problem-Solving Method
Friday	3407	3042	2585
Saturday	3513	2703	3055
Total	6920	5745	5640

Certain conclusions can safely be drawn on the basis of these findings. For example, the differences are small and the trends are inconsistent between the Tell and Listen and Problem-Solving methods with respect to the number of words required. However, the number of words spoken in the two Tell and Sell interviews is consistent, setting this method apart from the other methods. This suggests that either the person taking the role of Stanley in these interviews was exceptionally talkative or the interview style he used required more words. In any case, it is safe to conclude that the other two methods are not as time consuming as the Tell and Sell method. People often complain that they do not have time to listen, but the Tell and Listen method and the Problem-Solving approach, both of which require the nondirective skills of listening and responding to feelings, proved to be more economical in the number of words used than the more economical of the two Tell and Sell interviews.

The number of times that each person talked and the length of the speeches made by each also serve as measures of differentiation among the three methods. Table 8 shows the total number of words spoken by each, the number of times each spoke, and the average length of the speeches.

The interview styles clearly fall into three patterns as far as length is concerned. The amount of talking Stanley did decreased from the two Tell and Sell interviews through the two Tell and Listen interviews to the two Problem-Solving interviews. The average length of Stanley's

Table 8. Number of Interactions During Each Interview

Method	Tell and Sell		Tell and Listen		Problem-Solving	
Day	Fri.	Sat.	Fri.	Sat.	Fri.	Sat.
No. of words by Stanley	2735	2946	1614	1630	1138	1019
Number of speeches	22	32	25	26	38	33
Av. no. of words	124.3	92	64.5	62.7	29.9	30.8
No. of words by Burke	672	567	1428	1073	1447	2036
Number of speeches	21	31	25	26	37	32
Av. no. of words	32	18.3	57.1	41.3	39.1	63.6

speeches is almost identical for each pair of methods but distinctly different for the three methods. For the two Tell and Sell interviews, the average speeches made by Stanley were 124.3 and 92 words, respectively. Stanley's speeches averaged 64.5 and 62.7 words for the two Tell and Listen methods and 29.9 and 30.8 for the two Problem-Solving approaches.

The similarity in speech length for each method, coupled with the sharp differences among methods, brings up the question of whether speech length is controlled by the person who interviews or by the method he uses. It seems likely that both are contributing factors, because it would be improbable that the interviewer alone could exert so much control using different methods, even on the same individual.

There was no clear pattern for Tom Burke. Each of the Burkes talked little during the two Tell and Sell interviews and listened to Stanley's long speeches or was interrupted by him and could not make long speeches himself. During the Tell and Listen and the Problem-Solving interviews the Burkes made long speeches, in general approaching or exceeding the length of speeches made by the Stanleys. A most striking individual difference in the performance of the two role players was during the Problem-Solving interview. The average length of the speeches for one Burke was 39.1 and for the other it was 63.6. However, this approach might reasonably be expected to yield the biggest difference because it is the situation in which Burke is given the greatest freedom to talk and reveal his ideas. A person who has ideas and enthusiasm is likely to talk considerably more when encouraged than a less imaginative and less inspired person. Because the two Stanleys talked a similar amount in this interview, it seems quite probable that the difference in the two Burkes was due to their individual natures. The difference in Burkes is also very obvious for the other interviews.

How much an interview style tended to cause the interviewer to dominate the conversation is shown in Table 9. The interviews have been divided into three parts to show possible differences in Stanley's behavior in the early, the middle, and the later stages of the discussion.[2] Degree of domination was measured by the percentage of words spoken by Stanley.

Each of the three methods seemed to produce a fairly unique pattern.

---

[2]Stanley's speeches and Burke's responses were grouped as nearly as possible into equal number of speeches. For the first Tell and Sell interview, Stanley's twenty-two speeches were grouped 7-7-8; for the first Tell and Listen, the grouping was 9-8-8; for the first Problem-Solving, the grouping was 12-13-13; and for the last three interviews the patterns were 10-11-11, 8-9-9, and 11-11-11, respectively. Burke's speeches were grouped the same, except that the last third of the interview sometimes had one less speech than Stanley's, depending on whether Burke responded to Stanley's parting words.

The two Tell and Sell interviews showed Stanley speaking 80.3 and 83.9 percent of the words. This degree of domination was repeated with surprising uniformity in each of the thirds of the two interviews—the percentages of the six thirds falling within the 9-point range from 77.0 to 85.7. Stanley's domination occurred despite the fact that the two Tom Burkes differed greatly in their personalities and susceptibility to domination.

The patterns for the two Tell and Listen interviews were more similar to each other than were those of any of the other two methods. They showed Stanley doing slightly more than half of the talking, 53.0 percent during one interview and 60.3 during the other. In each case Stanley did less talking in the middle third than in the other two-thirds. This undoubtedly happened because the first third contained his introductory and warm-up remarks, while the last third included his summary and conclusion. At such times, the interviewer usually takes the dominant role.

The Problem-Solving interview was the only time Burke was induced to do more of the talking than Stanley, whose percentages for the two interviews were 44.0 and 33.6. Examination of the interview by thirds showed a trend for Stanley to talk more as the interview progressed. During the interviews, Stanley talked the least during the first third. Apparently, Stanley explored at first and then interacted with Burke. During the second Problem-Solving interview, Stanley allowed Burke to do approximately two-thirds of the talking, and this proportion remained surprisingly constant for all three parts.

Objective vs. Method

It is fairly clear from a study of the tables that the method assigned influenced the role Stanley played in the interview and seemed to exert

Table 9. Percentage of Words Spoken by Stanley

Method	Tell and Sell		Tell and Listen		Problem-Solving	
Period Covered	Total	By Thirds	Total	By Thirds	Total	By Thirds
Friday interviews	80.3	85.5	53.0	56.4	44.0	33.2
		77.4		48.5		48.5
		77.0		55.1		51.2
Saturday interviews	83.9	85.7	60.3	71.8	33.6	31.8
		82.3		50.8		32.1
		83.6		59.4		36.3
Both interviews	82.1	85.6	56.6	62.8	38.8	32.5
		79.8		49.3		38.6
		80.7		57.6		43.4

considerable control over his behavior. Because each method has an objective, the skills an interviewer will practice depend not only on his interviewing ability and knowledge, but also on the assignment he is given. Assuming two interviewers have the same repertoire of skills, one who is assigned the task of letting an employee know where he stands will practice different skills than one who is assigned the task of discussing an employee's job to obtain the employee's ideas for improving it. Whether an interviewer preaches or listens, dominates or draws out, explains or understands, is irritable or patient, depends partly on the objective he is asked to pursue, and although objectives determine skills, they do not necessarily cause the appropriate ones to be used.

However, the fact that an interviewer is given an objective and practices the proper skills in accordance with it does not necessarily mean that the objective pursued will be achieved. It is possible to seek one objective and achieve another, perhaps the opposite. It is possible also that some objectives can never be achieved, while others may be achieved incidentally or as by-products.

It would seem reasonable to expect that an employee's evaluation could be effectively communicated to him if that were the only objective, yet this was not always true. The interviewers recorded in this book often failed to achieve the objectives that characterized their methods. The fact that a judgment may be challenged causes an interviewer either to play down or to exaggerate a weakness. Since weaknesses in performance are more delicate matters to present than strengths, in most cases, much more time and many more words are spent discussing weaknesses, which causes the employee to feel more rejected by an appraisal than the superior intends.

Other Possible Ways To Achieve Accuracy

Rating forms mailed to employees to inform them of their standing might be a more accurate way of communicating an evaluation. However, this idea does not meet with favor among business executives because they consider it cold. Apparently, they want to hear the employee's reactions and hope to gain acceptance.

Some companies have attempted to make the appraisal of an employee more objective by combining several ratings made independently by persons qualified to evaluate the employee or by assigning committees to make the appraisal after discussing job performance. These methods reduce the "halo effect" and give support to the supervisor who must conduct the interview.

Whether the supervisor can do a better job of communicating the evaluation under such circumstances is not known, but the possibility that having the facts or proof in his favor may be a *disadvantage* should not be overlooked. It may be that group appraisals or evaluations based on objective measures such as observed behavior give the supervisor more confidence and make him less ready to listen to a subordinate's defense. The interviewee then is at a disadvantage because he has less opportunity to save face through rationalization.

When a supervisor's opinion is challenged, it is always wise for him to consider that his opinion or his standards may be in error. If he finds an error, a correction is in order and there is a chance for him to cooperate on the revision. If there is no error, failure to change his opinion creates a face-saving problem that can be resolved only by a change of some sort. A "correction" may be required regardless of whether or not an error is found. From the human relations point of view, it is best for an interviewer to drop a controversy over the "right" or "wrong" of an evaluation and go directly to the problem of finding an acceptable revision. Usually, only minor revisions are needed. The important point for the subordinate is that the person in authority is willing to make a change; thus he seems less threatening.

Another method for increasing the accuracy of an appraisal is to make use of objective measures of performance and to post them so every employee can see his comparative standing. However, the development of objective measures for many positions would be quite a chore and it is questionable whether management would seek such a plan.

Gaining the Employee's Acceptance

There seems to be a special management objective in holding an interview—obtaining the employee's acceptance of an improvement plan. Obtaining acceptance of a plan for improvement is more difficult when the reform requires a change in a person than when it requires a change in the job. Any criticism of a person tends to lead to a defensive attitude on his part; in the process of trying to correct an employee, a supervisor may make him rigid, hostile, and less ready to change than at the outset. Appraisals that stress performance are likely to have implications involving a person's judgment, personality, and attitude.

Various ways to gain acceptance of appraisals have been attempted. *Persuasion* or *selling* approaches represent appeals to reason. Although a person's wants and desires are considered, the choices made are assumed to be intellectual ones. *Counseling* or *therapeutic* approaches concern themselves with personal problems that may generate emotional resistance to the need for change. The counseling methods recognize the importance of the employee's feelings and the need to express and clarify them. Once the emotional obstacles are recognized and expressed, behavior changes follow. Because the true sources of resistance often lie beneath the surface or are reluctantly expressed, certain counseling skills are required.

When attempting to gain acceptance of a plan for improvement, either through counseling or selling, the interviewer assumes that the plan is a good one. If this is not the case, an additional cause for the employee's resistance is present.

One of the greatest merits of the Tell and Listen approach is that it neutralizes some of the bad feeling that is introduced by communication of the evaluation. The method utilizes some of the skills associated with nondirective counseling and may relieve the subordinate of some of the defensive feelings that an appraisal tends to arouse. However, it does not assure acceptance of the appraisal, and it may cause the employee to feel that a superior has changed his mind if he no longer insists on a change.

Listening may be in conflict with the objective of informing the employee where he stands, but if it results in the employee gaining insight into his own problems, both acceptance and communication of the appraisal may be achieved. Acceptance of an improvement plan and the accurate communication of an evaluation are not linked together; consequently, seeking to achieve one of these objectives may decrease an interviewer's chances of achieving the other.

In contrast, the major merit of the Problem-Solving method is that it has the single objective of improving job performance. The causes of poor job performance may be found in the person who holds the job (including his weaknesses, a misuse of his strong aptitudes, an inappropriate attitude, or lack of interest); the equipment with which he works; a lack of help from his superior; the activities of others; or any combination of these factors. A better job performance could undoubtedly be attained if an improvement in any one of these could be obtained. With many roads to improvement, the problem of gaining acceptance of one of them is simplified for an interviewer.

The success can be even greater if an interviewer uses the Problem-Solving method, forgets about the appraisal, and discusses the job and the employee's satisfaction. The possibilities of changing the job, the cooperation of fellow workers, and the kind of support that the supervisor can give are much less threatening and more profitable subjects for problem solving than are possibilities for changing the subordinate's performance. Once the subordinate freely engages in problem solving, he may see the need for making changes in his role. Opportunities for utilizing his strong abilities can be more profitable than those for overcoming his weaknesses. In some cases, this may require some changes in duties rather than in the employee.

Weakness of Problem Solving for Multiple Objectives

Obviously, a Problem-Solving interview will not (a) let the employee know exactly where he stands; (b) warn him; (c) evaluate the employee for promotional purposes or lateral transfers; (d) furnish a record of job performance; (e) obtain a record of ratings by various supervisors; and (f) supply higher management with an inventory of talent available. If any of these objectives is desired, additional procedures will have to be added to supplement the development plan.

Attempting to achieve one goal may also result in achieving others, but if several goals are sought at the outset, it is possible that none will be achieved fully. There can be but one goal if an interviewer wishes to create a favorable climate for effective problem solving. When several goals are sought, problem-solving activity loses its integrative function; thus, the first step for a superior approaching an interview is to settle on the major objective. Additional objectives achieved should be considered by-products.

Proponents of current appraisal programs claim they can fulfill the following needs: develop, motivate, reward, warn, justify merit increases, and recognize and give individual treatment to employees; force a superior to evaluate individuals, assess talent, talk to all subordinates about their work, and provide an inventory of talent and a promotion list; serve as a roster for merit increases; provide a means for seeing that no employee is overlooked; give the company and future supervisors a file of an employee's performance; train supervisors to objectively evaluate employees and to be aware of their training needs; and furnish records showing that each employee has been told where he stands. It is doubtful that a single method with the general scope of the standard appraisal plan can be successfully developed.

From the employee's point of view there are also many advantages to appraisal programs. Employees are entitled to know how their supervisors feel about their work and whether their performance adversely affects their future. Furthermore, if evaluations are pooled, employees can escape some of the harm a biased superior might have on their progress.

The value of an appraisal from the company's point of view resides not so much in *how well* any of these objectives are accomplished, but in *how many* of them are touched upon. To decide what kind of plan to use, a company must decide which of the many objectives it wants most to accomplish. There may be ways to achieve each of them, but no single plan will accomplish all of them. As a matter of fact, to try to accomplish the list of objectives mentioned above actually interferes with problem solving.

Often, the objectives that appraisal plans are said to achieve represent an after-the-fact justification or a rationalization of a solution already developed. Listing a multitude of objectives is characteristic of a sales approach where a cure-all remedy—one that is "good for whatever ails the company"—is announced. Instead of stimulating problem solving, it appeals to the harassed executive who wants a simple solution to all his problems.

Figure 3 is a graphic representation of the problems encountered when attempting to reach varied objectives with a single plan. Any approach that accomplishes a multitude of objectives is likely to have some unwanted side effects, such as loss of initiative, high personnel turnover, strained superior-subordinate relationships, loss of loyalty, poor upward communication, fear, conservative thinking, and the development of "yes men." The figure depicts undesirable effects (rectangles) distributed among the desired objectives (ovals). The *specific* plan approach is analogous to a rifle shot—limited in scope, relatively sure of achieving the goal, and least likely to achieve undesirable side effects. The *general* plan is analogous to the shotgun approach—it may attain a greater number of objectives, but the objectives may not be fully accomplished and unwanted results may be attained. If several objectives are desired, adopting several plans may be the answer, i.e., using several rifle shots and sighting on different specific targets with each shot.

When single objectives are desired, the possibilities are greatest because there are more ways to accomplish one objective than there are to accomplish any particular group of objectives.

If a group of managers is asked to select a method to achieve a particular goal, the members will contribute a list of possibilities or solutions in a few minutes because each objective can be approached from a variety of directions. There are many ways to develop employees, several ways to warn them, innumerable ways to motivate them, several merit recognition plans, a great variety of ways to select candidates for promotion, and many ways to improve "fair" treatment of employees. Many ideas suggested in a brainstorming session (Osborn, 1953, p. 317; Clark, 1958), if followed up, could be implemented and developed into fairly ingenious plans—certainly more effective than a single general plan.

Once a plan has been developed to achieve a given objective effectively, an employer can examine the by-products that can be achieved either directly or indirectly. Often, desirable by-products can be enjoyed if a few additional features that do not interfere with the major objective are

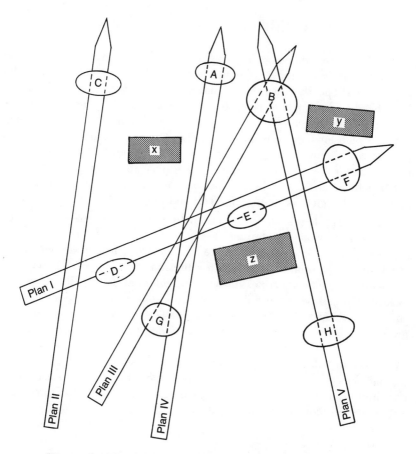

Figure 3. The Problem of Seeking Multiple Objectives
The ovals represent objectives, the rectangles represent unwanted side effects, and the arrows represent specific plans. The same objective may be reached from a number of positions, and the opportunity to choose from among several approaches is greater when there is a single objective. The by-products are different when the same objective is reached from different directions, and which by-product is preferred can determine final selection of a plan.

built into a plan. In this way, several desirable results can be attained using one plan. An employer can compare a variety of plans. The final choice should depend upon the pattern of by-products, both good and bad, as well as on the effectiveness with which alternative plans attain the main goal. It is important that the most important single goal be used as the starting point for problem-solving activity.

Avoid Supplying the Answers

When development of an employee is the primary objective of an appraisal program, those who make the appraisal usually supply the answers and specify ways the employee must change. The superior may feel that he is doing the subordinate a favor, not only because he has diagnosed the difficulty but also because he has furnished the remedy. When a plan for improvement is supplied, the problem of how to develop the individual employee is solved before the interview takes place; all that remains is for the superior to gain a subordinate's acceptance. It is apparent that this line of reasoning is not appropriate for the Problem-Solving method, although it is implied for Tell and Sell.

For a problem-solving discussion to occur, it is important for the interviewer to avoid even hinting that he has a solution in mind. If he can not help settling on a solution before the interview, it is desirable for him to return to the initial problem and ask himself why he wants the employee to change. Once he separates his own solution from the problem he wishes to solve, he will be better able to state the problem without criticizing the employee. Frequently, the employee will attempt to have the superior express his views about what should be done, but this occurs primarily because the subordinate suspects that the superior has an answer in mind and wants to "play safe." Problem solving can occur only when the subordinate ceases to be defensive and the superior is ready to accept the possibility that the job may be improved in a variety of ways, some quite different from those he has in mind.

Turning an Evaluation Interview into a Problem-Solving Session

If a company feels that the Problem-Solving approach has merit and that an evaluation is also desirable, there are a number of ways these two objectives can be combined.

One way is to call each employee in for an appraisal interview and to fill out the evaluation form jointly. The superior could raise questions such as how the employee felt he compared with others, what he felt his strengths were, and what aspects of the work he felt were most in need of improvement. It is important for the superior to remain open minded and to stimulate problem solving rather than to dominate the discussion. This approach depends on four assumptions:

1. Most employees are realistic and can evaluate themselves accurately;

2. A minority of the employees would either overrate or underrate themselves;

3. Employees who underrate themselves need encouragement, which can be given to them during the following year;

4. Employees who overrate themselves are immature and not able to take criticism. Only hard feelings would be created by challenging their unrealistic appraisals.

A second possibility would be for a superior to call a group meeting of subordinates and ask them to devise an evaluation plan and appraise each other. This would be possible only in cases where a number of persons reported to a given supervisor and were familiar with the performances of the others.

A third possibility would require that three or more persons familiar with the work of an employee appraise him and report the results to his superior. The superior would then interview the subordinate and tell him what the other people had said about his performance. The problem-solving aspect of this interview would be to try to find out what the raters used to form their opinions and what could be done so that they would have a more accurate impression. The superior, instead of standing in judgment, could support the employee.

Although this plan may sound somewhat ludicrous when first considered, it does supply the basis for cooperative problem solving, providing the superior can refrain from expressing personal opinions and does not take a position or reveal an evaluation.

Integrating Two Objectives of an Appraisal Plan

Even though an appraisal may not be essential for the development of an employee, it can serve as an aid in determining merit increases, lateral transfers, and promotions. Appraisals can be worthwhile for making an inventory of departmental talents to determine training needs or changes in hiring policy. To obtain an overall evaluation of a unit or department, it is necessary to make an analysis of individual abilities. For example, a company may find that many of its younger employees possess administrative abilities, while persons with high degrees of creative ability are approaching retirement. This finding would not indicate whether creative ability or administrative ability was more important; both could be essential. The goal in this situation would be to have a proper distribution of each type of ability in each department. The evaluation might indicate that in coming years a certain number of individuals with creative talents should be taken into the organization or that something should be done to increase interest along creative lines. If the balance between these abilities varies among departments, training and transfers would be in order. A few exchanges could result in improvement for all, much the way two ball clubs profit after a trade.

An inventory of talents can be taken with no concern about personalities. A balanced inventory may be achieved with a great variety of individual differences in talent. It is then unnecessary for each employee to have his weakness corrected because the strength of another will compensate. If variations in ability are respected, more attention and recognition can be given to strengths. An emphasis on superior traits is desirable because the greatest potential for development is present in the employees' natural aptitudes. If a company needs both creative and administrative talents, the best potential for improvement lies in fostering creative effort in those with high creative aptitudes, while giving executive training and responsibility to those with administrative ability. Naturally, the problem of proper rewards for different but essential and rare talents would have to be worked out to the satisfaction of those concerned.

Although the need for accuracy in the estimates or measures of abilities remains, an inventory summarizes the talents of employees without passing judgment on the individuals, and the need to interview the individual about an evaluation disappears. This is an advantage because the need to hold appraisal interviews often makes the supervisor inclined to appraise subordinates in a manner that will cause a minimum of unpleasantness. The supervisor may therefore be somewhat lenient in his appraisals of some employees, and the ratings may show less divergence than is warranted by the actual differences in employee performance. The removal of caution permits more accurate evaluations and encourages the interviewer to mention traits that are not subject to change and yet have a bearing on some assignments. For example, limited intelligence might be relevant to an appraisal that is used for determining an employee's promotability, but it would be inappropriate to bring up the question of intelligence during an interview intended to develop the employee.

Although an interview no longer is needed to communicate the appraisal, this does not mean that interviews can not be used to assist the superior in making an inventory. The superior can use the interview to locate interests and abilities that may not be utilized or be fully apparent. The supervisor can say, "I'd like you to tell me about anything you feel that I should know to make you more valuable to the company." This permits the employee to talk about correspondence school studies he may be undertaking, a personal problem he may have, community affairs he may be involved with, or anything about himself that he feels his superior may not have appreciated fully. The discussion can then proceed along lines described in the next chapter, which deals with problem solving.

Even if the interview is not designed to communicate an employee's appraisal, the employee may be anxious or ask about his progress. The real purpose of the interview will be undermined if the superior is trapped into making an appraisal. If the employer's true objective is an accurate assessment of talent, the superior can reassure the subordinate that the company is interested in locating employee interests and unused assets and ask the subordinate to describe his own talents. A discussion of employee interests and ideas should greatly aid the superior in an appraisal of subordinates, especially if he tries to understand their views and is a good listener. This approach to employee appraisal emphasizes strengths.

An appraisal plan that does not serve to communicate an evaluation may have as its objective (a) development, which would be accomplished by a Problem-Solving interview, to be discussed in the next chapter, or (b) making an inventory of employee talent, which could be accomplished by filling out a modified appraisal form or by a preappraisal interview, especially if the subordinate was asked to supply information he felt was relevant.

Two Relationships Between Appraisal and Interview

An appraisal plan ordinarily includes two activities: the appraisal of personnel and the conduct of interviews. These activities may be linked together or they may be independent. The upper part of Figure 4 shows a *dependent* type of relationship, in which the appraisal of the individual is the first step before an interview, which is a review of the appraisal. A number of objectives are anticipated by an interviewer and often are given as justifications for the appraisal program. Five common objectives are (1) to let an employee know where he stands; (2) to develop the employee; (3) to supply data for inventory purposes; (4) to warn or give recognition for individual performance; and (5) to supply management with data useful for promotions and transfers. The third and fifth objectives do not require an interview, but the first and fourth depend on one.

The third and fifth objectives can be reached independently, as shown in the lower half of the figure. In this type of situation, appraisal serves the objectives of inventory and promotion (or transfer). The appraisal can be made without concern for the coming interview. The topics for discussion at an interview can then be confined to the employee's needs and his ideas on job problems so that the development of the employee's performance can be the primary objective. An important by-product in this situation is improved communication, often a good substitute for one of the goals (letting the employee know where he stands). The goals of warning, letting an employee know where he stands, and having a record, however, appear to be lost if appraisal and interview are separated. If these

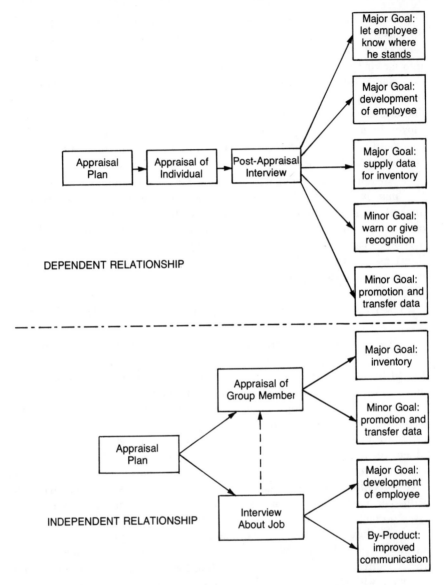

**Figure 4. Two Possible Relationships Between the Appraisal
of Personnel and the Conduct of Interviews**

The upper part of the figure shows a dependent relationship that exists when the appraisal plan is geared to achieve many objectives. The lower portion shows an appraisal as independent from an interview and the advantage of seeking one goal at a time. The dotted line between indicates that the appraisal will profit if it follows the interview.

objectives are deemed essential by a company, they may be incorporated in the day-to-day work relationship. However, the satisfaction gained from discussing job problems tends to give a sense of security to a subordinate so that the objectives that are sacrificed become less important.

Perhaps the ideal condition is to develop employees to the point where they no longer need praise and assurance from their superior but gain their satisfaction from successful experiences on the job. An employee's dependence on praise from above can be quite a burden in a management hierarchy.

The question of whether an inventory of talent should be integrated with the objective of merit increases and thereby serve as an appraisal of the individual remains unanswered. It would seem best to separate the evaluation of how an employee is doing on his present job from the estimation of how he would do on other jobs if promoted or transferred. The latter contributes most to the inventory and contains more opportunities for agreement. If an individual performance record is desired, it should either be part of a separate program or at least be recorded on a separate form and it should not be a secret document. The form could be filled in by the superior and his subordinate during a second interview or at the end of the interview. (The rationale for making the appraisal a joint activity will be discussed in the next chapter.) The addition of this objective (making a performance record) necessarily modifies the procedure because the superior begins to assume the role of a judge, especially when pay increases are associated with the interview. Sometimes it is wise for a superior to settle for a few important objectives rather than risk the ones attained in an attempt to achieve more.

Special Problems

Ideally, a superior should not criticize an employee during an appraisal interview, but this creates a problem of finding a way to correct certain personal habits or mannerisms that are annoying to everyone, a problem raised in almost any discussion of appraisals. An employee is entitled to be made aware of annoying mannerisms, and also a superior should not have to put up with really bad personal habits in a subordinate. However, the appraisal interview may not be the best vehicle for confronting such problems. The employee is likely to feel that he is being criticized for things that have little bearing on the job, which is a good point. An employee's post-interview reactions to an employer mentioning personal faults during the appraisal interview may be such comments as:

"You have to dress like the boss to get ahead around here."

"A person's work is judged by how often he takes a bath."

"I was told to watch my language around here, but I know someone who is really obnoxious and he was promoted."

If an employee's conduct is in poor taste, it might be better for a superior to find a suitable opportunity to raise the matter at an informal or casual meeting. To withhold a criticism until the annual appraisal interview is scheduled amounts to building the personal habit into the job performance—perhaps even making certain habits part of a job description.

Correcting antisocial personal habits may require a special time to discuss only the particular fault. An attempt should be made only after considerable thought and preparation by the supervisor, whose approach should be influenced by the nature of the fault, the kind of relationship he has with a subordinate, and the way the subordinate takes the criticism when it is broached. A specific plan would be more appropriate for each given individual than any procedure that could be described on these pages. Often it might be best to select a particular person, a friend of the employee, for example, to make the contact and bring up the matter.

When problems of dress, conduct, and etiquette are directly essential to performance on a job, such as for customer contacts, these matters can become part of a training program. Classes can be held to teach salespeople to dress in good taste and to learn courteous responses to insolent customer demands, if these skills are needed. In other cases, group meetings can be held to discuss ways to make customers feel more welcome, develop a list of good habits for better public relations, and offer suggestions on how minor annoyances in the group can be overcome. Group discussions utilize social pressure to determine the social values a group wishes to live by, and social pressure often means conformity. When bad habits are to be corrected, conformity happens to be desirable. When conformity is not desired, the discussion leader can use his position to encourage individuality.

CHAPTER TEN

The Problem-Solving Interview and Executive Development

When Development Is a Primary Objective

When the development of subordinates is one of the major objectives of the appraisal interview, it is desirable to eliminate any features that make an employee less receptive to change. An employee may not appreciate a program for improvement that is recommended to him and yet may be ready to adopt one that he plans with his superior. If the employee agrees on the changes, it is unnecessary to tell him of his appraisal, because an awareness of a weakness is not essential to development. The "telling" part of the interview is relevant only if it is assumed that knowledge is a first step in the development process. If it is assumed, however, that performance can be improved without correcting weaknesses, there is no need to communicate the appraisal.

In the analyses of the Problem-Solving interviews in Chapters 7 and 8, it was found that some part of the evaluation was communicated, even though this was neither verbalized nor a primary objective. If the separation between communicating an appraisal and developing an employee were more complete, the objective of development might be realized even more than it was in the transcribed illustrations.

The appraisal interview is but one of many ways to improve job performance. The potential use an organization has for a problem-solving discussion is the most important element in the appraisal plan. If joint problem solving can lead to better job performance, the important question is how to stimulate problem-solving behavior in an interview. More opportunities for problem solving are possible if the objective is restated as "getting a better job done with present personnel." A first step in this direction is the examination of some principles of problem solving (see Maier et al., 1975, pp. 104-105; Maier, 1973b, pp. 141-144; 616-628). If these principles can be utilized in an interview situation, they will help the superior to stimulate the thinking of a subordinate so that improvement can be a joint objective.

Procedure for Problem Solving

Determine Problem Conditions

There may be many paths to a given goal and a *problem situation* exists when an obstacle blocks progress; a *choice situation* exists when a choice must be made between two or more alternatives. Choice situations that offer only undesirable possibilities or equally attractive alternatives should be re-examined using problem solving to see whether the number of available choices can be increased. The essential difference between a problem situation and a choice situation (see Figure 5) is that in the former the alternatives must be thought out (the "idea-getting" process) and in the latter, a choice must be made from alternatives already known ("idea-evaluation" stage). Frequently, poor solutions to problem situations are accepted because there is a tendency to adopt the first solution that is found; poor choices are made because a selection is made from the poor alternatives offered and no others are sought. It is important to consider additional solutions in both choice and problem situations to avoid these traps.

Figure 5 shows the two types of situations diagrammatically. A problem situation exists in the upper half of the figure because progress toward a goal was disrupted by an obstacle, 0.

The problem of choosing an alternative route is diagramed in the lower half of the figure. The goal can be reached either by route ABC or route ADE. Since ABC is shorter, it would seem to be preferable.

Possible Oversights. In a problem situation there is a tendency to take the first solution that comes up and accept it as satisfactory because it reaches the goal. For example, the detour OQR reaches the goal by circumventing the obstacle. This tendency discourages the discovery of other

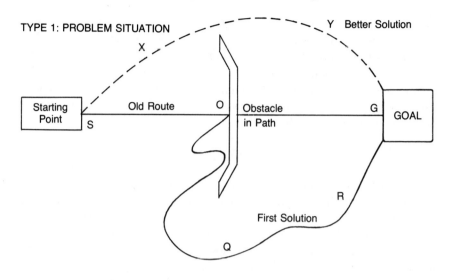

TYPE 1: PROBLEM SITUATION

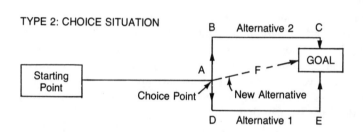

TYPE 2: CHOICE SITUATION

Figure 5. Two Types of Situations: Overcoming Obstacles and Choosing Between Alternatives

solutions, some of which may be superior to the first. For example, the route SXY reaches the goal in a more efficient manner and avoids the obstacle on route SOG.

Reactions to a choice situation are often limited because two or more solutions are plainly apparent and there is a tendency to choose one of them rather than seek additional alternatives. This is illustrated in the lower half of the figure by route AF, a possibility that was not apparent at the outset. The best route can be selected only when all alternatives are known and for this reason choice making should be delayed, even when good solutions are known and acceptable.

Both situations often exist and may require different types of problem solving. The first is idea gathering; the second is evaluation. Evaluation should be delayed in all cases until the idea-getting process has been carefully exhausted; evaluation inhibits the stimulation of new ideas because it confines the discussion to known alternatives.

In an experiment on resistance to change (Maier & McRay, 1972) it was found that innovative solutions could be increased if the leader continued the idea-getting process by merely asking for other alternatives when there was evidence of resistance.

Create a Favorable Climate

Certain conditions are conducive to problem solving, but others are unfavorable. Interferences must be removed before even an attempt at problem solving can be made. An interviewer not only must learn to detect unfavorable conditions, but also must create a favorable climate.

If an employee is emotionally upset, he is not in a problem-solving mood because he is inclined to blame circumstances outside himself and, in general, have a nonconstructive attitude. A person in this state can profit most from an interviewer who has an understanding attitude, but he should not be appraised or interviewed about job problems at such times, unless the early stages of the interview successfully remove his frustration. Under the best circumstances, at least ten percent of employees come to an appraisal interview apprehensively because approximately this many have some kind of emotional problem. However, the majority of employees will be ready for problem solving if something during the interview does not disturb them.

The superior plays a deciding role in determining the outcome of any discussion because he can state a problem in a variety of ways. The following principles serve as a guide for a supervisor promoting problem-solving behavior in an interview situation.

State the Problem in Situational
Rather than Behavioral Terms

Job situations rather than specific employee behavior should be discussed if cooperation is desired, and everything should be done to avoid references to personality. Failure to meet a deadline, for example, may be presented in two basically different ways:

1. "As you know, we have a lot of deadlines to meet in this business. I wonder if there is a way of fixing this job so that these deadlines won't creep up on us?" or

2. "You seem to be having difficulty meeting deadlines. I wonder if you have any ideas about how you can correct that?"

Although both of these statements present a problem, the second statement refers to the employee's conduct and will cause him to cover up faults and protect himself in some way. Defensive behavior will often occur even if the superior does not imply blame, recommend a correction, or imply that the employee is irresponsible.

It is not always easy for an interviewer to translate problems into situations, because he usually has a solution in mind when he talks to an employee. To overcome this, he must ask himself, "What is there in the job situation that causes me to be critical of this individual?" This allows the interviewer to focus on the result rather than the employee and helps locate the problem in the situation.

The role-play case in this book offered several opportunities for Stanley to state situational problems. It was apparent that Burke would have ideas on (a) reducing labor turnover among draftsmen; (b) improving communication among all supervisors reporting to Stanley; and (c) building morale and high standards in a group of subordinates. However, when Stanley was in the situation of *telling* Burke the appraisal, problems were expressed in behavioral terms such as (a) driving employees too hard; (b) failure to cooperate with fellow supervisors; and (c) poor human relations skills.

To practice stating problems in situational terms, a supervisor can write out a list of his subordinate's faults, ranging from irresponsibility to inability to relate to fellow workers. Then he can think of a specific time when the employee revealed one of these faults and try to translate the difficulty into situational terms. Attempts to do this with a few faults revealed by particular individuals in certain job settings will give a supervisor an idea of how the problem changes character when stated as a job difficulty, rather than a personality trait. If some cases do not lend themselves to this treatment, perhaps these exceptions can be reduced to a problem of fairness. The problem of deadlines might become "What do you consider a fair approach to our deadline problem?"

Any statement of a fairness problem must be sincere, and the subordinate must have every reason to believe that he is being asked to participate in setting a goal or determining a new method of measuring performance. He may not agree that counting deadlines missed is a fair measure of efficiency, but a score expressed in terms of the percentage of deadlines met might be accepted.

Express the Problem in Terms of Mutual Interest

Trust and confidence are enhanced when the activity in which people are jointly engaged is of interest to or leads to satisfaction for all. The nature of the interest or the gain need not be the same for everyone concerned; all that is necessary is for each of the participants to feel that everyone can profit from the activity, that it will be fair to all, and that no one will be able to take advantage of another. Thus problem solving is encouraged in an interview if the discussion is of interest to both the superior and the subordinate.

If a supervisor asks an employee to work harder for the good of the company or to show loyalty to the supervisor, he probably does not effectively involve the employee in the task. If, on the other hand, the superior says he is making a change for the sole purpose of helping the employee, there is still no guarantee the employee will cooperate. Generally speaking, people do not want to be obligated to others and will accept charity only as a last resort. An employer's dignity is not enhanced if he uses a paternalistic approach; in fact, frequently an employee's suspicion is aroused. Paternalism is effective only when a subordinate accepts an inferior status.

If both the company and the employee obviously stand to gain from an interaction, the interest of each is clear. The area of mutual interest can be the basis for cooperative discussion.

The way a superior states a problem can greatly influence the degree to which mutual interest is obvious to the employee. The following laudable objectives have little motivating value because mutual interest is not obvious: (a) persuading a worker to try out another's plan; (b) meeting deadlines that someone else sets; (c) following inspection practices planned by quality control; (d) covering up another's mistakes; (e) being loyal for the good of the company; (f) supporting the boss because that is the way the organization is set up; and (g) working hard so that the department will look good.

Statements such as the following raise doubts and suspicion in the employee's mind and tend to make him feel inferior:

1. "It's only because I want you to get ahead that I suggest you change your attitude."

2. "A person who cooperates around here will be rewarded."

3. "If you go along with this plan, I think I will be in a position to make it worth your while."

4. "This plan was set up for the good of the employees and has been arranged at considerable expense."

Offering a reward for cooperation is also an artificial way to introduce mutual interest because there is no essential connection between the reward and the act. However, when cooperation leads to greater job satisfaction, the connection is an inherent and natural one. Intrinsic motivation is always present when job interest is aroused.

There are many aspects of a work situation that are of interest both to the employee and to the company. The following mutually sought objectives are typical:

(a) making employees more safety minded;

(b) improving quality;

(c) scheduling to relieve pressure;

(d) making the job more interesting;

(e) improving employee morale;

(f) finding areas in which training is desired;

(g) setting production goals;

(h) determining the amount of freedom and responsibility desired.

Almost any aspect of the job is of mutual interest to the superior and the subordinate if it is expressed as a problem to be solved rather than a fault to be corrected. This does not mean that the subordinate will always refuse to change or improve, but if acceptance is to be assured, the change should be initiated from within the person who is to change. If the subordinate sees a need, the superior can place himself in a position to assist in any way he is able, and a cooperative and friendly relationship will be enhanced. On the other hand, if the superior initiates the change, he risks losing a good working relationship with the subordinate.

In most cases, a mutual interest is inherent if the superior indicates that he wants help with a problem. Only when he expresses dissatisfaction with the employee personally does a conflict arise.

Distinguish Between Solutions and Problems

One of the greatest difficulties for a supervisor to overcome is the fear that a subordinate either will be unaware of certain problems or will lack the ability to solve the job problems that he does recognize. Usually, the superior has a solution to a difficulty in mind before he talks to a subordinate, feeling that it is only fair that he should think of a remedy before criticizing. Often the superior's solution requires a change in the behavior of the subordinate. Sometimes the superior becomes so set on an idea that the problem changes into "How can I convince this subordinate to accept my solution," and a superior who begins with the best intentions gradually becomes an added barrier to communication.

If the superior has a solution in mind, it is unlikely that he will have the patience to conduct a problem-solving discussion. Sooner or later he will drop a hint of what he has in mind, or the subordinate may even do a bit of probing and ask if the supervisor has any suggestions.

To stimulate interest in true problem solving, the interviewer must state the problem so that a solution is not implied, confine his presentation to supplying needed information, and describe the difficulty in terms of the job. Once he has stated the problem, and this should be done briefly, the interviewer can ask for opinions and clearly reveal his desire to hear a variety of ideas from the employee. To refrain from supplying answers is not always easy. As a matter of fact, a superior often implies solutions and is unaware that he has expressed an opinion.

Examples of questions where a solution is implied follow:

1. "Do you have any ideas about why you don't have better cooperation?"

2. "Have you considered learning more about the technical features of this job?"

3. "What effect does a failure to meet deadlines in your unit have on others?"

4. "How would you handle this matter if you were in my shoes and were in charge of coordinating all units at your level?"

5. "What would you expect of a person in your job if you were in my place?"

These questions greatly restrict the freedom of an employee to problem solve because in each case a fairly specific remedy is implied. Suggestions and hints from a superior, even if unintentional, usually are perceived by the subordinate as a form of manipulation that may cause him to say things he thinks a superior wants to hear or cause him to become defensive and cautious.

The degree of freedom for problem solving can be increased in each of the foregoing examples by returning to the original problem. The superior can ask himself the following questions instead:

1. "Why is cooperation at that level important to me?"

2. "What makes me think that the technical requirements are not being met?"

3. "Why are deadlines so important to me?"

4. "Should my subordinate be concerned with my problem or should I be concerned with his?"

5. "How can I increase job interest among my subordinates?"

The answers to these questions will bring a supervisor closer to the origin of the problem and make more solutions possible.

Figure 6 illustrates how progress made toward a solution may actually decrease the number of opportunities for solving a problem. A person at decision point 1 has the possibilities of reaching the goal by routes A, B, C, and D. However, if he progresses to point 2, only three opportunities remain. By the time he reaches point 4, only one correct route is available to him. If the problem is not stated until point 4, there is a choice only between a right and a wrong way. At this point, it seems obvious to a superior that the subordinate should make the choice of a left turn (e.g., change his ways) to solve the problem. From his own position on the problem-solving path, he can not understand how the subordinate can disagree. However, if he took an objective look at the entire problem, from point 3 for example, he could see that it would be possible to follow route C and solve the problem in an entirely different way (e.g., modify the job so that the subordinate's behavior would be adequate). By going back to the original problem, it is often possible to discover still other solutions and to find routes that are shorter and more attractive. An exploration of a wider range of possibilities may cause either the subordinate to feel that he should make some changes himself or the superior to discover that the job should be altered.

Each route may have obstacles and advantages. Routes with obstacles that can not be overcome usually can be eliminated readily, but if things have progressed smoothly past several decision points, it is difficult for a decision maker to abandon his route. However, if there is an insurmountable obstacle at the end of route D, it is futile to spend time attempting to hurdle it.

The four problem formulations that follow are statements of the same problem, beginning with a specific suggestion of a solution and expanding to a broader statement of the same problem:

1. "What can we do to make you wear safety goggles?"

2. "What can we do to make you more aware of unsafe practices?"

3. "What can be done to remove some of the hazards in our work situation?"

4. "Do you have any ideas on how we can make this a safer place to work?"

The solution possibilities increase as the problem is stated in more general terms. The "use of goggles" may represent the greatest opportunity to reduce accidents, but if this is true the workers should also be able to discover the merits of the solution themselves. If there are other ways to increase safety, there is no essential reason for a superior to make the wearing of goggles paramount.

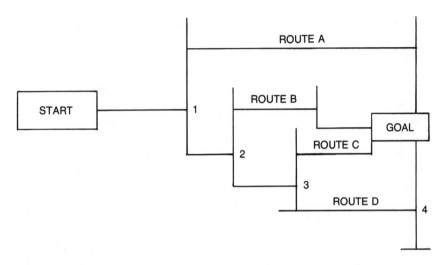

**Figure 6. The Starting Point of a Problem Is Richest
in Solution Possibilities**

As work on a problem progresses toward the goal, it becomes increasingly difficult for a decision maker to abandon the gains he has made, but he may be further from solving the problem than a beginner.

Principles, Skills, and Attitudes

Two important principles may serve as a guide to the interviewer. The first is that the process of *getting* or *generating* ideas for solutions to a problem must be separated from the process of *evaluating* the ideas. At the outset of a discussion it is important to present a number of possibilities for consideration without hearing evaluative opinions or passing judgment on any of them. Because judging inhibits creativity and freedom of thought, any poor ideas will be eliminated later anyway because they can not compete with good ones. If the superior discredits inferior ideas, he either stimulates defensive behavior or encourages capitulation and destroys participation.

A second principle concerns the introduction of variety in thinking. Various approaches to the problem and different methods for overcoming obstacles can be brought out by the use of questions. Often an employee is in a rut in his thinking and a question such as "Are there any other possibilities that we should consider?" will open up new channels of thought. (This question may be as relevant for the superior as for the subordinate.)

Encouraging the Subordinate To Participate

The degree to which the subordinate will become involved in a discussion of job problems depends on the interviewer's attitude, as well as his skills. Once a problem has been defined, the superior must have a receptive attitude during the interview.

Skill and attitude requirements include sensitivity to feelings, receptivity to ideas, an accepting and patient manner, the ability to reflect feelings (Rogers, 1942), the ability to restate an idea concisely, the knack of asking questions that stimulate thinking rather than threaten, and the ability to summarize. These skills can be used to advantage only when excessive time pressures are absent.

Training for skill development is different from learning facts and principles. The former requires practice and can not be learned from reading and listening to lectures. Role playing is one of the best off-the-job training methods for skill development; the ordinary classroom procedures are adequate for supplying information.

Need for a Receptive Attitude

There is a strong tendency for a superior to deflate poor solutions because he fears that they may be taken seriously. Consequently, he seldom waits for a subordinate to think of a variety of solutions. It is important for the interviewer to try to understand the situation in terms of the subordinate's point of view. Communication is possible only when each examines an experience with the same frame of reference. When the superior tries to find out what his subordinate thinks and feels, the first step has been taken. From this point, it is possible to move in unison to explore other problems. It is the superior's responsibility to do the major share of the understanding because the subordinate's job is under consideration and hence the subordinate is likely to feel threatened.

Once the interviewer understands basic skills and principles, it is important for him to consider the subject matter around which the problem-solving process may center. Content may vary considerably from situation to situation; some of the topics or problem areas will be discussed in the next section of this book.

Problem-solving discussions sometimes become deadlocked because there are two sides to a question and participants disagree over which is more important. Each person tries to bring issues that he considers relevant into the conversation and to dispute or minimize the points made by the other. This leads to a "yes, but" discussion. During this type of interaction, creative effort is used to refute points and little effort is made to resolve differences or reach an understanding.

The Two-Column Approach (Maier, Solem, & Maier, 1975, pp. 73-74) can make a valuable contribution when there is a dispute over facts, potential benefits, values, rights, justice, or risks engendered. The interviewer should suggest an exploration of the favorable (or unfavorable) aspects of an issue, starting with the points that the employee feels are most important. For example, if a subordinate opposes a change in work methods, the discussion would center on what could go wrong if such a change were made. All ideas should be accepted and listed until this side of the issue is completely exhausted.

Once he has covered his side, an interviewee will be more ready to examine the other side of the question. Again, he should be expected to make all the contributions and none should be volunteered by the superior. The employee may be hesitant at first, but gradually he will develop a fair list of facts or arguments supporting a viewpoint opposed to his initial one.

When both sides of a problem have been explored by one individual, there is some assurance that the issues raised are pertinent, and these can serve as the appropriate material for problem solving. The problem can be stated in terms of how best to keep or capture the advantages and yet experience as few of the disadvantages as possible. Problems which involve a violent conflict of interest can become a source of mutual concern if an attempt is made to resolve the question in terms of maximizing gains and minimizing losses.

Content of Problem-Solving Discussions

Employee-Initiated Problems

If discussion centers around problems that concern the subordinate, there is good assurance that the subject will be of mutual interest; the discussion will lead to situational factors; and opportunities for the superior to reveal personal biases will be reduced. Asking the subordinate about problems, therefore, is a good introductory approach. The following is an example: "As you know, we have these meetings every so often so that we will force ourselves to take a look at the overall features of our jobs. How has your job been going since our last talk?"

A little later it might be appropriate to ask, "Have you run into any problems or difficulties that it might be worth our while to examine? Perhaps we can make some changes that will make things work out to greater satisfaction for you or your group."

Exploratory questions should be sufficiently general to avoid giving the impression of prying into private affairs or cross-examining. Such questions lead to the discovery of areas of concern for the employee and tend to uncover problems and demonstrate a sincere willingness to discuss them. A general or vague question allows the interviewee to bring up a wide range of problems and gives him freedom to select those of concern and importance. Specific questions often are threatening. Only when an employee has a high degree of confidence and the appropriateness of a specific topic has been well established is it advisable for a supervisor to use a specific line of questioning. Pointed questions may establish factual details, but an employee's interest in details comes later, when all threat has been removed.

If a subordinate feels free to suggest that the superior or the company should make some changes, it is especially important for the superior to listen. At no time should he become defensive, because he will gradually become involved in an argument. Recognizing one's own defensive behavior is one of the most advanced skills in human relations training.

Determining Employee Interests

An employee may feel he has no special problems but may still dislike some aspects of his job. Even though company policy may state that a job can not be changed to suit the desires of the employee, it is well for a supervisor to consider any likes or dislikes, because they may throw light on the employee's job performance. Jobs and assignments may be altered to suit the employee's interests better, which will lead to a matter of mutual interest, increased job satisfaction.

When a subordinate is given a chance to discuss personal preferences, the effect may be to increase his acceptance of undesirable features of the job because these often are outweighed by the desirable ones. Even if this does not occur, the employee may still feel better because a problem has been shared. However, the greatest potential lies in the possibility that the employee may achieve a better perspective on his own strengths and weaknesses. Discussing unpleasant aspects of a job often leads to the discovery of anxieties and concerns the employee may have about his ability to perform satisfactorily. Insight into a problem like this may stimulate an employee's desire for training, and the superior can be helpful in this respect. However, if the superior suggests the training for a subordinate, he places himself in the role of a judge and the subordinate covers up or rationalizes deficiencies. It is psychologically very different for the employee to request assistance or training than for the superior to make the diagnosis and suggest the remedy.

When the subordinate has emotional problems that interfere with his work, it is possible that he will recognize and face these if given the opportunity during a nonthreatening discussion. Such a discovery may cause him to appreciate his need for therapy and the question of how best to obtain this can become the subject for problem solving. The discovery of strengths also is important because this knowledge is necessary for confidence building. An employee is at his best when realistically confident of the things he is able to do. An insecure person tends to perform at less than peak potential.

Company Problems and Goals

It is only natural that the problems of most vital concern to a superior are those with which he is actually involved. Nevertheless, it is best for a supervisor to delay a discussion of these until the employee has had a chance to voice his own concerns and to demonstrate that he is in a problem-solving state of mind. Problems can be introduced by requesting the subordinate's help. Because his vantage point is different from that of the superior, he may have certain personal feelings, opinions, or knowledge about the reactions of others. If problems are stated in situational terms, they are of interest to the subordinate as well as the superior, because both are concerned with doing the job efficiently. Furthermore, an employee is always interested in participating in decisions that concern his work situation, and he likes a chance to demonstrate his ability.

Questions about goals or quotas that must be met, reasonable targets, company requirements to meet new competition, changes in markets, etc., can be presented as problems to an employee who is expected to take some form of action, and the request for help should and can be sincere. Through the sharing of company needs and expectations, the subordinate develops a better feeling for the larger operation, so this discussion contributes to his growth, as well as to his greater sense of responsibility and motivation. At the same time, the superior gains the benefit of the subordinate's thinking, which is of special value because it represents upward communication, one of the most needed and least developed forms of communication.

The process of sharing problems does not mean that goals and specifications can not be imposed from above. The truth is that this will occur in any case. The problem is how to discover which portions of the solution have been predetermined by the higher authority so that the rest of the problem can be solved. For example, a 10-percent cut in budget may be imposed with the expressed desire to maintain the same quality of service. Questions of how best to make the cut, what effects it will have, what changes in service might be necessitated, etc., all remain areas in which discussion and problem solving can take place. (Whether or not an arbitrary decision such as this is wise is another matter that need not conflict with the process of sharing other problems or portions of the same problem.) Often, areas for problem solving are overlooked because attention is focused on what has been decided rather than on what still is undecided. It is necessary for a leader to spell out the freedoms as well as the limitations.

When several employees report to a given superior, it is more efficient and more creative to discuss matters of concern to all in a group meeting, rather than to hold separate interviews. If separate interviews are held to discuss group problems, it should be made clear that solutions reached in any of the interviews must be contingent upon what occurs in the interviews with each of the other employees.

Discussion of Job Perceptions

A person who occupies a management position perceives a subordinate's job as consisting of certain duties and responsibilities; restricting the subordinate's freedom to a certain degree; requiring certain initiating actions; requiring the subordinate to work with certain individuals and to cooperate with others; and demanding certain special abilities and not making use of others. The manager may judge a subordinate's success or failure in the job more by performance in some of these areas than in others. If several subordinates working on parallel jobs (e.g., a group of office managers in the sales department) wrote job descriptions, there could be a high degree of disagreement among them and none might agree with the superior's.

When a superior judges performance, he is likely to base his evaluation on the way he perceives a subordinate's job rather than be influenced by the subordinate's perception, yet the subordinate's perception directly influences job performance. A superior does not necessarily have the same impression of the duties, responsibilities, etc., required of the job as the person who occupies it and may be influenced by his own position and experience. If he supervises a job he once held, he may continue to view it as he did. Generally speaking, a superior is a better listener, is more prone to delegate, and has a more open mind when supervising a job he never has performed.

Which job perception should be used to measure performance presents a major source of difficulty in job appraisal. Research on this subject reveals frequent and wide discrepancies (Maier, Hoffman, Hooven, & Read, 1961).

Findings show differences in perception of:

(a) actual duties covered by the job description;
(b) relative importance of the duties;
(c) time required to perform various duties;
(d) company goals;

(e) ability requirements for the job;

(f) obstacles encountered on the job.

The degree of disagreement varies greatly, depending on the superior-subordinate pair studied, as well as on the uniqueness and complexity of the job. In general, staff jobs, newly created jobs, and service jobs show greater discrepancies than production jobs, but the differences in most cases are sufficiently marked to create communication barriers.

A difference in job perception that has considerable emotional overtones has to do with the subordinate seeing a job as constantly changing while the superior sees it as relatively static. This seems to be true especially if the superior once held the job.

The problem of job perception is even more complex because the superior changes his perception of a subordinate's job depending on who fills it; company needs at the time; the presence or absence of pressures for economy; and a shortage or an abundance of opportunities for advancement for the employees reporting to him.

Barriers to Communication

There is also a general reluctance by subordinates to discuss job problems with their superiors. Whether or not they see the superior as too busy, uninterested, or too critical can not be inferred, but it is a rare superior who is aware of the existence or the extent of this comunication problem. Most of them feel that they are quite accessible.

Because various opportunities for misunderstanding are present, it is wise for a superior to devote some interview time to an exploration of the job, the ability requirements, the relative importance of various duties, and the time needed for each. The superior should have the employee describe his views and explore minor discrepancies later. The superior can change the job description to cover some additional responsibilities. By suggesting that some job changes need to be made, a supervisor avoids criticizing the way the job has been done and instead focuses constructive attention on future operations. Because only activities in the future are subjects for discussion, this is the most practical approach to moving a subordinate's job perception nearer to the superior's.

After the job has been discussed in terms of the present situation, it is desirable for the participants to explore an ideal future situation. This leads to ways a job can be modified to make it more desirable, assuming that money and time are not limiting factors. A consideration of ideal conditions gives an employee an opportunity to discuss such things as the need for an assistant so he can devote more time to supervising; a desire to have a restudy made of standards; some pet methods for improving inspection; or the advisability of holding meetings with peers to discuss related problems with the superior. Often the subordinate's suggested improvements are in line with those the superior would like to make. Any suggestions can become a source of ideas for improvements that are of mutual interest. Sometimes the subordinate requests changes the superior might hesitate to suggest because he fears they may create resentment. For example, the suggestion that the subordinate needs an assistant or a change in his responsibilities, if initiated by the superior, might create anxiety and defensiveness; but if requested by the subordinate, any of these changes would tend to improve good will.

Naturally, all ideal conditions can not be met and, generally, the subordinate does not expect this, but the problems in a work situation are more acceptable to him when they have been discussed. When the superior tries to understand, it is possible for the subordinate to accept present difficulties with greater tolerance. The subordinate is more willing to discuss problems and express desires when he feels that the superior is trying to be helpful and is not evaluating his performance in terms of unrealistic goals. Similarly, when the superior is aware of the obstacles under which an employee must operate, he is more able to evaluate the total situation and plan for the future.

Influences of Job Perceptions

In the case study used in this book to illustrate the three approaches to the appraisal interview, Stanley and Burke were given certain facts in common on their role sheets. These were Burke's high productivity, exceptional creativity, and superior technical knowledge; the high turnover in his unit; his failure to tell Drake of a design change; and his unwillingness to take some routine jobs. From Stanley's point of view, Burke appeared to be a technical genius with a problem relating to people. The turnover suggested his poor relations with subordinates; the Drake incident revealed lack of consideration for peers; and his reluctance to accept assignments made him a problem for superiors. Stanley had to overemphasize the importance of Burke's technical knowledge; he suspected that Burke drove subordinates too hard in order to explain why Burke's unit had such high productivity.

However, for Burke, the same facts added up to an entirely different interpretation. Burke saw himself as a developer of employees whose extensive technical knowledge gave him the ability to train and whose creativity inspired his workers. Burke thought the turnover occurred because he trained his workers so well that they received better job offers elsewhere; preoccupation with his job caused him to forget to inform Drake; and the need to have challenging jobs to keep employees from

leaving was a good reason for requesting these jobs. Conflicting perceptions of Burke's job performance led to disagreement about areas for
improvement and about the fairness of the appraisal.

Only through effective problem solving involving two-way communication can these differences be brought out and a solution be developed
in role play. Possible solutions in the situation include changing Burke's
job so he is a part-time consultant for the section, with Frank Dobbs
serving as supervisor during his absence; trading junior designers with
Drake; having group meetings to give out assignments; giving anyone his
choice of an assignment whenever the previous job is completed; checking
out pay scales and potential promotions; making Burke more sensitive
to the needs of fellow supervisors; and expanding Burke's duties to include
helping others. The possibilities include changes in Burke's job, Burke's
duties, Stanley's method of operation, and Burke's attitude. Most of these
possibilities could increase Burke's performance, and one or more could be
practical and acceptable to both parties.

Influences of Personality

Although a person's basic personality is stabilized fairly early in life,
changes do occur. Favorable changes are associated with (a) increased
maturity; (b) improved security; (c) healthy group attitudes; (d) the development of self-confidence; and (e) relief from frustration. Each of
these represents a gradual process, such as improved emotional adjustment, rather than a sudden change, so it is apparent that attempts to
make a person over in an appraisal interview by way of requests, demands, or threats are likely to fail. These techniques may even aggravate
the very condition a supervisor wishes to correct.

The following example of a personality change that was recommended
in an appraisal of an employee may clarify this point. In this case, the
weakness stressed was an assistant superintendent's "inability to make
up his mind." The appraised person procrastinated in a variety of ways
and often seemed to go to great lengths to avoid making a decision. The
superior was very dominant and there was little doubt that he contributed
to the condition he described as a "weakness" in his subordinate. Other
available information indicated that the worker had the knowledge and
intelligence to assume responsibility for making important decisions.
Critical evaluation of the behavior pattern as a whole suggested that he
was insecure. If this diagnosis was correct, it meant that correction would
depend upon increasing the employee's security. Telling him about his
weakness would not increase his security and could heighten the insecurity.

Clearly, as personality changes can not be suggested or demanded, a superior must distinguish between the kind of behavior that an employee can control and the kind over which he has no control, although even when obviously controllable behaviors are considered, certain difficulties arise. For example, good manners can be taught, but the question is whether the process would be less threatening if they were taught by group training methods instead of by supervisors.

When an employee's personality traits are considered with the intention of making an appraisal, the lack of a desirable characteristic results in a devaluation of the individual. A person who is appraised as having an inability to make decisions may be perceived either as an indecisive person or as a person who has many characteristics, one of which is that he does not make decisions readily. If a supervisor is not making an evaluation, many traits that would seem to be weaknesses in an employee would not seem disturbing or undesirable. For example, there are occasions when a person can enjoy someone's performance on the piano, despite certain inaccuracies, but if the person were hiring a performer these same faults would become central. The problem of devaluing an individual in an interview because he lacks a certain trait is discussed further on pages 190-192.

Distinguishing Between Strengths and Weaknesses. "Weaknesses" are often the same traits as "strengths" except that they are seen from a different perspective. The following pairs of statements refer to the same basic traits and seem to be either strengths (a) or weaknesses (b):

(1a) "The thing I like most about Jane is her honesty. You can depend on what she says to you."

(1b) "Jane's worst trait is her bluntness. She often lacks tact because she is so brutally frank."

(2a) "Bob's best characteristic is that he is so easygoing. Nothing seems to upset him."

(2b) "Bob's worst characteristic is that he can not be depended upon. He is always late for engagements and does not seem to mind keeping others waiting."

(3a) "Debbie has a lot of drive and initiative. She always has a job done on time. That's what I like most about her."

(3b) "What I like least about Debbie is the way she puts on the pressure. She's a hard taskmaster."

(4a) "Tom's best characteristic is his ability to get along with people. Everyone likes him."

(4b) "Tom's main trouble is that he wastes time talking to people."

This list could be expanded many times and illustrates that if a supervisor is successful in correcting weaknesses he may also be tampering with strengths.

Both successes and unfortunate reactions have come from attempts to correct behavior. The risk factor is always present. Unless it can be removed, it may be more advisable to seek methods other than appraisal interviews to reform or correct an employee.

An employee's personality traits or behavior should not become part of the discusssion except and insofar as they are brought in by the subordinate. If the subordinate does bring up something of this kind, the superior should turn the questions raised into a problem and avoid giving advice. Responses such as "You feel you don't have the cooperation you deserve" or "Deadlines sort of get you down, is that it?" may be appropriate restatements of issues raised by the subordinate; when so stated they can become topics for problem solving. The superior should avoid passing judgment; he should neither agree nor disagree, but try to help explore the problem the subordinate has raised rather than try to come up with a solution.

Determining Aspirations. The superior must know an employee's needs to interpret properly his job performance or his attempts at self-improvement. The employee's present job performance and the assistance he can be given to prepare for the future hinge upon this knowledge; thus an important topic during a problem-solving discussion is the employee's ambitions or hopes. These vary according to an employee's past experiences of success and failure, as well as outside pressures, such as the views and accomplishments of associates.

Sometimes a superior incorrectly assumes that an employee wants to move ahead and criticizes the employee for not preparing for a higher job. On other occasions, a supervisor may correctly make the same assumption and criticize an employee for being too ambitious and for trying too hard to move ahead. Often the supervisor's judgment is influenced by conditions—either a shortage of openings or a shortage of personnel to fill the existing openings—but in nearly every case the employee's performance rating on his present job is influenced by his superior's opinion of his promotability.

When discussing an employee's aspirations in the company it is important for a supervisor to do more than list them. Aspirations have a motivating value only when they are consistent with the person's ability and training and when they are in line with what the company has to offer. The question of an employee's future clearly is a topic for problem solving. It should be of mutual interest because both superior and subordinate stand to gain from the coordination of company and personal interests.

Determining Promotability. It is clear that a person's expectations for the future may influence his present performance, but satisfactory performance does not necessarily reveal a desire for promotion. If performance on the present job and promotability are made part of the same evaluation process, an inconspicuous source of error and misunderstanding is present. If appraisal forms are used, the treatment of an employee's performance and his estimated potential for other positions should appear on separate pages or on separate forms. To reduce the tendency to be critical of an individual whose behavior and interests do not make him a candidate for promotion, it is desirable for a supervisor to separate the discussion of performance on the present job from potential ability and interest in other jobs.

Face-saving problems also must be considered in connection with promotions. Extrinsic motivational pressures, such as those exerted by family, the desire for a higher standard of living, and the expectations of fellow workers, place a satisfied employee at a disadvantage. If he denies an interest in promotion it is interpreted by fellow workers as "sour grapes" and being by-passed can then be considered a form of failure or rejection. A discussion of these problems with an employee can lead to the development of ways in which he can stay on a job and not lose face. This is an area in which a superior can be a real help and prevent employees from accepting positions that are unsuitable to their interests and welfare.

CHAPTER ELEVEN

Improving Superior-Subordinate Relations

The Problem of Delegation

Need for Delegation

As companies grow, the responsibilities of supervisors gradually increase so that work load pressures force them to share some duties with assistants or subordinates; thus work pressures alone make delegation a welcome solution to the superior, even if he does not feel the need for technical aid that an assistant might give in certain areas.

Subordinates favor more delegation of responsibility from above and welcome the opportunity to reduce the work of their superiors. Without real delegation they lack the freedom to adapt their own efforts to changing circumstances and miss the satisfaction and motivation that "being on one's own" can give. Middle-management personnel are practically unanimous in feeling that they would like more complete delegation and that their decisions would be better if they were given more freedom of action to make decisions.

What seems to be a popular move is not always taken, which indicates that there is more to the problem than appears on the surface. Subordinates may think their decisions would be better, but superiors apparently fear

178

that decisions would not improve; subordinates could not handle the power; blame for poor decisions made from below would be on their shoulders; or they could not keep up with the way things would be run by their subordinates. When a superior has full confidence in a subordinate's ability and loyalty, he feels most free to delegate authority, so establishing confidence and trust becomes part of the problem.

Many opportunities for misunderstanding are implicit with delegation. Frequently, it is not clear just how much is delegated; the extent of delegation may vary from day to day and be influenced by job pressures and moods. Variations both in the degree to which a duty is delegated and in the number of duties that are delegated are possible, and some forms of delegation may be more desirable than others. A knowledge of the stages of delegation may remove the communication problems that exist and suggest to a supervisor how to proceed as the subordinate develops and acquires job knowledge and judgment.

The first thing a superior delegates is a *set of duties*. The subordinate is allowed to perform the duties without direct supervision and is judged in terms of *how well* the job is done, rather than by *how* it is done. Usually, the superior decides which duties will be delegated; too often, the selection is made in terms of what the superior dislikes doing himself or what is least important. Obviously, delegation in terms of what the subordinate likes or feels is important leads to the best motivation on his part. If the employee is not ready to assume responsibility for certain duties that he wishes to undertake, his lack of experience need not be a crucial argument against delegation, as training can be undertaken.

The Stages of Delegation

Stage 1. The delegation of duties without the right to make decisions is shown as Stage 1 in Figure 7. It represents the minimum degree of withdrawal of supervision and may be emotionally easiest for a subordinate because decisions and solutions are backed by the supervisor's judgment, but it fails to make use of the subordinate's problem-solving ability.

Stage 2. The second stage of delegation permits the subordinate some voice in determining the outcome; he is either allowed or expected to recommend changes, but must gain approval from the superior. The desire to prevent the superior from exercising veto power serves to restrain the subordinate from using freedom and initiative and causes some diversion of attention from the problem at hand to ways of making suggestions that will please the superior.

This stage has the advantage of protecting the quality of decisions and the disadvantage that problem solving or decision making under these conditions is stifled and problems fail to stimulate the subordinate's

Stage	Nature of Delegation	Character	Example
1	Duties only	No opportunity to plan job routine or procedure	Superior has drafts-man draw plans according to speci-fications
2	Duties plus decision making requiring superior's approval	Decisions encouraged that anticipate superior's thinking	Subordinate suggests changes in lighting; superior holds veto power
3	Duties plus partici-pation in decision making	True participation	Departmental work planned during conference
4	Duties plus full decision making	Full delegation	Subordinate expected to handle coffee breaks the way he thinks best

Figure 7. Stages of Delegation
There are two dimensions in the delegation process: the number of activities dele-gated and the extent to which a given activity is delegated. Delegation begins when supervision is withdrawn.

imagination. Confining a subordinate's responsibility to making recom-mendations is practiced primarily because the superior does not wish to delegate completely until it is safe to do so. Actually, the subordinate's recommendations may be of inferior quality because the subordinate does not concentrate fully on the problem at hand when he has to be concerned with earning the superior's approval. Most of the difficulty, however, is because the superior and the subordinate each favors his own ideas.

Stage 3. In the third stage of delegation, the superior and the sub-ordinate solve problems together. This can be accomplished better if all subordinates involved in the problem work together as a team and the superior conducts the discussion. However, it can be done with a dis-cussion between the superior and one subordinate, as illustrated in the Problem-Solving interview. The quality of the solution is protected be-cause the experiences of two or more persons are pooled.

A Problem-Solving interview gives a superior a good opportunity to determine whether the subordinate is ready to assume the responsibility of full delegation. It also serves to develop the subordinate, as it gives him a chance to analyze a problem with the aid of good questions from a superior. Finally, the interview makes it possible for both to reach a decision on how much delegation can be given so that each can have the optimum satisfaction and protection necessary.

Stage 4. Full or complete delegation is the goal or end stage in the delegation process. At this point, the subordinate has been given a free rein in decision making and makes final decisions. To achieve this, the superior must be ready to give up any right to reverse a subordinate's decisions and must support the decisions once they are made, whether or not he feels they are good or bad. Willingness to support a subordinate's decisions does not free a superior of responsibility, because he did make the decision to delegate the responsibility to a particular employee. In exchange, the superior has the benefit of the subordinate's best thinking.

Although a subordinate is given the freedom to make decisions, his performance is still subject to criticism. Whether or not he receives a favorable evaluation must depend on the total effect or outcome and measurable indices such as production, quality, service, labor turnover, morale, etc., not on the superior's agreement or disagreement with the particular decisions that are made. If the total effect is poor, it can mean that the superior did not choose an employee well; but, if the total effect is excellent, it can mean that the superior has done a good job placing and developing the subordinate. A superior must be willing to gamble that a subordinate can do a better job when left alone than when supervised. A superior who attempts to "play it safe" makes the subordinate an appendage to himself.

Naturally, the most advanced stage of delegation represents a big emotional step for a superior and he must "feel his way" through the stages. Discussions with associates in similar situations, role playing, and on-the-job tryouts are ways to deal with some of the feelings of stress aroused by the implications of full delegation. An employer's concern needs to be finding opportunities to increase the amount of responsibility that a given supervisor now delegates.

Because the different stages of delegation require quite different work relationships between a superior and a subordinate, it is important that the stages of delegation be clearly understood by both, and that they be reviewed regularly either to reaffirm or to alter them.

Finding Areas To Delegate

The first thing a superior needs to do to increase delegation is to examine his own involvement in various aspects of the job. If the superior supervises a job he once held, he will probably have considerable

difficulty delegating because he is inclined to think that his way of operation was best. Because familiarity with the details of the way a job was
performed in the past may make a superior opinionated, the first areas he
should delegate are those in which he feels least qualified.

He may still find it necessary to examine his personal biases and his
feelings about possible decisions to determine whether he is ready to delegate. If a superior finds himself unable to accept responsibility for a subordinate's decisions, he should break the area down into smaller parts; he
may find that he can grant full delegation for the administration of coffee
breaks, but may wish to put a ceiling on the total time allowed so any
change in time would require his approval. In this manner, the subordinate may be given full delegation in a small area and the superior still has
the protection that he feels is necessary.

Most activities can be circumscribed so that full freedom can be given
within specific boundaries. The nature and location of the boundaries
should be made clear in every case and re-examined periodically either
to reassure the subordinate of the extent of his freedom or to examine
opportunities for adapting changes.

As a superior experiences satisfaction with a program of delegation,
he can increase the duties delegated as well as the number of subordinates with whom he shares responsibility. He should do this gradually and
with caution, however, so that he does not become disillusioned. Failure
may result in frustration and cause the most tolerant and understanding
supervisor to become rigid and autocratic, destroying a superior-subordinate relationship that took years to develop.

Preparing Subordinates for Delegation

A subordinate who is learning a job can be initiated into Stage 1 as
soon as he has the basic skills to carry out the work. Stages 2 and 3 should
follow shortly, as the employee develops confidence. Stage 3, the better of
the two procedures, requires more time but can serve as the transition to
full delegation.

Full delegation can be the subject for a discussion during which the
subordinate can clarify his interests and degree of confidence, and the
superior can describe his biases and special ways of doing things. Out of
this discussion should emerge some clearly defined areas of responsibility
the subordinate wishes to have and the superior is happy to grant. If in
some cases full delegation is given while in others certain conditional
restraints remain, these differences should be made clear.

There are two dimensions where delegation may be increased: the
degree of delegation and the amount of responsibility or the number of

activities delegated. Figure 7 shows that various activities may be at different stages of delegation. The most desirable pattern is for a subordinate to have full authority for at least some activities. Ten duties at Stage 3 would indicate less progress in a delegation program than two duties at Stage 2, six at Stage 3, and two at Stage 4.

Meaning of Full Delegation

When delegation is complete, there is more freedom for problem solving, which not only allows flexibility to develop solutions but also permits considerable overall planning in a unit or department about company goals.

Although an employee's decisions may be interdependent and supplementary, this may not be apparent to someone who is unfamiliar with the employee's thinking. A superior might not see the relationship between two consecutive decisions and consequently would be unable to evaluate them. For this reason, the performance of a responsible supervisor can not be evaluated in terms of isolated decisions. For example, a baseball manager can not be judged by the pinch hitters he selects at a given moment or in a given game, but must be evaluated in terms of more remote and more objective criteria, such as games won by coming from behind, games lost by one run, etc. No one can say he made a wrong choice on a given occasion without knowing all the facts that were at his disposal.

The industrial manager's performance also must be evaluated in terms of objective measures, such as quality, inventory, production costs, labor turnover, absenteeism, morale, etc. The standards used for evaluation should be known to all and should be accepted by those who are evaluated. If the criteria are questioned, they should be re-examined and subjected to group problem solving so that everyone in question has a voice in determining the way performance is measured. It is important for the criteria to be consistent.

An evaluation based on objective criteria is not a matter of opinion, and the person measured need not be told how he is doing. Usually, he will know this better than anyone else.

If Delegation Does Not Work

If the end results of delegation are unsatisfactory, the superior may have to reverse the process or make changes in personnel. It is the superior's responsibility to assist the subordinate if he needs help; furnish training if this seems appropriate; transfer an employee if this is practical; increase or decrease the area of responsibility if the nature of the job permits; or follow any number of other possible alternatives. When it is apparent that neither the employee nor the job can be changed, a new kind of decision must be made.

Sometimes threat is used as a last resort, which suggests that it is more likely to be effective than the methods described previously. However, if an employee fails to improve as a result of a Problem-Solving interview, it is questionable whether threat of discharge will be effective. The number of management-caliber employees who profit from fear-induced motivation is so small that one can assume that an employee who must be threatened is not worth reforming. It seems more practical to exchange the employee for another rather than to continue with methods that are unpleasant to administer.

Attitudes Conducive to Problem Solving

Attitudes can influence the outcome of problem-solving activity. The initial approach a person has to a problem frequently depends on the feeling he has about the problem, as well as on the circumstances that created it. Whether he sees problems as sources of frustration or as opportunities, as things to get out of the way or as things to be sought after, as the product of someone's error or as the opportunity to cooperate, depends on his attitude. Attitudes are not based on knowledge or special skills. They can not be adopted at will but are acquired gradually through a process of making them part of one's faith and system of values.

The following attitudes represent those that are conducive to problem solving in the setting of a developmental interview. It is likely that these same attitudes would be helpful in other problem-solving situations, and some of them actually have been isolated from the analysis of problem-solving behavior in group situations. Some of the attitudes described below may seem logical and may be intellectually acceptable to a person, but still may be difficult to translate into action. Others may be questioned because they are in conflict with those already held. (For a report on a variety of studies, see Maier, 1970.)

Seeing Differences as Opportunities

Conflicts of opinions and ideas may be seen as undesirable because they lead to disputes; however, they can also be seen as stimulants for invention. Whether a conflict will lead to an argument or to creative effort depends largely upon the viewpoint of the conference leader in a group situation or the superior during an interview.

If disagreement is undesirable, it is played down and efforts at reconciling differences are encouraged. Compromise tends to be a common and happy result in such cases because each participant or faction gives up something to gain something else. Obviously, the nature of the problem and the kinds of solutions under dispute determine whether a compromise can be a logical integration of two patterns of thought. A compromise, as an intermediate position, can be superior in quality to either of the initial solutions, but the major virtue of compromise is that it encourages acceptance and permits face saving. Compromises are most easily reached when the differences are quantitative rather than qualitative and when only two points of view are in conflict.

Suppose, however, that honest disagreement is seen as interesting and desirable because it can lead to creative discovery. In this situation, disagreement is something to seek out, and an assumption is made that conflicts can never be resolved by avoiding an issue, but only by meeting and dealing with it.

Typically, a compromise is designed to deal with disagreements when solutions to a problem are in conflict, but by then it may be too late to permit participation in an inventive or creative settlement. If differences are apparent and are respected from the outset, the process of arriving at a solution that best resolves the differences can be a cooperative process.

In a role-play experiment dealing with overcoming resistance to change (Maier, 1953), it was found that new solutions were reached only when the situation was approached as a problem. A choice between two obvious alternatives characterized the outcome when attempts were made to play down differences. In this experiment, the conflict was between the supervisor, who wanted each employee to perform on the job he was best able to do, and three employees who wanted to exchange jobs to reduce boredom.

Disagreement about what constituted efficient work patterns and how boredom affected the workers was inevitable in this case, and when this was not recognized by the role players, a conflict between two possible solutions developed: either to discount boredom and concentrate on efficiency or use a less efficient but less boring method. However, when a Problem-Solving approach was taken from the outset, the facts and the fears were dealt with in proper perspective. More than a third of the solutions integrated two possible solutions for a new method of work. Each of the new solutions had a creative and individual character, suited to the persons involved in the discussion.

The leader plays a decisive role in seeing that differences of opinion are considered and respected. In another experiment (Maier, 1950) it was found that the solutions were inventive only when the leader respected and encouraged differences. The quality of solutions (Maier & Solem, 1952) was better even if a discussion leader's function was minimal. His presence seemed to prevent majority views from dominating by permitting minority opinions to be heard. It was evident also from this experiment that minority viewpoints, when respected, could serve to improve, but not lower, the quality of decisions, because logic was on the side of quality. When the minority view was wrong, opportunity for its expression failed to reduce the quality of the group product, and when sound evidence was on the side of the minority, the majority tended to think more effectively.

To further test the value of differences of opinion in upgrading the solution process, Hoffman (1959) and Hoffman, Harburg, and Maier (1962) compared the problem-solving ability of two types of four-member groups—those with similar personality scores and those with dissimilar scores. They found the nonhomogeneous groups were more inventive. Although this type of research raises many questions, it supports the theory that differences in thinking should be encouraged and used for constructive purposes. It is apparent that leaders and managers can use their talents either to discourage or to encourage disagreement. Discouraging disagreement may lead to conformity and lack of creativity, and disagreement can lead to inventive solutions, if the conflict is used constructively.

Although the preceding experiments dealt with small-group situations rather than interviews, it seems probable that the same principles apply to an interview. Actually, the interviewer is relatively more influential than a discussion leader and for this reason it is especially important for him to play a constructive role. In a group situation, individual members often compensate for the limitations of a leader (Heyns, 1948).

Assuming Better Ways Can Be Found

An invention, a process, a work plan, or anything that has been developed in the past can be viewed with respect and admiration, but this may prevent the viewer from re-examining every product or plan with the goal of improving it. Those who admire what has been accomplished may fail to see opportunities for problem solving that a person who feels less awe for previous ingenuity may discover.

A conservative attitude about the past is less conducive to problem solving. A certain amount of dissatisfaction with the past is desirable to initiate opportunities for solving problems and to delay the evaluative process. This does not mean that radicalism is conducive to problem solving. Discontent and frustration turn to hostility; changes promoted under such conditions are destructive in nature and stand in contrast to constructive change produced with the critical help of an innovator (Maier, 1942). The conservative attitude also has value, providing it is the result of healthy caution, rather than stubbornness generated from fear and insecurity. Conservatism, when it stems from appreciation of existing merit, serves as a restraining influence on the innovator who may be so intent on creative insights that he loses track of certain practical considerations. The ideal condition is to have the right combination of these two opposing attitudes.

It is desirable to approach situations in search of problems and then to view problems as opportunities to explore and invent. However, there must also be an evaluation of and a selection from the contributions. Evaluation and selection can be used separately as supplementary functions in improving problem-solving behavior. The danger is that the evaluation will occur too soon and stifle creative problem solving.

An interviewer can stimulate a critical attitude in a subordinate during a Problem-Solving interview by periodically inviting suggestions on ways to improve the job (Maier & Sashkin, 1971). This request must be repeated from time to time because the way a job has been done in the past becomes a habit for the employee. After he has been on the job for a period of years, the employee is in danger of running the job on a routine basis; it may take new blood or good questions from a supervisor to break up the routine. The most important thing is that suggestions for improvements, when elicited, receive an understanding hearing by the interviewer.

Respecting Feelings as Well as Facts

Feelings often are overlooked in problem-solving discussions because emphasis is placed on the correctness of a solution or the wisdom of a decision rather than on the acceptability of the solutions or decisions for the individual who must execute them. But human beings are influenced by their feelings as well as by facts, and feelings often determine the facts a person will consider and those he will reject (Maier & Lansky, 1957). Although purely intellectual decisions have a place, it is unrealistic to regard them as superior because the emotional elements have been eliminated. The importance of feelings depends upon the nature of the problem, and problems with people make such data relevant.

In an interview situation, a superior can do a great deal to upgrade the problem-solving process by revealing interest in the subordinate's feelings and by freely expressing his own feelings. If feelings are taken at face value and do not become the basis for a rationalizing process where irrelevant facts are brought into the picture, communication and constructive effort should benefit materially.

Frequently, too much concern with "rightness" or "wrongness" complicates the decision-making process, so that instead of solving a problem an interviewer takes a step in the direction of another problem. Danielson and Maier (1957) demonstrated that a disciplinary issue could be settled at any one of several stages, but that the best results were obtained if the guiding objective was "better future performance" rather than "evaluation of past performance."

If a supervisor attempts to fix blame, he may encourage dishonesty and then must decide what to believe. If the employee admits guilt, the supervisor must decide whether to reward for honesty or punish for guilt. If the supervisor believes that punishment is justified, he must decide whether he wishes to pay the price of reduced loyalty and a possible grievance procedure to see that justice is done. This requires many minor decisions, each fraught with the possibility of an error in judgment.

Emphasis on the Problem, Not the Solution

Much resistance to new methods is based on an employer's fears— the fear that errors may not be noticed unless they are pointed out; the fear that violations of a rule will be repeated unless punishment is inflicted; the fear that poor ideas may not be discarded unless a responsible person points out fallacies; and the fear that good ideas may not be discovered unless an experienced person brings them out. The fear is usually disproportionate to the danger. A supervisor can do a good deal to upgrade the thinking of an individual or a group without actually determining the decision. Some of the methods for stimulating and evaluating ideas have already been discussed, but a certain attitude seems to support the skills already mentioned—being problem minded instead of solution minded.

Most people are solution minded and strive to attain answers even before they have the problem in focus. They answer questions and offer advice long before they understand the reasons for the questions or the requests for advice. However, problem solving and the supply of appropriate information can be increased if interest and concern with the problem itself can be stimulated. An interviewer or a conference leader may find it necessary to bring a discussion back to the problem repeatedly to prevent premature solutions. Lengthening the period of focus on a problem, therefore, is an important contribution a superior can make to upgrade the thinking of subordinates.

Guidelines for the Interviewer

Allowing Freedom for a Subordinate

A Problem-Solving interview should not have an agenda, although a superior may devote some time to refreshing his memory on the subordinate's accomplishments and matters discussed on previous occasions. It also may be wise for him to speculate on some of the problems that might come up during the interview and to consider how to state problems in *situational* terms. An interviewer should not be anxious without a set of notes to follow, however, as most of his planning should go into preparing to conduct a Problem-Solving interview in which the subordinate will do most of the talking. The course of the interview should be guided by the subordinate's wishes and knowledge; the content of the discussion will be determined by developments.

Being Sensitive to Feelings

The problems, interests, and emotional concerns of employees vary considerably and an interviewer must be sensitive to whatever feelings lie behind what an employee says. Sometimes the most important feelings will not be obvious, but the interviewer should be ready for any possibility and conduct the interview accordingly. Some employees may state their ideas clearly and yet may not reveal their true feelings or may describe what is a temporary emotional state. A superior must not jump to conclusions at any step of the interview.

Making Use of Feedback

Sensitivity to the feelings of a subordinate permits an interviewer to profit from the "feedback" that every interpersonal relationship affords. Although feelings can be expressed in many ways, with experience the feedback can be understood with a surprising degree of accuracy. Like the experienced driver who knows how to apply the brakes on a slippery pavement by adapting foot pressure to the way the car responds, the sensitive interviewer can detect when questions are threatening and change an approach accordingly.

Because no two employees have the same problems or solutions, it follows that the most profitable and individualized interaction will occur if the employer makes use of the many opportunities offered in every interview situation to understand and respond to veiled expressions of fears, hostilities, insecurities, hurt feelings, inferiorities, defenses, pride, status needs, rejections, etc.; but these opportunities will be lost unless the interviewer is alert and uncritical.

Some of the greatest obstacles to increased sensitivity to feelings are the following:

(a) the tendency to follow a prearranged plan;

(b) failure to understand that rank is a barrier to communication;

(c) thinking of a reply instead of trying to understand;

(d) fear that the interview may not lead to a constructive experience;

(e) the tendency to judge another by the situation rather than by his behavior.

These obstacles may be the result of previous habits of thinking; they do not result from a need for complex skills. The development of sensitivity is relatively easy once any interferences are removed. The interviewer will have made a good beginning when he (a) successfully avoids such habits as planning the interview, answering questions, and jumping to conclusions; (b) has had a few successful experiences to gain the necessary confidence to reduce anxiety about outcomes; and (c) pays attention to the other person's feelings rather than tries to put himself in the other person's place. When an interviewer has a new point of view, he can acquire the skills of listening actively, respecting pauses, reflecting feelings, restating ideas, asking general exploratory questions, asking stimulating questions, and summarizing periodically with relative ease.[3]

Improving Adjustment Through Job Interest

Good emotional adjustment requires the development of interests outside the self. Naturally, internal concerns will detract from outside interests, but a well-adjusted person, once secure in a job, should be interested in the surroundings. One of the main contributions that problem-solving techniques can make to an employee's development is directing attention to the job situation and thereby stimulating an interest in the surroundings. As a subordinate participates in solving problems in the environment, he becomes increasingly involved in things other than himself.

Comparative and Asset Values

Comparative Values. When assessing an employee's worth, an employer often evaluates positively for abilities the employee possesses and devaluates for those he lacks, comparing each employee with others along a scale of strengths and weaknesses. This approach to appraisal gives each employee a *comparative value*.

Strengths or special abilities can seem to be part of the employee's value as a person and any loss or shortage in ability lowers his worth as a person when a comparative approach is used. When comparative values are used as adjectives, less worth is associated with the person whose traits fall below average. Appraisals tend to promote this comparison and

---

[3]The reader may extend his sensitivity training by carefully studying the transcribed interviews in Chapters 3 through 8 from time to time. New insights emerge even after the material has been examined many times.

an employee is rated lower when he is judged to possess traits that fall below standards of expectation. If a supervisor describes an employee as irresponsible, indecisive, or insecure, he devaluates him as a person because these are usually considered personality traits. With a comparative approach to appraisal, any of the employee's traits that fall below others tend to be seen by the interviewer as weaknesses that need correction.

Past experiences of devaluation are perhaps the reason why employees are hurt when even minor weaknesses or errors are mentioned during an interview. The reason many interviewers mention such things is to make the employee a better person, but the employee may feel that he is not doing well enough at the present time. He may experience feelings of rejection, inadequacy, or incompetence at the slightest mention of his contribution to an error that was made.

Asset Values. Another way to look at an employee's strengths is to consider them *asset values*. A beautiful painting is an asset, yet a house that lacks such a painting is not devaluated. Responsibility may be a desirable trait and a distinct asset, but a person who lacks this trait need not be devaluated. Just because certain traits are admired does not make their absence a fault.

The Problem-Solving approach to employee development tends to promote asset values rather than comparison values because the potential contribution that an individual can make to a department is discussed, not how the employee compares with others. If a job can be made unique (and no two jobs need to be identical) and if it is discussed in relation to the employee's own special interests, the employer's tendency to compare disappears. If the discussion leads to a consideration of job problems, even the asset values of the employee fade into the background and only the job-related issues come to the fore. With the job itself as the topic for discussion, an interviewee need not fear devaluation.

When There Is a Need To Compare. Although devaluation of an employee often leads to poor adjustment on his part, this does not mean that comparison is always undesirable. Frequently, a comparison of employees and their abilities must be made, especially when people are hired, transferred, and promoted.

Failure to win in competition is not necessarily a devaluation, but it frequently is experienced that way. However, it does not follow that there is something wrong with an employee who is not chosen for an assignment. Experiences of failure and devaluation are not a function of what happens to a person but rather of the way he interprets them. A person who is considered for a promotion and does not receive one may experience either failure because he was unable to win the promotion or success because he was among those who were considered. The latter interpretation would mean a healthier adjustment and place the person in a better mental state to compete successfully the next time. Too often people fail to face problems because they fear devaluation (see Dembo, Leviton, & Wright, 1956). Anything a superior can do to prevent devaluation when interviewing subordinates and anything he can do to turn problems into obstacles to be overcome will lead to satisfaction and acceptance of reality on the subordinate's part.

An Overview of the Problem-Solving Interview

If the Problem-Solving interview is to be used in connection with an appraisal program, some of the objectives associated with such a program will either have to be sacrificed or covered by some other plan. Some of the objectives that the Problem-Solving approach may either neglect or eliminate, as well as some of problem solving's special merits, are discussed in the following sections.

Some Deficiencies

Deficiencies may be evident either from undesirable results or from failure to achieve desired objectives. To some extent, objectives are a personal matter, and the nature of a deficiency may vary from one company to another. The deficiencies below depend largely on the perceived objectives of an appraisal.

No Provision for Letting Employees Know Where They Stand. If this objective is desirable, some supplementary method for objectively communicating an employee's comparative standing would have to be developed or a procedure for obtaining the subordinate's cooperation in making the appraisal would be needed.

However, the need for letting employees know where they stand might seriously be questioned. Whenever we have raised the question to groups of managers, a majority of them indicated they wanted to know what the boss thought of them, but this does not necessarily mean that they really wanted to know all the facts or that such knowledge would benefit them. As a matter of fact, the employees who said they did not know where they stood usually were the least capable. It is possible that the desire to know where one stands is an indication of insecurity. If the Problem-Solving interview developed security, the need for letting employees know where they stand would disappear. However, the Problem-Solving interview has no built-in security and this lack should be evaluated and remedied if it seems to be a serious loss in a particular situation.

No Company Record To Prove an Employee Has Been Told He Must Improve. Although there are times when a record is highly desirable, such situations arise infrequently. Because this is a special problem and applies to only a few individuals, it does not seem to be an essential feature for a general program designed to cover all of a company's personnel. A supervisor needs to develop a specific procedure for dealing with employees who are incompetent and for whom improvement through training and transfer are of doubtful value.

No Opportunities To Praise an Employee. Praise might be given without interfering with the main purpose of the interview, but a superior must consider the interpersonal relationship developed during a cooperative problem-solving interaction and the relationship created when a superior praises a subordinate. The latter situation tends to exaggerate rank difference and assume the existence of a dependent relationship in which the superior is a kindly paternalist, but nevertheless a judge. This situation motivates a subordinate to please the boss rather than to think through a problem.

However, praise from a superior does not always stimulate a dependent relationship. In problem-solving discussions, persons of equal rank react to the ideas of others with interest and make evaluative statements by referring to ideas as "good" or "bad." This "give and take" is healthy, but seems to lose its value in a problem-solving setting if praise for a participant becomes so prominent that it motivates that person to seek more praise.

Although it is more preferable to praise for merits than to criticize for faults, at best, praise is an extrinsic form of motivation. The intrinsic motivation produced by job interest is the best motivator to promote cooperation. This type of inner motivation is what is expected at the middle-management level and higher.

Insofar as praise and recognition have a value in superior-subordinate relations, they seem most appropriate in day-to-day interactions. Recognition can be attached to specific acts as they occur rather than be withheld for some formal meeting, when it would tend to remove spontaneity. For this reason, the discussion of the content of a Problem-Solving interview (pages 168-174) contains little mention of the need for recognition.

No Record of Appraisals for Inventory and Promotion Purposes. If the Problem-Solving interview is part of a company program for employee development, the appraisal of individuals is not one of its by-products. To obtain appraisals that are useful for other purposes, it is necessary either to supplement the Problem-Solving interview or to introduce a special program. (This problem is discussed on pages 151-153.) It is important not to introduce a program that violates the basic values of the Problem-Solving approach, and it is possible to increase the accuracy of the merit-rating process by properly separating the appraisal process from the interview procedure.

Desirable By-Products

Because the development of the employee on the job is the main objective of the Problem-Solving interview, this interview method is expected to be superior to the other two for employee development. It is expedient to examine some of the desirable by-products that naturally follow from its use. Some of the important ones are the following:

A Desirable Form of Motivation. If a job is modified to suit an employee's special aptitudes and interests, the work will be more interesting to him. Any increase in interest constitutes a form of *intrinsic* motivation.

Intrinsic motivation can also be sparked by the removal of unfavorable attitudes, fears, and questions of fair treatment or reasonable assignments that may detract from the pleasantness of a job. If employee relations are improved or if some alterations, often very minor ones, are made in the job itself, many negative feelings about the job will disappear.

To locate points of interest or irritation it is necessary to explore the job from the point of view of the subordinate. Of the three interview types examined, the Problem-Solving interview seems most appropriate for this function.

An Increased Sense of Responsibility or the Motivation To Execute Decisions That Have Been Made. Decisions are most likely to be effectively carried out when they are fully accepted. There are various degrees of acceptance, but the acceptance of a decision is more complete for a person who has participated in reaching it. Participation in a discussion is not enough; the satisfaction of influencing results and other people seems to be needed for full acceptance (Marquis, Guetzkow, & Heyns, 1951, pp. 55-67). When an employee has a real influence on the way a job is done, he feels a direct responsibility for its success.

Security on the Job and Status in the Company. When an employee participates in solving job problems that are important to him, instead of feeling that he is working for a boss and dependent upon a superior's acceptance, he feels that he is running the job. Successful operation of a job, rather than a successful relationship with a superior, becomes the dominant factor. Because a capable individual feels that he has more influence over a job than over a superior, he can experience a certain amount of control over his environment. An incompetent employee, on the other hand, may need some support from a superior to experience a satisfying degree of security. The willingness of superiors to recognize and accept below-average performance may be an essential supplement to job security for many employees, and the question of employee transfer can be a matter for problem solving if an employee can not handle a particular job.

More Effective Use of the Subordinate's Capabilities and Thinking. During a Problem-Solving interview, the employee's views not only are welcome but are actively solicited. Ideas initiated from below can be an important source of innovation and invention, not only because of the youth and enthusiasm that may be present in the lower echelons, but also because young people are less likely to be bound by past traditions and former ways of thinking. Past experience has many lessons to contribute, but it also causes thinking habits to become entrenched. A source of creative problem solving is available to any organization when it uses the thinking available in lower ranks.

A Higher Degree of Communication. Decisions made by superiors and passed on to subordinates as assignments frequently are criticized because those who must execute the decisions misunderstand certain details of the decision, see no reason for the change, or feel that better alternatives were overlooked. A subordinate feels no responsibility for interpreting a decision for the benefit of others because he feels obligated to do only that which he thinks is included in his assignment. Consequently, assignments may be inadequately executed because they were incorrectly transmitted to others in a unit. Through problem solving, communication is improved with respect to the specific nature of the decisions made, the reasons for the decisions, and the alternate decisions rejected.

Frequently, before decisions are implemented, conditions change so that the decision no longer is appropriate. Nevertheless, a subordinate may be inclined to execute such a decision because it is the safe thing to do. Often the blindness shown is equivalent to an attendant awakening patients to give sleeping pills. When decisions are reached jointly, however, communication is sufficient to permit an employee some element of judgment that may forestall the execution of decisions that for one reason or another have ceased to be appropriate.

No amount of added detail while passing a decision down the line can result in the complete communication that occurs when a decision is made jointly. Neither party by himself could find or anticipate the richness of possibilities available, yet these are by-products of participation in problem solving.

The communication of problems and decisions is facilitated by a discussion in which each member freely expresses his views; also, communication of attitudes, objectives, differences in interpretation of the problem, and personal interests or fears is improved. Because each of these factors is associated with emotions, better problem solving requires that they be accurately communicated. Formal communication methods characteristically screen out emotional factors or hide them with intellectual rationalizations.

Quality of Solutions Upgraded. With joint problem solving, two different viewpoints and two pools of experience are combined, a distinct asset when both participants have ability. Of course, a compromise between good and poor thinking may lower quality, but the Problem-Solving interview does permit the utilization of divergent viewpoints, which can lead to invention as well as a reduction of oversights.

Under the best conditions, the Problem-Solving interview should be a learning experience for both participants; when this occurs, satisfaction is optimal.

Fewer Undesirable By-Products

Besides having desirable by-products, the Problem-Solving interview avoids some of the undesirable by-products of standard appraisal interviews. The Problem-Solving interview:

Prevents Emotional Conflicts that Frequently Start when a Superior Attempts To Change a Subordinate's Personality or Behavior. These conflicts are the source of defensive behavior, and often both participants are frustrated so that neither has a constructive experience. When this occurs, new problems are created and the superior-subordinate relationship may be permanently strained.

Reduces the Likelihood of Subordinates Becoming "Yes Men" and Promotes Independent Thinking. A subordinate who tries to please the boss contributes little to the welfare of the organization; it is questionable whether this type of employee is desired, even by an insecure superior. Frequently the superior who develops "yes men" is so busy trying to oversee a job that he is unaware of the degree to which he dominates subordinates. Job pressure serves to increase any given supervisor's tendency to act in an authoritarian manner. The remedy for the harassed superior is delegation.

Reduces the Number of Face-Saving Situations, Because the Job, Not the Person, Is the Center of a Discussion. Because losing face is extremely degrading for everyone, people are more aware of their own needs to save face than of similar needs in other people. Often the most difficult obstacle to overcome is created by the participants' attempts to deal with a problem objectively. How to save face soon outweighs the real problem and many opportunities to solve problems are wasted when the question of who is right is raised.

CHAPTER TWELVE

Implications and Applications of the Problem-Solving Approach

Two pervasive themes in the preceding chapters are job performance and ways of dealing with employees' individual differences in behavior, attitudes, values, and feelings. In short, the focus was on employee development.

Employee development is an ongoing process, based on a respect for individual differences as well as an expectation of high performance standards. It is our contention that the problem-solving model explored in various contexts throughout the last three chapters provides a viable approach to developing people and organizations.

The Need for Quality and Acceptance

Careful research in the area of problem solving (Maier, 1963) has yielded two dimensions that correlate reliably with a decision's effectiveness: *quality* and *acceptance*.

The *quality* of a decision depends on the decision maker's respect for and utilization of the known facts (external reality). *Acceptance* of the decision refers to how favorably the implementers of the decision react to it. A high-quality decision that does not have the full support of the persons who are expected to implement it may lack the necessary support to insure its success. Thus, decisions may be ineffective because they lack quality, acceptance, or both.

The required degree of quality and acceptance varies with each decision. At one extreme are easily accepted decisions in which quality is very important. For example, setting the price on a product must take into account such facts as cost, competition, and marketing opportunities, yet salespeople readily accept the price that is set by the company. At the other extreme are decisions in which quality is of minor importance but which require full attention to acceptance of the decision. For example, the allocation of a new truck to a repair crew presents a problem of perceived fairness if each member feels he is most deserving. When the leader has the crew members participate in making this decision, there tends to be a redistribution of trucks so that all members stand to gain from the introduction of a new truck (Maier, 1952, pp. 231–232). Invariably the worst truck is discarded, but the decisions vary greatly from one crew to another. Such situations tend to be tailored to fit the values, attitudes, and personalities of the crew members.

The problem of achieving both quality and acceptance is complex because the quality of a decision depends on the wisdom of the decision maker (a combination of his knowledge and intelligence), and acceptance of a decision depends on the affected persons' being allowed to participate in the decision. Because wisdom and participation are not conditions for all decision making, it is necessary to use expertise in some situations, participation in others, and a combination of the two in others. The Problem-Solving interview (applied to group situations) is an effective way to achieve quality decisions and at the same time to gain acceptance through participation. Superior-subordinate problem solving applies not only to the appraisal situation, but whenever a superior wishes to influence a subordinate's performance on a new project, gain a subordinate's acceptance of a change, set priorities, or have a subordinate accept unpleasant tasks or endure hardships.

In the role-play interviews, Stanley's suggestion that Burke help his fellow supervisors was not acceptable because Burke felt it was not his job to give technical assistance to other units; he thought other units should have routine assignments so they would not need his help. Burke felt that refusing assignments that lacked challenge was justified; it was not his intention to try to avoid work or to deprive others of assignments they found preferable. He felt no need to change his supervisory procedure because he felt that turnover was healthy under the circumstances. None of the solutions Stanley had in mind had Burke's full acceptance, yet Burke would have to implement them. Stanley thought he would show favoritism by following Burke's suggestions for distributing assignments, but he could have found ways to avoid the issue of favoritism. Having Stanley give out assignments in group meetings, giving Burke a special group, or making Burke available as a consultant were solutions that had the potential of being acceptable to both parties.

Decisions requiring a high degree of both quality and acceptance require problem-solving skills. When the need for quality is high and gaining acceptance is not an obstacle, decisions can successfully be made by superiors alone. Because such decisions need only to be clearly communicated, the Tell and Sell method is appropriate. Decisions requiring acceptance when quality is not seriously endangered call for joint participation, and the problem must be stated without offending or blaming. Tell and Listen may be an acceptable method in these cases. As the need for both quality and acceptance increases, the Problem-Solving approach becomes more and more feasible.

Problem Solving Deals with Particulars

Much failure in communication stems from statements that are too general and have one meaning for the speaker and a somewhat different one for the listener. For example, if a group of managers is asked whether they believe in delegation, practically all of them will answer in the affirmative. However, if a situation is described in which B, a subordinate to A, discharges a good employee who has been insubordinate, and the group is asked whether A, B's superior, should have been consulted first, the group will request specifics (Maier, 1952, pp. 110–118). Questions may cover what the employee refused to do, how B made the assignment, and whether the job was in the employee's job description. Soon, many other details of the situation will be considered. The group will now be divided and most participants will refuse to give a "yes" or "no" answer to the initial question. The discussion will tend to be productive, however, and the questions of how much authority A should have delegated to B and under what conditions exceptions should be made will usually be agreed upon.

Another general question on which managers tend to disagree is whether an organization should allow by-passing. Some consider by-passing a violation of the chain of command and are against it; others consider an open-door policy a necessity and favor it (Maier, 1973b, pp. 580–582). Each person will describe situations that favor his own position. Again, a specific situation, such as a case in which a subordinate needs to communicate with his boss's superior to receive a transfer, produces a much better discussion. If the subordinate's immediate superior opposes the request for a transfer and the subordinate is highly qualified, what should be done? This question promotes considerable discussion. The basic problem is how a subordinate can by-pass without causing organizational problems. This same question applies to by-passing both up and down the organizational hierarchy and readily leads to specific solutions that can be generalized to other situations, although similarities and differences must always be considered when generalizing. Questions of honesty, authority, and who is right require the same treatment.

Many questions have to be answered by both yes and no. Specific circumstances and the values of the persons concerned can not be ignored. In role play, no two groups will arrive at the same conclusions, even using the same role-play case. What is accepted as fair by one group may be rejected by another. Each group tends to come up with an acceptable solution depending on the personalities of those involved and on the skills of the leader. On the whole, more than 80 percent of the participants in any one situation will consider their group's solution fair.

The same principle applies to all superior-subordinate relations. A decision that is effective for one person may be a failure for another. Decisions involving people must be tailored to fit their personalities and values, and this requires two-way communication and the process of searching together, using the skills of problem solving.

Searching Together for a Solution

When two or more people meet to discuss a problem, it is not uncommon for each to have a solution in mind. If the interviewer has a solution, he is likely to use a Tell and Sell approach. If the solutions of two or more persons differ, a conflict arises and participants try to persuade one another, each selecting facts that support his own solution. The only alternatives discussed are the ones that each brought to the meeting, and hard feelings often are the result.

Suppose two people want an orange and only one is available. Each feels he should have the orange. Once the conflict is established, a compromise seems the only alternative. Each person could have half an orange. But if the problem is probed to discover why each wants the orange, it may be that one wants the juice and the other wants the skin. In this situation, each can achieve his full goal.

If an interviewer reaches solutions prematurely, he may find he has a new problem—gaining the acceptance of a subordinate. If acceptance is necessary and persuasion does not work, a supervisor may resort to force, especially if he is in a position of power.

The best time for a supervisor to consider the importance of acceptance is before deciding on a solution. One of the best ways to gain acceptance is to return to the basic problem, list the possible solutions, and suggest a search for additional ones with an employee (Maier & McRay, 1972). Basically, problem solving involves searching together to find ways to reach goals that are of mutual interest. Once the alternatives have been listed, agreement can be reached on one solution, which then becomes a decision. Some decisions are of poor quality because no good solutions were generated, others are poor because a good selection was not made. The advantage of searching together and selecting together (evaluation process) is that the possibility of both quality and acceptance is maximized (Maier, 1970).

Further Applications of the Problem-Solving Approach

Management by Objectives

Over the last two decades an entire management philosophy has been built around the technique of setting goals or objectives that are quite specific and time-bound. Management by Objectives (MBO), first suggested by Peter Drucker (1954), introduced a method by which a superior and his subordinate could plan the subordinate's performance objectives for the coming year (or some specified period). The plan has evolved largely through writers such as Odiorne (1965) and has been supported by the American Management Association. MBO is based on the assumptions that if work groups and individual organization members can work together to specify short-term objectives, numerous positive outcomes will result. In addition, individuals involved in setting their own objectives and in working through barriers that impede their being met are more likely to accomplish those objectives effectively.

MBO is also based on a number of assumptions pertaining to an individual's work needs. Among these are:

(a) the individual's desire to know what his boss expects in terms of performance;

(b) the individual's need to have access to required resources—skills, technology, advice, help—that enable him to perform effectively;

(c) his need for adequate feedback from his boss about his performance;

(d) his felt needs for support, training, development, and an opportunity to grow in the job;

(e) his needs for positive reinforcement for effective performance;

(f) his need for realistic expectations around improved performance.

Given the MBO approach and some of the employee's work needs, the importance of using a Problem-Solving approach when setting objectives is clear. How the superior and subordinate interact—in other words, the skill and communication involved—is the determining factor in the success of the program. Because both successes and failures have been reported (Ivancevich, Donnelly, & Lyon, 1970), it is apparent that the procedure itself is not the answer.

Quality and acceptance must play an important role in MBO programs if they are to be successfully implemented. It is vitally important that both subordinate and superior accept and support goals that are agreed upon; both must psychologically "own" the decision if the objectives are to be reached. The goals reached are often contingent upon the dimension of quality—accurate data—and whatever additional resources the person needs to reach the goal.

The MBO program has merit because goals are agreed on by both parties—the employee and his superior—and success is measured by how well the subordinate performs in meeting the goals set.

An important point is that to compare actual accomplishments with goals set earlier, the goals must be measurable. For example, "doing better" has been found to be too vague a goal. Also, uncontrollable factors and economic conditions often change the fairness of goals, so subordinates' complaints often mention overemphasis on quantitative features (Raia, 1966).

Another problem with the MBO program is how to agree on the goals. One subordinate may wish to impress a superior by setting high goals, but he may then delay the time when he will be held accountable. Another may set low goals so that he can readily attain them, receiving his satisfaction at the time for accountability. But the most common problem (in this author's observation) is the tendency for a superior to dominate the goal-setting situation by mentioning what others are planning, what the company is planning, or by "selling" certain of his own plans to the subordinate.

Such dominance by the superior leads to overt resistance to change on the part of the subordinate, as seen in the role-play interviews. MBO aims to minimize resistance to change by taking a Problem-Solving approach and explicitly examining the need for change in situations, in persons, or in work units. The employee's participation in an MBO program is an explicit recognition of the fact that individuals or groups are more likely to commit themselves to performance goals if they are highly involved in and have impact on situations that bear directly on their work. Again, the dimensions of quality and acceptance are paramount.

MBO programs have had wide appeal because executives can be briefed in half a day on the basics, but skill in administrating the program requires considerable training. This point is usually too readily passed over or not appreciated by the promoters themselves. Superiors can not effectively motivate subordinates unless intrinsic incentives are introduced. The Problem-Solving interview style is an essential requirement of any program that involves setting goals, planning proficiency measurement, or supplying input from below. Without full participation by the employee, MBO can follow the same fate as the traditional appraisal interview in that too many dread it and honest opinions are omitted, but once the interviews have been held, employees relax and forget them.

Organization Development

The Problem-Solving approach provides much of the impetus for any program that qualifies as *organization development*. Currently, there is considerable debate about what exactly constitutes this relatively new field in which behavioral science knowledge is applied to planned organization change. Sherwood (1972, p. 153) provides the following definition: "Organization development is an educational process by which human resources are continuously identified, allocated, and expanded in ways that make these resources more available to the organization and, therefore, improve the organization's *problem-solving* capabilities." The end product, or the ongoing product, of successful OD is effective problem solving between individuals and in groups. A number of specific "building blocks" of OD make improved problem solving their focus. The phases of organization development include sensing and diagnosis, team building, intergroup relations, and organization goal setting. Each relates to some dimension of problem solving: identification; clarification; brainstorming; choosing workable, realistic solutions; action-step planning; or follow-up.

A major characteristic of OD is that it relies heavily on *learning by doing* to solve problems. Such learning includes the utilization of numerous skills: communication, openness and explicit expression of ideas and feelings, and working through individual and group conflict. The Problem-Solving approach outlined in previous chapters is a central asset to this process. Because growth requires stimulation, an effective superior serves as a stimulator, not a supplier, of ideas.

The major strategy of OD is to have individuals make interventions in the ongoing process of the organization in such a way that human resources are optimally tapped. A Problem-Solving approach facilitates this happening. Group problem solving requires an integrative process, and serving as an integrator is a major role of the group leader.

Employee Counseling

The major objective of counseling is to help individuals learn to manage their lives more effectively. Often, it is difficult, if not impossible, to separate an employee's personal life from his work life because they are so interdependent. Thus, it falls on the supervisor's shoulders to facilitate an employee's *personal* development in addition to his *job* development.

As corporate officials more and more assume additional responsibility for the personal development of their employees, there is an increasing need for supervisors to learn basic helping and counseling skills. Once again, problem solving is a viable approach for the supervisor to utilize during counseling interactions with employees. Listening, accepting feelings without criticism, respecting personal interests, and searching together for alternative solutions are relevant skills.

Conflict Resolution

Conflicting Goals. Conflicts between superiors and subordinates, workers at the same level, parents and children, or teachers and students often involve conflicting goals that can be integrated if they are discussed and mutually respected during a problem-solving discussion.

Filley (1975) treats conflict as the opposite of problem-solving behavior. True conflicts arise when the goals or objectives of the parties involved are opposed. For example, labor and management may have different objectives for the distribution of profits. In cases like this, representatives of opposing parties usually meet with solutions and strategy already prepared. Each participant does his problem solving prior to the meeting. The representatives need to find a common goal, such as the survival of the company or how to increase productivity, although too often the conflict is considered basic by both participants and no attempt is made to locate mutual interests.

If no mutual interest can be found, the conflict can lead to strikes, mutual hard feelings, the subjugation of one or the other party, or a compromise solution that is not satisfactory to either side.

Conflicting Solutions. Conflict may also arise, not because the goal is disputed, but because each party has a preferred solution. In such cases, additional alternatives should be searched for jointly so that problem solving can begin. The Problem-Solving interview situation reported in this book brought to the surface many solutions of mutual interest; the Tell and Sell and the Tell and Listen interview methods did not surface goals of mutual interest.

Lack of Communication. Some conflicts are more imagined than real. Unless there is full communication (both up and down the organizational hierarchy and between related work units), conflicts are often a matter of faulty perception, hypersensitivity, or misunderstanding. Rank often creates a communication barrier. For example, a superior's failure to praise an employee for a good job after he has seen the employee smoking in the rest room is viewed by the employee as a reprimand. Frequent discussion of problems seems to be the best way to reduce potential imagined conflicts.

Resentment of Behavior. Finally, there are conflicts not among goals or solutions but because certain behavior is resented. For example, an employee may be a problem because his superior thinks he makes too many personal phone calls; yet the superior may not wish to discharge the employee because he does more work than anyone else. If the employer passes a rule forbidding personal calls, some employees may rebel or quit. In a situation like this, the employer needs to define the problem and decide why the behavior in question should stop. If the calls are made during a lunch break, he may complain that the company lines are giving busy signals; if the calls are shortened, he still may object because they are excessive. If the employer's objection can be specified it may be that a solution is possible, although the true reason may be the employer's rigid attitude. Very often in situations of this kind, the objections brought up originally are not the most basic ones (which, incidentally, the employer may not realize), and conflicts based upon unreal objections need to be explored in an atmosphere in which feelings are respected so that true feelings can come to the surface. The Problem-Solving interview's emphasis on dealing with feelings is relevant for conflicts of this type.

Summary

Effective problem solving has been presented in this and previous chapters as a healthy, productive, growth-inducing way for individuals to relate to one another. It is the type of interaction that lends itself to many day-to-day situations both inside and outside formal organizational settings. Individual growth is at its core, and for growth to occur, needs and goals must be understood and then met through behavior that is responsible and responsive to the individual's needs.

Importance of the Person

Numerous concepts have been explored and researched in the area of problem-solving behavior. Theories, skills, techniques—each has been considered in some depth. In the final analysis, however, the most viable force is the personal, *human* dimension. A manager, a teacher—anyone responsible for supervising the work of another—is effective in his particular job role only to the degree that he is effective as a *person*. The ability to feel empathy for another, to see things from another person's point of view, is critical to effective management. Allowing others to have their own values and goals is also crucial if managers and employees are to optimize their human resources.

Two additional dimensions central to personal effectiveness are *congruence* and *flexibility*. A *congruent* person is aware of himself and his own needs and is cognizant of how his behavior affects others. He is also able to communicate what he thinks and feels. A *flexible* person remains open to influence from others and is open to a re-examination of his own perceptions of reality.

Managers and people who report to them are by definition interdependent: what each does affects the others. If managers focus on their own personal development as well as that of the employees reporting to them, the effects will be synergistic.

Importance of Skills

A reoccurring theme of this book is the need for skills that promote growth and effectiveness. Managers must continually improve their ability to *listen*, to *express* themselves, to *observe* what goes on around them, to *respond* to those with whom they interact, and to *intervene* when, in their judgment, it makes sense to do so.

To grow and to increase one's effectiveness entails taking risks with other people. To more fully integrate the personal attributes, skills, techniques, and theories presented in these pages challenges one to take some of those risks to develop in a nonstatic way.

References and Readings

References

Burke, R. J., & Wilcox, D. S. Characteristics of effective employee performance review and development interviews. *Personnel Psychology*, 1969, *22*, 291-305.

Clark, C. H. *Brainstorming*. Garden City, N.Y.: Doubleday, 1958.

Danielson, L. E., & Maier, N. R. F. Supervisory problems in decision making. *Personnel Psychology*, 1957, *10*, 169-180.

Dembo, T., Leviton, G. L., & Wright, B. A. Adjustment to misfortune—A problem of social-psychological rehabilitation. *Artificial Limbs*, 1956, *3*, 4-62.

Drucker, P. *The practice of management*. New York: Harper & Row, 1954.

Filley, A. C. *Interpersonal conflict resolution*. Glenview, Ill.: Scott, Foresman, 1975.

Heyns, R. W. *Functional analysis of group problem-solving behavior*. Ann Arbor, Mich.: University of Michigan, 1948. (Mimeographed)

Hoffman, L. R. Homogeneity of member personality and its effect on group problem-solving. *Journal of Abnormal and Social Psychology*, 1959, *58*, 27-32.

Hoffman, L. R., Harburg, E., & Maier, N. R. F. Differences and disagreement as factors in creative group problem solving. *Journal of Abnormal and Social Psychology*, 1962, *64*, 206-214.

Ivancevich, J. M., Donnelly, J. H., & Lyon, H. L. A study of the impact of management by objectives on perceived need satisfaction. *Personnel Psychology*, 1970, *23*, 139-151.

Katz, D., Maccoby, N., & Morse, N. C. *Productivity, supervision and morale in an office situation*. Ann Arbor, Mich.: University of Michigan Institute for Social Research, 1950.

Kay, E., Meyer, H. H., & French, J. R. P., Jr. Effects of threat in a performance appraisal interview. *Journal of Applied Psychology*, 1965, *49*, 311-317.

Maier, N. R. F. The role of frustration in social movements. *Psychological Review*, 1942, *49*, 586-599.

Maier, N. R. F. The quality of group decisions as influenced by the discussion leader. *Human Relations*, 1950, *3*, 155-174.

Maier, N. R. F. *Principles of human relations: Applications to management*. New York: John Wiley, 1952.

Maier, N. R. F. An experimental test of the effect of training on discussion leadership. *Human Relations*, 1953, *6*, 161-173.

Maier, N. R. F. *Problem-solving discussions and conferences: Leadership methods and skills*. New York: McGraw-Hill, 1963.

Maier, N. R. F. Assets and liabilities in group problem solving: The need for an integrative function. *Psychological Review*, 1967, *74*, 239-249.

Maier, N. R. F. *Problem solving and creativity: In individuals and groups*. Monterey, Calif.: Brooks/Cole, 1970.

Maier, N. R. F. Prior commitment as a deterrent to group problem solving. *Personnel Psychology*, 1973, *26*, 117-126. (a)

Maier, N. R. F. *Psychology in industrial organizations* (4th ed.). Boston: Houghton Mifflin, 1973. (b)

Maier, N. R. F., Hoffman, L. R., Hooven, T. C., & Read, W. H. *Superior-subordinate communication in management* (Research Study 52). New York: American Management Association, 1961.

Maier, N. R. F., & Lansky, L. M. Effect of attitude on selection of facts. *Personnel Psychology*, 1957, *10*, 293-303.

Maier, N. R. F., & McRay, E. P. Increasing innovation in change situations through leadership skills. *Psychological Reports*, 1972, *31*, 343-354.

Maier, N. R. F., & Sashkin, M. Specific leadership behaviors that promote problem solving. *Personnel Psychology*, 1971, *24*, 35-44.

Maier, N. R. F., & Solem, A. R. The contribution of the discussion leader to the quality of group thinking. *Human Relations*, 1952, *3*, 155-174.

Maier, N. R. F., Solem, A. R., & Maier, A. A. *The role-play technique: A handbook for management and leadership practice*. La Jolla, Calif.: University Associates, 1975.

Marquis, D. G., Guetzkow, H., & Heyns, R. W. A social psychological study of the decision-making conference. In H. Guetzkow (Ed.), *Groups, Leadership, and Men*. Pittsburgh, Pa.: Carnegie Press, 1951.

Meyer, H. H., & Kay, E. A comparison of a work planning program with the annual performance appraisal approach. *Behavioral Research Services Report No. ESR 17*. General Electric Company, 1964.

Meyer, H. H., & Walker, W. B. A study of factors relating to the effectiveness of a performance appraisal program. *Personnel Psychology*, 1961, *14*, 291-298.

Odiorne, G. *Management by objectives*. New York: Pitman, 1965.

Osborn, A. F. *Applied imagination: Principles and procedures of creative thinking*. New York: Charles Scribner's, 1953.

Raia, A. P. A second look at management goals and controls. *California Management Review*, 1966, *8*, 49-58.

Read, W. H. Upward communication in industrial hierarchies. *Human Relations*, 1962, *15*, 3-15.

Roethlisberger, F. J., & Dickson, W. J. *Management and the worker*. Cambridge, Mass.: Harvard University Press, 1939.

Rogers, C. R. *Counseling and psychotherapy*. Boston: Houghton Mifflin, 1942.

Sherwood, J. J. An introduction to organization development. In J. W. Pfeiffer & J. E. Jones (Eds.), *The 1972 Annual Handbook for Group Facilitators*. La Jolla, Calif.: University Associates, 1972.

Further Readings*

Balinsky, B. Some experiences and problems in appraising executive personnel. *Personnel Psychology*, Summer 1964, *17*, 107-114.

Barrett, R. S. Performance suitability and role agreement: Two factors related to attitudes. *Personnel Psychology*, 1963, *16*, 345-357.

Barrett, R. S. Explorations in job satisfaction and performance rating. *Personnel Administration*, 1964, *27*, 14-21.

Barrett, R. S. The influence of the supervisor's requirements on ratings. *Personnel Psychology*, 1966, *19*, 375-387. (a)

Barrett, R. S. *Performance rating*. Chicago: Science Research Associates, 1966. (b)

Barrett, R. S., Taylor, E. K., Parker, J. W., & Martens, L. Rating scale content: I. Scale information and supervisory ratings. *Personnel Psychology*, 1958, *11*, 333-346.

Bartlett, C. J. The relationship between self-rating and peer ratings on a leadership behavior scale. *Personnel Psychology*, 1959, *12*, 237-246.

Bass, B. M. Reducing leniency in merit rating. *Personnel Psychology*, 1956, *9*, 359-369.

Bassett, G. A. *Practical interviewing*. New York: American Management Association, 1965.

---

*The readings list was prepared for this volume by Professor R. J. Burke, York University, Downsview, Ontario.

Bassett, G. A., & Meyer, H. H. Performance appraisal based on self-review. *Personnel Psychology*, 1968, *21*, 421-430.

Bayroff, A. G., Haggerty, H. R., & Rundquist, E. A. Validity of ratings as related to rating techniques and conditions. *Personnel Psychology*, 1954, *7*, 93-112.

Beckwith, E. F. Take the guesswork out of performance rating. *Supervisory Management*, 1965, *10*, 4-7.

Benjamin, R., Jr. A survey of 130 merit-rating plans. *Personnel*, 1952, *20*, 289-294.

Bentley, C. H. Performance ratings—What next? *Public Personnel Review*, 1950, *11*, 119-125.

Best, W. H. Some new directions in personnel appraisal. *Personnel Psychology*, 1957, *34*, 45-50.

Bittner, R. H. Developing an industrial merit rating procedure. *Personnel Psychology*, 1948, *1*, 403-432.

Black, J. M. Appraising employees: Tell them the truth. *Supervisory Management*, April 1963, *8*, 37-38.

Blake, R. R. Reexamination of performance appraisals. *Advanced Management*, 1958, *7*, 19-20.

Blake, R. R., & Mouton, J. S. Power, people and performance reviews. *Advanced Management*, 1961, *24*, 13-17.

Boyd, B. B. Why dread performance appraisal? *Supervisory Management*, January 1963, *8*, 4-8.

Brown, G. E., Jr., & Larson, A. F. Current trends in appraisal and development. *Personnel*, 1958, *34*, 51-58.

Brumback, G. B. A reply to Kavanagh's "The content issue in performance appraisal: A review." *Personnel Psychology*, 1972, *25*, 567-572.

Brumback, G. B., & Vincent, J. W. Jobs and appraisal of performance. *Personnel Administration*, 1970, *33*(5), 26-30.

Bucklow, M. Reviewing employee rating. *Bulletin of Industrial Personnel Practices*, 1950, *6*(4), 3-15.

Bucklow, M. Staff reporting—A new look at the halo effect. *Personnel Practices Bulletin*, 1960, *16*(4), 1-17.

Buel, W. D. Items, scales, and raters: Some suggestions and comments. *Personnel Administration*, 1962, *25*, 15ff.

Burch, W. Annual employee reviews. *Personnel Journal*, June 1963, *42*, 284-285.

Burke, R. J. Characteristics of effective performance appraisal interviews. *Training and Development Journal*, 1970, *24*, 9-12.

Burke, R. J. Why performance appraisal systems fail. *Personnel Administration*, 1972, *35*, 32-40.

Byrt, W. J. The construction and review of an appraisal scheme for professional staff. *Personnel Practices Bulletin*, 1960, *16*(1), 1-19.

Campbell, J. P., Dunnette, M. D., Arvoy, R. D., & Hellervik, L. V. The development and evaluation of behaviorally based rating scales. *Journal of Applied Psychology*, 1973, *57*, 15-22.

Carroll, S. J., & Tosi, H. L. The relation of characteristics of the review process as moderated by personality and situational factors to the success of the "management by objectives" approach. *Academy of Management Journal*, 1969, *12*, 139-143.

Carroll, S. J., & Tosi, H. L. Goal characteristics and personality factors in a management-by-objectives program. *Administrative Science Quarterly*, 1970, *61*, 295-305.

Carroll, S. J., & Tosi, H. L. *Management by objectives: Applications and research*. New York: Macmillan, 1973.

Carron, T. J. Simplification of employee appraisal programs. *Journal of Industrial Psychology*, 1965, *3*(4), 81-90.

Caskey, C. C. A positive approach to appraisal of performance. *Supervision*, August 1967, *29*, 11-12.

Chew, W. B., & Howell, L. E. New light on trait rating. *Personnel*, 1960, *37*, 42-45.

Clingenpeel, R. E. How employees feel about performance appraisal. *Personnel*, 1962, *29*, 70ff.

Cohen, B. M. A new look at performance appraisal: The specimen check-list. *Human Resources Management*, 1972, *11*, 18-22.

Coleman, C. J. Avoiding the pitfalls in results-oriented appraisals. *Personnel*, November-December 1965, *42*, 24-33.

Cooks, D. The impact on managers of frequency of feedback. *Academy of Management Journal*, 1968, *11*, 263-277.

Cotham, J. C., & Cravens, D. W. Improving measurement of salesman performance. *Business Horizons*, 1969, *12*, 70-78.

Covner, B. J. The communication of merit ratings: A philosophy and a method. *Personnel*, 1953, *30*, 88-98.

Cozan, L. W. Forced-choice: Better than other rating methods. *Personnel*, 1959, *39*, 80-83.

Creswell, M. B. Effects of confidentiality on performance ratings of professional health personnel. *Personnel Psychology*, 1963, *16*(4), 385-393.

Cummings, L. L. A field experimental study of two performance appraisal systems. *Personnel Psychology*, 1973, *26*, 489-502.

Cummings, L. L., & Schwab, D. P. *Performance in organizations: Determinants and appraisal*. Glenview, Ill.: Scott, Foresman, 1973.

Dailey, W. W. Needed: A new manifesto for performance evaluation. *Personnel Administration*, July 1961, *24*, 41-46.

Dayal, I. Some issues in performance appraisal. *Personnel Administration*, January 1969, *32*, 27-30.

Doiron, R. C. The personnel evaluation process. *Journal of Systems Management*, 1970, *21*, 37-41.

Dooher, M., Marquis, J., & Marquis, V. *Rating employee and supervisory performance: A manual of merit-rating techniques*. New York: American Management Association, 1950.

Dunnette, M. D. Managerial effectiveness: Its definition and measurement. *Studies in Personnel Psychology*, 1970, *2*, 6-20.

Evans, J. W. Emotional bias in merit ratings. *Personnel Journal*, 1950, *28*, 290-291.

Farson, R. E. Praise reappraised. *Harvard Business Review*, 1963, *41*, 61-66.

Fear, R. A. *The evaluation interview*. New York: McGraw-Hill, 1958.

Feinberg, M. R. Performance review: Threat or promise. *Supervisory Management*, May 1961, *6*, 2-12.

Feinberg, M. R. Performance appraisal and executive morale. *Management Record*, June 1961, *23*, 25-31.

Finn, R. H. Is your appraisal program really necessary? *Personnel*,1960, *37*,16-21.

Finn, R. H. Pitfalls in performance appraisal. *Supervisory Management*, July 1962, *7*, 43-45.

Fiske, D. W. Variability among peer ratings in different situations. *Educational and Psychological Measurement*, 1960, *20*, 231-292.

Fitzgerald, T. H. Appraisals: Personality, performance and persons. *California Management Review*, Winter 1965, *8*, 81-86.

Flanagan, J. C. The critical incidents technique. *Psychological Bulletin*, 1954, *51*, 327-358.

Flanagan, J. C., & Burns, R. K. The employee performance record: A new appraisal and development tool. *Harvard Business Review*, 1955, *33*, 95-102.

Fogli, L., Hulin, C. L., & Blood, M. R. Development of first-level behavioral job criteria. *Journal of Applied Psychology*, 1971, *55*, 3-8.

Ford, G. B. Build a winning team with better appraisal. *Supervisory Management*, December 1964, *9*, 14-17.

Fraser, J. M. Setting standards for appraisal. *Personnel*, July 1968, *1*, 24-26.

Freeberg, N. E. Relevance of rater-ratee acquaintance in the validity and reliability of ratings. *Journal of Applied Psychology*, 1969, *53*, 518-524.

French, J. R. P., Kay, E., & Meyer, H. H. Participation and the appraisal system. *Human Relations*, 1966, *19*, 3-20.

Glickmann, A. S. Is performance appraisal practice? *Personnel Administration*, 1964, *27*, 28-35.

Gluck, H. R. Appraising managerial performance. *Personnel Journal*, March 1964, *43*, 137-140.

Grant, D. L. Are personality trait factors a desirable feature of performance rating plans? *Personnel Administration*, May 1963, *26*, 56-59.

Grela, J. J. Work sheet helps supervisors talk constructively with employees. *Personnel*, 1955, *33*, 417-422; 424.

Gruenfeld, L. W., & Weissenberg, P. Supervisory characteristics and attitudes toward performance appraisal. *Personnel Psychology*, 1966, *19*, 143-151.

Gunderson, E. K., & Ryman, D. H. Convergent and discriminant validities of performance evaluations in extremely isolated groups. *Personnel Psychology*, 1971, *24*, 715-724.

Hagerty, P. E. Why not take the "rating" out of performance rating? *Public Personnel Review*, 1955, *16*(1), 39-44.

Hall, W. B. Employee self-appraisal. *Personnel Journal*, 1950, *29*, 134-136.

Hall, W. B. Employee self-appraisal for improved performance. *American Management Association, Personnel Service*, 1951, *140*, 29-34.

Hanson, P. G., Morton, R. B., & Rothaus, P. The fate of role stereotypes in two performance appraisal interviews. *Personnel*, 1963, *16*, 269-280.

Harris, C. R., & Heise, R. C. Tasks, not traits—The key to better performance review. *Personnel*, May-June 1964, *17*, 60-64.

Hathaway, R. K. Straight talk on performance appraisal. *Supervisory Management*, April 1966, *11*, 4-6.

Hayden, S. J. Getting better results from post-appraisal interviews. *Personnel*, May 1955, *33*, 541-550.

Heier, W. D. Implementing an appraisal-by-results program. *Personnel*, 1970, *47*, 24ff.

Hersey, R. As others see us. *Personnel*, 1962, *39*, 8ff.

Hollander, E. P. The friendship factor in peer nominations. *Personnel Psychology*, 1956, *9*, 435-447.

Hollander, E. P. Validity of peer nominations in predicting a distant performance criterion. *Journal of Applied Psychology*, 1965, *49*, 434-438.

Hoppock, R. Can appraisal counseling be taught? *Personnel*, 1958, *135*, 24-30.

Howard, R. C., & Berkowitz, L. Reactions to the evaluators of one's performance. *Journal of Personality*, 1958, *26*, 494-507.

Howe, D. R. Effective performance rating. *Personnel*, 1952, *30*, 328-338.

Hughes, C. L. Why goal oriented performance reviews succeed and fail. *Personnel*, June 1966, *44*, 335-341.

Hughes, C. L. Assessing the performance of key managers. *Personnel*, January 1968, *45*, 38-43.

Huse, E. F. Performance appraisal—A new look. *Personnel Administration*, 1967, *30*, 3ff.

Huttner, L., & O'Malley, T. R. Let them know. *Personnel Psychology*, 1962, *15*(2), 179-186.

Ivancevich, J. M. The theory and practice of management by objectives. *Michigan Business Review*, 1969, *21*, 13-16.

Johnson, E. P. New kind of performance review emphasizes executives' development. *Personnel*, 1954, *33*, 131-133.

Kallejian, V., Brown, P., & Weschler, I. R. The impact of interpersonal relations on ratings of performance. *Public Personnel Review*, 1953, *14*, 166-170.

Kavanagh, M. J. The content issue in performance appraisal: A review. *Personnel Psychology*, 1971, *24*, 653-668.

Kay, E., & Huse, E. F. Try this approach to appraisal. *Supervisory Management*, 1966, *11*, 4-8.

Kay, E., Meyer, H. H., & French, J. R. P. Effect of threat in a performance appraisal interview. *Journal of Applied Psychology*, 1965, *69*, 311-317.

Kellner, A. D., & Loser, R. G. Successes and failures in executive performance planning. *Personnel Administration*, 1965, *28*, 18-24.

Kellogg, M. S. Coaching appraisal: A tool for better delegation. *Supervisory Management*, 1965, *10*, 14-21. (a)

Kellogg, M. S. The ethics of employee appraisal. *Personnel*, July-August 1965, *33*, 33-39. (b)

Kellogg, M. S. *What to do about performance appraisal*. New York: American Management Association, 1965. (c)

Kellogg, M. S. *Closing the performance gap*. New York: American Management Association, 1967.

Kelly, P. R. Reappraisal of appraisals. *Harvard Business Review*, May-June 1958, *36*, 59-68.

Kelly, P. R. What is wrong with performance appraisal? *Purchasing*, 1960, *49*, 80-81.

Kindall, A. F., & Gatza, J. Positive program for performance appraisal. *Harvard Business Review*, 1963, *41*, 153-166.

Kirchner, W. K., & Dunnette, M. D. Identifying the critical factors in successful salesmanship. *Personnel*, 1957, *34*, 54-59.

Kirchner, W. K., & Reisberg, D. J. Differences between better and less effective supervisors in appraisal of subordinates. *Personnel Psychology*, 1962, *15*, 295-303.

Kirk, E. B. Performance appraisals: Formal versus informal. *Personnel*, 1963, *42*(4), 184-187. (a)

Kirk, E. B. Results-centered appraisals. *Personnel*, November 1963, *42*, 495-498. (b)

Kirk, E. B. Appraisal participation in performance interviews. *Personnel*, January 1965, *44*, 22-25.

Knauft, E. B. Construction and use of weighted checklist rating scales for two industrial situations. *Journal of Applied Psychology*, 1948, *32*, 63-70.

Knight, F. B. The effect of the acquaintance factor upon personal judgements. *Journal of Educational Psychology*, 1923, *14*, 129-142.

Laudsepp, E. Performance appraisals that motivate individual development. *Management Review*, 1961, *56:M*, 62-70.

Lawler, E. E. The multitrait-multirater approach to measuring managerial job performance. *Journal of Applied Psychology*, 1967, *51*, 369-381.

Lawshe, C. H., Kephart, N. C., & McCormick, E. J. The paired comparison technique for rating performance of industrial employees. *Journal of Applied Psychology*, 1949, *33*, 69-77.

Lawton, E. C. Is group appraisal the best way to evaluate top executives? *Personnel Administration*, March 1959, *22*, 30-32.

Leete, J. F. "Pen," a new twist on employee performance review. *Personnel*, October 1967, *46*, 572-575.

Leskovic, E. W. Guide for discussing performance appraisal. *Personnel*, March 1967, *46*, 150-152.

Lewis, A. E. Making appraisals pay off. *Supervisory Management*, June 1967, *12*, 18-20.

Lopez, F. M. *Evaluating employee performance*. Chicago: International Personnel Management Association, 1968.

Machaver, W. V., & Erickson, W. E. A new approach to executive appraisal. *Personnel*, 1958, *35*, 8-14.

Maier, N. R. F. Three types of appraisal interview. *Personnel*, 1958, *34*, 27-40.

Mayfield, E. C. Management selection: Buddy nominations revisited. *Personnel Psychology*, 1970, *23*, 393-407.

Mayfield, E. C., & Carlson, R. E. Selection interview decisions: First results from a long-term research project. *Personnel Psychology*, 1966, *19*, 41-53.

Mayfield, H. In defense of performance appraisal. *Harvard Business Review*, 1960, *38*, 81-87.

McConkey, D. D. Measuring managers by results. *Personnel*, December 1962, *41*, 540-546.

McConkey, D. D. Judging managerial performance. *Business Horizons*, 1964, 7(3), 47-54.

McConkey, D. D. Results approach to evaluating managerial performance. *Advanced Management Journal*, October 1967, 32, 18-26.

McCormick, R. Can we use compensation data to measure job performance behavior? *Personnel Journal*, 1972, 51, 918-922.

McGregor, D. An uneasy look at performance appraisal. *Harvard Business Review*, 1957, 35, 89-94.

Meyer, H. H. Performance appraisal interviews communicate both ways. *Personnel*, 1955, 34, 6-8.

Meyer, H. H. The validity of the in-basket test as a measure of managerial performance. *Personnel Psychology*, 1970, 23, 294-307.

Meyer, H. H., Kay, E., & French, J. R. P., Jr. Split roles in performance appraisal. *Harvard Business Review*, 1965, 43, 123-129.

Meyer, H. H., & Walker, W. B. Need for achievement and risk preference as they relate to attitudes toward reward systems and performance appraisal in an industrial setting. *Journal of Applied Psychology*, 1961, 45, 251-256.

Moon, G. G., & Hariton, T. Evaluating an appraisal and feedback training program. *Personnel*, 1958, 35, 36-41.

Morrisey, G. L. *Appraisal and development through objectives and results*. Reading, Mass.: Addison-Wesley, 1972.

Moulton, W. H. Performance appraisal: Let the facts speak for themselves. *Supervisory Management*, September 1962, 7, 8-12.

Nagel, B. F. Criterion development. *Personnel Psychology*, 1953, 6, 271-289.

Noland, R. L. Theoretical foundations of the appraisal interview. *Public Personnel Review*, 1967, 28(2), 93-95.

Novit, M. Performance evaluation and dual authority: A look at group appraisal. *Management of Personnel Quarterly*, Spring 1969, 1-9.

Oberg, W. Make performance appraisal relevant. *Harvard Business Review*, 1972, 50, 61-67.

Odiorne, G. S. *Personnel administration by objectives*. Homewood, Ill.: Richard D. Irwin, 1971.

Patton, A. How to appraise executive performance. *Harvard Business Review*, 1960, 37, 63-70.

Paul, R. J. Employee performance appraisal: Some empirical findings. *Personnel*, 1968, 47, 109-114.

Payne, B. L., McNair, M. P., Jr., & Kelly, P. R. Appraisal of managers and management development. *Management Record*, March 1961, 23, 8-17.

Planty, E. G., & Efferson, C. E. Counseling executives after merit rating or evaluation. *Personnel*, 1951, 27, 384-396.

Prather, R. L. Job profiles, performance evaluation and career progress. *Personnel Journal*, 1969, 48, 513-522.

Quinn, J. L. Bias in performance appraisals. *Personnel Administration*, 1969, 32, 40ff.

Raia, A. P. Goal setting and self-control. *Journal of Management Studies*, 1965, 11, 24-53.

Randle, C. W., & Monroe, W. H. Better ways to measure executive performance. *Business Management*, 1961, 19, 64-66.

Raudsepp, E. Guidelines for developing employee potential. *Supervisory Management*, April 1967, *12*, 46-48. (a)

Raudsepp, E. Performance appraisals that motivate individual development. *Management Review*, 1967, *56*, 62-70. (b)

Richards, K. E. Some new insights into performance appraisal. *Personnel*, 1960, *37*, 28-38.

Roadman, H. E. An industrial use of peer ratings. *Journal of Applied Psychology*, 1964, *48*, 211-214.

Rosen, A. Congruence of staff nurses' self-ratings of performance with supervisor's ratings. *Nursing Research*, 1967, *16*(4), 368-371. (a)

Rosen, A. Performance appraisal interviewing evaluated by proximal observers. *Nursing Research*, 1967, *16*(1), 44-50. (b)

Ross, P. F. Reference groups in man-to-man job performance ratings. *Personnel Psychology*, 1966, *19*, 115-142.

Rothaus, P., Morton, R. B., & Hanson, P. C. Performance appraisal and psychological distance. *Journal of Applied Psychology*, 1965, *49*, 48-54.

Rowe, K. H. Management appraisal and development. *Management International Review*, 1966, *4*, 68-75.

Rowland, V. K. *Evaluating and improving managerial performance*. New York: McGraw-Hill, 1970.

Schrader, A. W. Let's abolish the annual performance review. *Management of Personnel Quarterly*, 1969, *8*, 293-299.

Schultz, R. S. How to appraise people. *Supervision*, 1967, *29*(11), 5-7.

Shelton, H. W. Mutual rating: The key to employee participation. *Advanced Management*, March 1948, *13*, 1-6.

Sheridan, A. J., & Carlson, R. E. Decision-making in a performance appraisal situation. *Personnel Psychology*, 1972, *25*, 339-351.

Siegel, A. I., Schultz, D. G., Fischi, M. A., & Lanterman, R. S. Absolute scaling of job performance. *Journal of Applied Psychology*, 1968, *52*, 313-318.

Sindall, J. W. Employee appraisal works two ways. *Administrative Management*, September 1967, *28*, 51-52.

Sloan, S., & Johnson, A. C. New context of personnel appraisal. *Harvard Business Review*, November 1968, *46*, 14-16.

Smith, J. P. Personal behavior in the performance appraisal interview. *Advanced Management*, January 1968, *33*, 56-62.

Smith, P. C., & Kendall, L. M. Retranslation of expectations: An approach to the construction of unambiguous anchors for rating scales. *Journal of Applied Psychology*, 1963, *47*, 149-155.

Sokolik, S. L. Guidelines in the search for effective appraisals. *Personnel*, November 1967, *46*, 660-668.

Spriegel, W. R. Company practices in appraisal of managerial performance. *Personnel*, 1962, *39*, 77-83.

Stone, T. H. An examination of six prevalent assumptions concerning performance appraisal. *Public Personnel Management*, 1973, *2*, 408-414.

Sutermeister, R. A. Basic problems in evaluating employee performance. *Hospital Administration*, 1966, *11*(3), 9-16. (a)

Sutermeister, R. A. Custom-tailor your appraisals. *Supervisory Management,* December 1966, *11,* 27-29. (b)

Taff, J. P. Why do performance appraisal programs go sour? *Personnel Administration,* May 1959, *32,* 50-52.

Taft, R. The ability to judge people. *Psychological Bulletin,* 1955, *52,* 1-23.

Taylor, E. K., & Wherry, R. J. A study of leniency in two rating systems. *Personnel Psychology,* 1951, *4,* 39-47.

Thompson, D. W. Performance reviews: Management tools or management excuse. *Personnel Journal,* 1969, *48,* 957-961.

Thompson, P. H., & Dalton, G. W. Performance appraisal: Managers beware. *Harvard Business Review,* 1970, *48,* 149-157.

Thorndike, E. C. A constant error in psychological ratings. *Journal of Applied Psychology,* 1920, *4,* 25-29.

Thorton, G. C. The relationship between supervisory and self appraisals of executive performances. *Personnel Psychology,* 1968, *21,* 441-455.

Tiffin, J. Six merit-rating systems. *Personnel,* 1959, *37,* 288-291.

Tomb, J. O. Getting your money's worth out of executive performance appraisal. *Controller,* December 1960, *28,* 580-582.

Tosi, H. L., & Carroll, S. J. Some factors affecting the success of "management by objectives." *Journal of Management Studies,* 1970, *7,* 209-223.

Trickett, J. N. Management appraisals: A key to management self development. *Personnel,* 1955, *32,* 234-245.

Uhlaner, J. E. Human performance effectiveness and the systems management bed. *Journal of Applied Psychology,* 1972, *56,* 202-210.

Waggoner, W. G. Getting back into focus on performance ratings. *Personnel,* 1954, *33,* 17-18.

Ward, W. H. The "it's your business" approach to ratings. *Personnel Psychology,* 1961, *14,* 183-191.

Weingarten, J. Hard look in employee appraisal. *Management Review,* October 1966, *55,* 41-45.

Weitz, J. Selecting supervisors with poor ratings. *Personnel Psychology,* 1958, *11,* 25-35.

Wetjen, J. F. Performance appraisals: A study of systems used to appraise employee performance. *Training and Development Journal,* 1968, *22,* 46-56.

Whisler, T. L. Performance appraisal and the organization man. *Journal of Business,* 1958, *31,* 19-27.

Whisler, T. L., & Harper, S. F. (Eds.) *Performance appraisal: Research and practice.* New York: Holt, Rinehart and Winston, 1965.

Whitlock, G. H. Application of the psychophysical law to performance evaluation. *Journal of Applied Psychology,* 1963, *47*(1), 15-23.

Wickert, F. R., & McFarland, D. E. (Eds.). *Measuring executive performance.* New York: Appleton-Century-Crofts, 1967.

Wolfe, E. W. Staff evaluations: A key to more effective performance. *Journal of Rehabilitation,* 1960, *26*(4), 9-22; 37-38.

Zander, A. F. (Ed.) *Performance appraisals.* Ann Arbor, Mich.: Foundation for Research on Human Behavior, 1963.

Zander, A., & Gyr, J. Changing attitudes toward a merit rating system. *Personnel Psychology*, 1955, *8*, 429-448.

Zavala, A. Development of the forced-choice rating scale technique. *Psychological Bulletin*, 1965, *63*, 117-124.

Index